Working with Children and Young People Who Have Displayed Harmful Sexual Behaviour

also of interest is Dunedin's

PROTECTING CHILDREN AND YOUNG PEOPLE SERIES

Sharon Vincent, *Learning from Child Deaths and Serious Abuse in Scotland* (2010)

Anne Stafford, Sharon Vincent and Nigel Parton (eds) *Child Protection Reform across the United Kingdom* (2010)

Kate Alexander and Anne Stafford, *Children and Organised Sport* (2011)

Sharon Vincent, *Preventing Child Deaths: Learning from review* (2013)

Julie Taylor and Anne Lazenbatt, *Child Maltreatment and High Risk Families* (2014)

Caroline Bradbury-Jones, *Children as Co-researchers: The need for protection* (2014)

Sharon Vincent (ed.), *Early Intervention: Supporting and Strengthening Families* (2015)

Jane Appleton and Sue Peckover (eds), *Child Protection, Public Health and Nursing* (2015)

Julia Seng and Julie Taylor (eds), *Trauma Informed Care in the Perinatal Period: Growing forward* (2015)

Deborah Fry, Patricia Lannen, Jennifer Vanderminden, Audrey Cameron and Tabitha Casey, *Child Protection and Disability: Methodological and practical challenges for research* (2017)

Cheryl Burgess, Ruth McDonald and Sandra Sweeten, *Effective Family Support: Responding to what parents tell us* (2018)

See www.dunedinacademicpress.co.uk for details of all our publications

Working with Children and Young People Who Have Displayed Harmful Sexual Behaviour

Stuart Allardyce
National Manager of Stop it Now! Scotland

Peter Yates
Lecturer in Child and Public Protection, Edinburgh Napier University

EDINBURGH ◆ LONDON

Published by Dunedin Academic Press Limited
Head Office: Hudson House, 8 Albany Street, Edinburgh EH1 3QB
London Office: 352 Cromwell Tower, Barbican, London EC2Y 8NB

ISBN: 978-1-78046-068-0 (Paperback)
         978-1-78046-584-5 (ePub)
         978-1-78046-576-0 (Kindle edition)

British Library Cataloguing in Publication data
A catalogue record for this book is available from the British Library

Typeset by Makar Publishing Production, Edinburgh, Scotland
Printed and bound by CPI Group (UK) Ltd, Croydon, CR0 4YY

Contents

Acknowledgements

We would like to extend particular thanks to Julie Taylor for her endless enthusiasm, encouragement and invaluable guidance and support throughout the writing of this book. We are also grateful to our families for their infinite patience. All errors are our own, but we would like to thank the following generous colleagues for their comments, feedback and expert advice on particular sections of the book: Stephen Barry, Kevin Creeden, Donald Findlater, Sarah Graham, Richard Ingram, Lorraine Johnstone, Angela McCann, Ethel Quayle, Phil Rich, Berit Ritchie, Rowena Rossiter and Lisa Thornhill. We also wish to sincerely thank the many children and young people we have worked with over the years, along with their families, from whom we have learnt so much. This book is dedicated to them.

The authors

Stuart Allardyce is a qualified social worker who has specialised as a practitioner and manager in working with children and young people who have displayed harmful sexual behaviour for more than fifteen years. He is national manager of the child protection charity Stop it Now! Scotland. Additionally, he is chair of the National Organisation for the Treatment of Abusers (NOTA) Scotland, chair of the NOTA UK and Republic of Ireland Policy and Practice Committee and a trustee of White Ribbon Scotland. He is an associate at the Centre for Youth and Criminal Justice at Strathclyde University.

Dr **Peter Yates** is a lecturer in child and public protection at Edinburgh Napier University. He is a qualified social worker with more than ten years' experience of child protection, having worked in a local authority children and families practice team followed by four years as a senior practitioner within a specialist service for young people who have displayed harmful sexual behaviour. His particular research interests within this field include sibling sexual abuse and victim crossover, and he has published and presented at international conferences on these subjects.

Foreword

Sexual abuse is currently high on the societal agenda in many countries of the world. In the UK, as in the USA, a string of high-profile cases involving 'celebrity perpetrators' has brought the widespread nature of sexual harassment and sexual abuse firmly into the public consciousness. All national jurisdictions across the UK have ongoing or recently concluded public inquiries into historical abuse, though the course of these inquiries has so far proved to be far from straightforward.

While media attention given to recent high-profile cases may have increased the number of people coming forward to disclose their experiences of abuse, one of the problems with most of the public discourses that have emerged so far about sexual abuse is that they have tended to reinforce a stereotypical image of adult paedophiles preying on vulnerable children. Consequently, the very significant proportion of all child sexual abuse perpetrated not only by adults but also by other children has been downplayed. Even when reports of child- and adolescent-perpetrated child sexual abuse gain media attention, it is within a frame that presents the children as mini versions of adult sex offenders, or 'paedophiles in waiting'. The reality is somewhat different. In the largest UK study of 700 children and young people who had sexually abused others, we found that 50% had themselves been victims of sexual abuse and 50% had experienced physical abuse or domestic violence in their backgrounds (Hackett *et al.*, 2013). For many, their histories of abuse and their own offending behaviour were part and parcel of an enmeshed experience of trauma, neglect and pain. When seen through this lens, we need to respond to them as much as children in need of protection as children in need of criminalisation.

Lack of awareness of the issue of children and young people who harm others sexually promotes a distorted and stereotypical view of child sexual abuse, overplaying some risks (such as 'stranger danger') and underplaying others (for example, that most risk of sexual harm to children exists within families by people of all ages known to them). Failing to understand the specific needs of children and young people who present with harmful sexual behaviour also means that they are more likely to receive inappropriate criminal justice responses, such as sex-offender registration or community notification policies designed with adult sex offenders in mind but then applied by default to minors. Such measures, being inherently adult focused, at best fail to provide a balanced response to the issue of harmful sexual behaviour and, at worst, they may cause irreparable developmental damage to children who are drawn into their requirements (Pittman, 2013).

This book addresses this important topic with sensitivity. The authors start by exploring the important topic of how emotions, attitudes and values may impact on the professional response to the problem of children and young people's harmful sexual behaviour. They examine harmful sexual behaviour in the context of childhood sexualities, address the question of why such behaviour emerges in childhood and what the professional system can do to focus its assessment and intervention responses and to prevent the problem from occurring. At a time when a better-informed picture about the realities of child sexual abuse is urgently needed, this book provides a vital part of this complex jigsaw.

Professor Simon Hackett

Professor of Child Abuse and Neglect, Durham University and
Chair of NOTA UK and Republic of Ireland

Introduction

While estimates of prevalence vary between countries, around 19% of girls and 8% of boys worldwide will have experienced contact sexual abuse by the age of eighteen (Pereda *et al.*, 2009b; Stoltenborgh *et al.*, 2011). Impact varies from individual to individual, but a range of studies show that sexual abuse in childhood is associated with substantially compromised mental and physical health outcomes that can endure into adulthood (e.g. Davidson and Omar, 2014; Irish *et al.*, 2009; Kisiel *et al.*, 2014; Sawyerr and Bagley, 2017). Child sexual abuse is, therefore, increasingly being recognised as a widespread public health concern in contemporary society.

There is also growing awareness among researchers and childcare professionals that not all sexual abuse is perpetrated by adults. Since the 1990s various studies have shown that a significant proportion of child sexual abuse is perpetrated by children under the age of eighteen. Indeed, Hackett *et al.* (2016) estimate that at least one-third of all sexual offences against children in the UK are committed by other children.

Understanding that children and young people can be perpetrators as well as victims of sexual abuse is a challenging notion for both professionals and the public. It is a social issue that raises many questions that are difficult to answer, such as:

- How should this behaviour be conceptualised when displayed by children and young people?
- What are the most effective responses to situations where children and young people have acted in these ways?
- How do we prevent this form of abuse occurring in the first place?

This book sets out to answer these questions.

Children's rights and harmful sexual behaviour

We believe that many incidents involving sexual abuse perpetrated by children and young people are serious crimes, and proportionate management of the genuine risks that these individuals present will be necessary. However, drawing on the definition of childhood set out in the United Nations Convention on the Rights of the Child (UNICEF, 1989), we also believe that those under the age of eighteen who display this behaviour need to be seen as children first and foremost. Throughout this book we use the term 'young people' when referring to individuals aged 12–18 and 'children' when referring to individuals below the age of twelve. Nonetheless, we believe that all individuals under the age of eighteen are children, and as such deserve particular protection from harm and abuse. Preventing children and young people who have displayed harmful sexual behaviour from abusing further victims is a key safeguarding goal. However, children and young people who have displayed this behaviour also need to be protected, and – like their victims – have a right to nurture, respect, family life, education and social inclusion. We contend that responses to children and young people who have displayed harmful sexual behaviour need to be embedded in a robust children's rights perspective, even when their actions have caused considerable harm to others.

It may appear obvious to state that children are different from adults, with distinct needs and vulnerabilities arising from their developmental status. Nonetheless, it remains the case that children and young people who have displayed harmful sexual behaviour are often responded to in ways that are shaped fundamentally by the assessment and risk management of adult sex offenders. This is partly because research and practice focusing on this client group emerged in the 1980s as an adjunct to clinical practice with adult sex offenders. Since then, research has conclusively shown that children and young people represent a distinct population from adults who commit sexual offences, and pathways into – and out of – this behaviour are very different for children when compared to adults (Lussier and Blokland, 2014; McKillop *et al.*, 2015). There is now a large body of scientific evidence to support the view that children and young people who have displayed harmful sexual behaviour are not 'mini adult sex offenders'. Over the last twenty years, this has led to the evolution of practice approaches that recognise the importance of the developmental status of this client group. However, this progress in relation to direct practice is continually compromised by insensitive policy and legislation which, each year, results in ever-growing numbers of children and young people being criminalised for issues relating to sexual misconduct.

Recorded sexual crime has been rising steadily in both the UK and other countries for many years, which may, in part, relate to a growing confidence on the part of victims in reporting sexual crime to relevant authorities (Bentley, 2017; Office for National Statistics, 2017a). In line with this trend, contemporary situations where a young person sexually abuses a child or peer are accordingly more likely to be reported to the police now than they were in the past. The number of reported sexual offences by a child against another child rose in England and Wales by 71% between 2013 and 2016 (BBC, 2017) and increased by a further 7% between 2016 and 2017 (Youth Justice Board/ Ministry of Justice, 2018). Additionally, while the number of UK children in custody for sexual offences is small, the percentage of children serving prison sentences where the primary offence was a sexual crime rose from 5% in 2010 to 8% in 2015 (Janes, 2016). Such increases are not unique to the UK and are occurring in other jurisdictions such as Australia (Australian Board of Statistics, 2017). Many of these crimes committed by children and young people in the UK are of the utmost seriousness: 15% of rapes in England and Wales in 2016 involved a perpetrator under the age of eighteen (Criminal Justice Statistics, 2017). Some, however, are lesser infractions: 35% of juvenile sexual offences in 2016 attracted a caution, indicating that they were below the level of seriousness requiring prosecution (Bateman, 2017).

There are several factors that may account for the rise in recorded sexual crime involving children and young people. Over the last ten years, there has been growing public debate about how access to pornography, sexual messages and gender stereotyping – especially online and via social media – may be affecting the social and sexual development of children and young people, introducing them to sexual experiences at increasingly early ages and influencing cultural norms, particularly with respect to the normalisation of sexual violence against women and girls (Papadopoulos, 2010; Bailey, 2011). Alongside this has been considerable media coverage of young people coming to the attention of the police because of sharing self-produced sexual images – the phenomenon adults call 'sexting' (Cooper et al., 2016). We cannot exclude the possibility that more children and young people are now displaying this behaviour than ever before. However, it seems just as probable– if not more likely– that growing anxieties and uncertainty among adults about what constitutes

normative childhood sexual development and behaviour (particularly in relation to online conduct) are contributing to a climate where childhood sexual
behaviour is increasingly monitored, policed and responded to as problematic
or abusive.

This upturn in the reporting of youth sexual crime occurs in the context of
increasingly punitive approaches in many countries to the management of sex
offenders in the community. Since the 1990s, we have seen the development
of sex-offender registration in Anglophone jurisdictions such as the US and
the UK along with the introduction of community notification processes, resi-
dence restriction requirements, preventative orders and multi-agency public
protection arrangements. Young people convicted of sexual offences are regularly drawn into these processes, leading to stigmatisation and experiences
of shame for many children and their families (Pittman, 2013). These processes were developed to monitor and supervise adult offenders and were never
designed with the needs of children under the age of eighteen in mind. It is
often the case that processes implemented to protect the public place significant limits on where a child may live and attend school, as well as dictating who
they spend time with. All of these are key factors influencing positive social
development in childhood and adolescence (Rigby *et al.*, 2013b).

A recent UK study of the lived experiences of youth justice practitioners
working with this client group paints an abject picture of how some agencies
stigmatise young people and how this can impact on young people's sense of
self-worth. As one professional put it:

> [some] wanna just cut them off ... cut them out of school, so then
> they lose that social 'how to be normal with females or males,' ... no
> longer can you be anywhere without an adult or a staff member so
> again just drumming in all those 'I am deviant,' [messages] so then
> what my kids start to do is 'I'll stay home, can't go nowhere, school
> don't want me, youth clubs don't want me, nobody wants me' (Myles-
> Wright and Nee, 2017, p. 14).

Similarly, Hackett *et al.* (2015) describe the case of a twenty-four year old
man charged with a sexual offence at age seventeen and assessed at the time as
being at low risk to prepubescent children. After several years of stability and
positive progress in his life, he and his wife were devastated when their newborn

daughter was placed on the child protection register because of concerns that he presented a sexual risk to her. Stillman (2016) also describes several children and young people in the US convicted of sexual offences experiencing regular harassment and discrimination, including a twelve year old girl placed on the sex offender registry for twenty-five years. All of these cases underline the fact that children and young people who have displayed harmful sexual behaviour are increasingly being drawn into a criminal justice system that is strongly associated with stigmatisation, labelling and poor outcomes across the life course (McAra and McVie, 2010). The disproportionate use of measures such as these represent a clear denial of their rights as children.

The increasing difficulty we have as a society in responding proportionately to children and young people who have displayed harmful sexual behaviour, and in accepting their developmental status as children above all else, is ultimately a social justice issue (Letourneau and Miner, 2005; Zimring, 2009). Furthermore, a key finding in the emerging literature is that the social and sexual development of many of these children has been affected by factors such as childhood adversity, trauma, learning disability and developmental delay (McKillop *et al.*, 2015). This trend, therefore, represents the drawing of children and young people who are often already troubled into a system that is essentially iatrogenic, in which their treatment unintentionally causes them further harm. This is not to underplay the seriousness of harm these individuals have caused others, and the promotion of community safety through the prevention of further victimisation is also a fundamental social justice issue. However, we need to be mindful that young people in need can easily move from 'care' status to 'criminal' status, and by relabelling them as 'sex offenders' we embark on a dehumanising process where they are ultimately defined as 'former' or 'ex'-children (Whyte, 2008).

Use of language

Language does not passively reflect our environment; rather it is a key tool in constructing and making sense of our world. It is also one of the principal ways we communicate our values and ethical priorities. In writing this book we have paid close attention to the use of language throughout. Accordingly, we have deliberately eschewed the term 'juvenile sexual offender', which is commonly used in the international literature to describe this population. Instead we adopt the rather unwieldy term 'children and young people who have displayed harmful sexual behaviour'. We have made this choice for several reasons.

Although criminal justice responses are inevitable in some cases, the term 'juvenile sexual offender' will often be a misnomer as many of these children and young people are never charged with an offence, either because their behaviour never comes to the attention of adults or because it is dealt with as a child welfare or protection matter. Moreover, the labelling of young people as 'sex offenders' is profoundly stigmatising. With identity formation being a key aspect of child and adolescent development, it is unhelpful to use terminology that pathologises the individual and creates an identity defined precisely by what we do not want them to become. It is more difficult to change one's identity than it is one's behaviour, and being labelled a juvenile sexual offender will rarely help people feel more socially anchored as part of their community as they move into adulthood and try to become responsible citizens and positive contributors to our society (Dewhurst and Nielsen, 1999).

There is no consistent or universally agreed meaning of the term 'harmful sexual behaviour', but throughout we draw on the following definition:

> Sexual behaviours expressed by children and young people under the age of 18 years old that are developmentally inappropriate, may be harmful towards self or others and/or be abusive towards another child, young person or adult (Hackett *et al.*, 2016 p. 12).

The use of the past tense in the phrase 'children and young people who have displayed harmful sexual behaviour' is intentional. Although practitioners often talk about working with individuals 'with harmful sexual behaviour', the clear intention of any intervention is to put the behaviour in the past. Moreover, for most children the behaviour is already in their past, as the vast majority desist from such behaviour through natural maturation (Caldwell, 2016). Although risk reduction is an important goal in working with this client group, we believe that helping individuals – as well as their families and communities – safely to move on from lives defined by harm and abuse should be the focus of interventions. These are children first and foremost; the reason that we are working with them may be because they have abused others, but it does not define them, and nor should it be the sole focus of our interventions.

Purpose and structure of this book

In this book we critically appraise relevant theories, research, policy and practice guidance in relation to working with this client group. We have tried to contextualise this literature within the wider fields of child development, child protection studies, criminology, child and adolescent mental health and research into therapeutic work with children and young people. We argue that many of the practice responses to harmful sexual behaviour significantly misunderstand the nature of the challenges presented by working with these children and young people because they remain rooted in adaptations of approaches to working with adult sex offenders. We also argue that reflecting on the social contexts of sexual harm – what we do when we define actions as harmful, and the meanings we place on the notions of sexual abuse and sexual offending in contemporary society – is vital if we are to develop methods that genuinely contribute to positive outcomes for children and young people.

This book is aimed at practitioners and managers as well as students, academics and researchers in fields such as social work, child protection, law, psychology, health, psychiatry, education, law enforcement, counselling and psychotherapy. It will be relevant to those who work with children up to the age of eighteen, but it may also be of interest to those who mainly support adults involved with sexual offending who wish to explore developmental perspectives in their work with young adults. We write as practitioners working in a UK context, but we have reflected the international nature of this issue.

Chapter 1 considers how social attitudes and values influence practice with this client group and examines the implications for reflective practice and staff support. Chapter 2 offers an overview of research on normative sexual development in the emerging field of childhood sexualities and explores the implications of this literature for how practitioners identify harmful sexual behaviour in pre- and post-pubescence. Chapter 3 provides an overview of descriptive studies of this population, drawing on emerging trends such as the move from small, clinical studies to larger data sets and the increasing internationalisation of research. Chapters 4, 5 and 6 chart a shift from 'traits based', psychologically orientated views of children and young people who have displayed harmful sexual behaviour to more contextual and sociologically orientated conceptualisations of this issue in recent discussions of aetiology, assessment and intervention, respectively. Chapter 7 considers the dimensions of gender, age, developmental background and victim type, and how attention to these variables can help practitioners target assessment and intervention approaches in more effective and individualised ways. Chapter 8 reviews the literature on online harmful sexual behaviour, and our concluding chapter explores emerging debates about the prevention of harmful sexual behaviour. Each chapter ends with a summary of key learning points for practitioners.

A final note of caution. This book is not comprehensive and should be considered by readers as a map to help them navigate this developing field of childcare and forensic practice. For professionals, it should not be seen as a substitute for detailed guidance or high-quality training and support. Much can be learnt from a book, but engaging with children and young people who have displayed harmful sexual behaviour requires interpersonal sensitivity, relationship skills and self-awareness. As practitioners, we, like many others, have found involvement with this client group immensely rewarding and enriching. We have also benefited from knowledgeable and sensitive supervision and external consultancy, supports we consider necessary if professionals are to reflect on their own practice and to consider issues around impact. This work is emotive and can elicit profound and searching questions for practitioners about a range of themes including risk, parenting, power, crime, social justice, gender relationships, sexual thoughts and feelings, consent, intimacy and the nature of childhood itself. We hope this book has a role to play in orientating professionals to the key issues and debates in this field. However, it is not an alternative to the invaluable learning that is gathered through direct practice, opportunities for constructive self-reflection, observation of professionals more knowledgeable than oneself, and engagement with the lived experiences of service users.

Chapter 1

Attitudes and values

Introduction

In a recent UK study, a group of young people convicted of sexual offences were asked about their views of themselves. One young person said he did not think of himself as a sex offender, but believed others saw him that way. 'I don't like it', he commented, 'I want to try and get a normal life. I can have one, sort of, but it is hard' (Janes, 2016, p. 255).

By contrast, another recent study refers to a fourteen year old boy described in a practitioner's report thus:

> He identified strongly with the label of 'sex offender' and the negative emotions that encompassed that label. He became withdrawn during treatment and he made a number of negative comments about himself. He was not able to separate himself from his label (Hackett *et al.*, 2015, p. 249).

Labelling, and the assumptions that go with it, are some of the key challenges in working with this client group and can influence direct practice in many ways. The sexual abuse of children can transgress our core personal and social values. In this chapter we explore the attitudes and values that underpin labelling, and some of the powerful emotions that can be experienced by professionals undertaking work with these young people. We examine how these feelings can relate to social attitudes to sex offenders generally, and to children and young people who have sexually abused specifically. We explore how these feelings and attitudes can impact on practice, particularly when working with client resistance and managing risk. We discuss barriers to engagement with parents, and conclude with a discussion of the importance of reflective practice and supervision when working with this client group.

Initial responses to harmful sexual behaviour

CASE SCENARIO

Jane has been the social worker for Harry (thirteen) and Sophie (six) for nine months. When Jane first became involved with the family, Harry rarely attended high school and Sophie arrived at primary school most mornings unwashed and wearing dirty clothes. Their mother, Mary, was drinking too much and her boyfriend was violent towards her. Mary herself had been in care as a child and found the demands of being a parent challenging. Over several months, Mary ended the relationship with her boyfriend, reduced her drinking and showed improvement in the care of her children. Jane had recently decided in supervision that it would be appropriate to close their case.

Jane then received an unexpected phone call from Mary. She sounded very distressed and told Jane that her next-door neighbour had visited that morning. The neighbour had angrily accused Harry of sexually abusing Eva, the neighbour's five year old daughter. The neighbour said that, yesterday afternoon, Eva had been playing with Sophie in their back garden after school and Harry had joined them. Harry took Eva behind a bush and told her that he wanted to 'show her what grown-ups do when they love each other'. He put his hand between her legs, under her clothes and then put his finger 'right inside her flower'. She told him this hurt and asked him to stop. She ran home and was very upset, but was only able to tell her mother what happened the following morning when she refused to go to school. Mary says that she thinks the allegation is malicious because she recently fell out with her neighbour. She cannot believe that Harry would have acted in this way.

This scenario is fictional, but such situations regularly come to the attention of child welfare services. A recent Freedom of Information request revealed that 32,452 reports were made to police in England and Wales between 2012 and 2016 involving alleged sexual offences by children against other children. This represents an average of more than twenty-two initial concerns of this nature every day (Barnardo's, 2017).

Receiving a call like this is demanding for even the most experienced of practitioners. During the call, Jane will need to listen to intimate details of sexual conduct that may be abhorrent and upsetting to hear. She will have to gather information to ascertain what steps need to be followed to investigate this serious allegation thoroughly and to safeguard all of the children involved. She will also need to pay careful attention to her relationship with Mary, as a positive outcome for the children will require Jane to respond to the mother's distress and confusion in a calm and containing manner.

Jane has worked with Harry for some time. Some immediate questions that may be prompted for her might include:

- Were there warning signs that she could have picked up on that might have prevented the incident happening in the first place?

- Is the behaviour experimental and opportunistic or is it more ingrained and planned, and perhaps an indicator of more deep-seated problems?
- How much of a risk is Harry to other children, now and in the future?
- Is it safe for Harry to remain living at home? Does he present an ongoing risk to Eva, or even Sophie, his own sister? Might he already have abused Sophie?
- How safe will Harry be within his own community further to this allegation?
- How can these families continue to live together safely as neighbours?
- Why has Harry acted in this way? Does this mean that he has been sexually abused himself? And if he was abused, who abused him and is he still at risk?

A disclosure of this nature will typically lead to an investigation involving police and social work, necessitating interviews with Eva as the alleged victim and Harry as the alleged perpetrator of a serious crime. It is likely that Sophie will also be interviewed and that she and her brother may be separated while further assessment is undertaken. Practice situations such as these are rarely emotionally neutral. While hearing about the allegation, Jane may experience various feelings such as anxiety, sadness, loss, disgust or anger. During the investigation, she will need to remain alert to potentially competing and conflicting feelings of sympathy and antipathy towards different participants. These feelings are not always easily predictable, and Jane may, at different times, feel sympathy towards Eva for the distress that she has experienced, or anger because of the problems her allegations cause for Harry. Jane may also be angry with Harry for what he has done, or feel sorry for him on the basis of the abuse she thinks that he may have experienced in order for him to have acted in this way. During a home visit to explain the legal situation, plan interviews with the children and negotiate a safety plan, a variety of competing feelings may similarly be evoked in relation to Mary herself and to the victim's mother. How practitioners respond to situations such as these, and the safeguarding decisions they then make, can be influenced in various ways by the feelings that they experience.

Public and professional attitudes towards sex offenders

Attitudes and values have an important role to play in how professionals respond to practice situations. Because of this, understanding something about social attitudes towards sex offenders and to child sexual abuse can provide a useful backdrop to understanding the influences on professional decision-making in cases where children and young people have acted in sexually abusive ways.

Research suggests that – more than any other type of crime – sexual offences against children are perceived by the public as particularly heinous (Brown, 2009). They can elicit a range of powerful emotions including fear, moral outrage, disdain and disgust (Bastian *et al.*, 2013; Salerno *et al.*, 2010). These feelings may be grounded in empathy and compassion for a particular child who has been victimised, but they can also relate to more general social attitudes about sex offenders and crimes against children. These attitudes appear natural to us, but are influenced by factors such as personal experiences, political rhetoric, the media, and the views of our family, friends, work colleagues and community rather than an empirically grounded understanding of the factors relating to the sexual abuse of children.

The media commonly depicts sex offenders who have abused children as 'evil monsters' or 'predatory paedophiles', with coverage typically focusing on high-profile – but relatively rare – serious cases. These tragic situations usually involve the sexual murder of children, the predations of celebrities, serial offences committed in institutional settings or unusual cases such as those involving female sex offenders. These depictions obscure the picture that emerges from empirical research, which reveals that most sex offenders are adult or adolescent males, are known to their victims, and usually do not sexually reoffend (McCartan, 2010). Exceptional cases, therefore, significantly distort public understanding of risk, community safety and the likelihood of rehabilitation for most offenders (Fox, 2013).

Research into how sexual crimes are reported in the media has often focused on how this kind of coverage influences public attitudes and values (Soothill and Walby, 1991; Cowburn and Dominelli, 2001; Wilson and Silverman, 2002). One recent study, for example, found that British readers of tabloid newspapers (which often use hostile language when representing sex offenders) expressed significantly more negative perceptions about sex offenders than readers of broadsheet newspapers (Harper and Hogue, 2015). The view that many members of the public have of sex offenders – particularly those who abuse children – as subhuman, parallels treatment of other socially vilified groups (e.g. economic migrants, people who are homeless, members of the Roma community). This process of dehumanisation can easily lead to the legitimisation of draconian legislation and the denial of human rights. In a UK study of social attitudes, Viki *et al.* (2012) found that the more members of the public perceived sex offenders as lacking uniquely human traits, the more likely they were to endorse interventions such as extended custodial sentences, chemical castration, exclusion from society and even capital punishment.

The professional values and codes of ethics of most helping professions attach importance to the notion of human dignity and support the promotion of human rights (e.g. Scottish Social Services Council, 2014). Nonetheless, professionals are not immune to the feelings and biases described above, which can result in tensions between professional and personal values in practice situations. Several studies have shown that, in the absence of working with or receiving specific training about sex offenders, professionals may also have negative attitudes and stereotypical views towards this client group (Craig, 2005; Hogue and Peebles, 1997). Professionals may, therefore, also make assumptions about the general levels of risk posed by sex offenders, the typical dynamics involved in the sexual abuse of children and the likely outcomes of rehabilitation, which are driven by inaccurate stereotypes and which can impact on decision-making in practice.

Public and professional attitudes towards young people who have displayed harmful sexual behaviour

These attitudes towards sex offenders are mirrored in surveys examining public attitudes towards young people who have displayed harmful sexual behaviour. For example, studies of undergraduates in North America have found pessimistic attitudes concerning whether young people charged with sexual offences could ever be rehabilitated (Sahlstrom and Jeglic, 2008; Rogers and Ferguson, 2011), while a US study of 125 undergraduates found that feelings of disgust provoked by a fictional vignette featuring the sexual assault of a fifteen year old girl by a seventeen year old boy correlated with a range of assumptions about the seventeen year old such as whether he had low levels of empathy (Stevenson *et al.*, 2015). Furthermore, Kernsmith *et al.* (2009), in a US telephone survey of 733 members of the public, found that 71% were afraid of adolescents who had been charged with a sexual offence and 85% supported the idea that they should be on the sex offenders register.

These feelings and thoughts are often shared by professionals, such as Jane, the social worker in the case study given earlier in this chapter. A small study of the experiences of eighteen counsellors in the US and Australia working with this client group found that feelings of confusion, guilt and disgust were common (Chassman *et al.*, 2010). A larger study of thirty-four US school counsellors found stereotypical and negative attitudes towards these young people, generally grounded in knowledge that was hearsay, anecdotal or subjective (Morgan *et al.*, 2016). Although it did not survey attitudes and values, a much larger UK study of childcare practitioners and managers (n=578) found that two-thirds felt they had relatively low confidence in working directly with this client group, with many reporting feeling 'upset' (40%), 'anxious' (36%) and 'worried' (25%) when thinking about their experiences with these young people (Clements *et al.*, 2017).

This picture in relation to the views that both professionals and the public can have of children and young people who have displayed harmful sexual behaviour is complicated further by fundamental issues relating to how we conceptualise childhood. Since the 1990s, media coverage of exceptional cases involving youth violence (such as the 1993 murder of two year old Jamie Bulger by two ten year old boys in Liverpool) has led to considerable scrutiny of the meaning of childhood and the capacity of children to act in ways that can be seen as 'evil' (Muncie, 2014). This reflects a tendency in modernity to construct children in one of two ways: as innocent, vulnerable and in need of care and protection, or as threatening, dangerous, and in need of strict discipline (Brownlie, 2001; Jenks, 2005). In addition to these binary constructions of children as either inherently innocent or dangerous, since at least the nineteenth century the primary boundary between constructions of childhood and adulthood has been the experience of adult sexuality (Angelides, 2004; Gittins, 1998). Childhood is often considered to be a period of sexual innocence, and children who transgress the boundaries of innocent childhood through sexual activity might quickly be cast as a 'dangerous' child (Gittins, 1998). These binary constructions of childhood play out in legislative and policy contexts in various ways. The fact that most states adopt an age of consent that marks the legal age at which a person is considered to be competent to consent to sexual acts, while also holding any child below that age responsible for abusive behaviour that may result in them being prosecuted for committing a sexual offence, would be a clear example of this.

These binary constructions can also result in stereotypical thinking, hindering the capacity of professionals to appreciate complexity, and to recognise the specific needs and circumstances of children they are working with. In particular, it can lead to two principal responses to situations in which children are alleged to have displayed harmful sexual behaviour. On the one hand, attempts may be made to preserve the notion of children as vulnerable, innocent and lacking the capacity to be abusive. Barbaree and Marshall (2008) suggest that adolescent sexually abusive behaviour is often dismissed as 'boys being boys', and that professionals can misinterpret abusive situations as young people experimenting or being involved with sexual play. Similarly, in a study of social workers' retrospective accounts of decision-making in cases involving sexual behaviour between siblings, Yates (2017b) found that social workers often framed children as vulnerable and intending no sexual harm to others, and children's sibling relationships as non-abusive and of intrinsic value. It was not within the social workers' underlying perspective of sibling relationships to consider them a possible context in which abuse could take place. When confronted by sibling sexual behaviour that might reasonably be regarded as abusive (entailing, for example, large age-gaps or use of force), the social workers often engaged in a number of mechanisms to maintain their perspectives of children and of sibling relationships. These mechanisms included doubting that the sexual behaviour had happened, resisting labelling the behaviour as abuse, and overlooking the potential emotional impact of the sexual behaviour on the victim in their decision-making. On the other hand, children and young people displaying harmful sexual behaviour may so contravene our expectations of what it means to be a child that they risk not only being cast as a dangerous child but also losing the 'protective cloak of childhood' altogether (Woodiwiss, 2014, p. 147). They may, therefore, be seen as a 'mini-adult sex offender', subject to all of the dehumanising stereotyping of sex offenders outlined above. Yates (2017b) found some evidence of this, particularly in cases involving older adolescents who were perceived by professionals to express no remorse for their behaviour. Jane will, therefore, need to be acutely aware of her spontaneous feelings and attitudes to children and young people who have displayed harmful sexual behaviour and how they can impact on her judgements as she engages with Mary and Harry further to Eva's allegation.

Direct practice with young people and their families

Professionals report that they often find building a trusting relationship with a child or young person who is understandably reluctant to discuss their sexual behaviour a considerable challenge (Clements *et al.*, 2017). A study by Bankes (2006) demonstrates how recurring patterns of unconscious processes between the worker and the young person who has acted in an abusive way can affect how the worker engages with their client and their capacity to remain attuned to them. Eleven UK practitioners who worked with this client group consented to have sessions with clients videoed. In reviewing transcripts of those sessions, practitioners were able clearly to identify moments where they felt frustrated, anxious, resentful and antipathetic towards the young person. These correlated with points where they thought the young person was not taking responsibility for their behaviour, which they saw as evidence of his being unable to self-manage risk. The transcripts showed that these moments coincided with times when practitioners used more interrogative styles of questioning, spoke much more than their client, interrupted silences and ignored cues when the young person was introducing new, relevant themes to the session. Bankes describes this as the 'responsibility avoidance syndrome', a process whereby the young person appears not to be taking responsibility for their behaviour, which then leads unconsciously to the practitioner feeling the burden of prevention of further abuse shifting from the client to them. This arouses anxiety and frustration, which is acted out in more persecutory ways of working. These processes may lead to further disengagement from the client, which Bankes describes as a 'spiral of avoidance' (Bankes, 2006, p. 256) (see Figure 1.1).

The question of responsibility avoidance also arises in working with parents. Clements *et al.* (2017) found that many practitioners described challenges in working with parents who deny that their child has acted in a harmful sexual way or who conceptualised the behaviour in a different way from professionals. One healthcare professional succinctly articulated their frustrations in the following way:

> [when working with parents] 1. There is usually a background of likely abuse, 2. this background is strongly denied by the parent, who 3. insists the child is autistic (Clements *et al.*, 2017, p. 18).

The picture that emerges from research is more complex and diverse. Parents in these situations respond in a variety of ways to finding out that their son

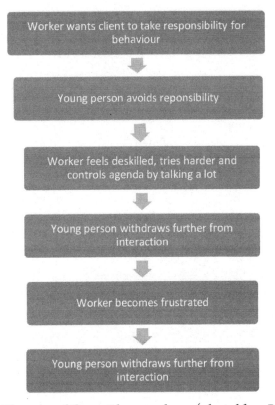

Figure 1.1: The responsibility avoidance syndrome (adapted from Bankes, 2006).

or daughter has sexually harmed another child. Hackett *et al.* (2014), in a UK case file review analysing the responses of 117 parents to this kind of situation, found initial feelings of anger, shock, guilt and fear were common. Longer-term responses ranged from parents being entirely supportive of their child, through to outright rejection (usually where the victim was a close family member such as a sibling or cousin), with many parents reporting strong feelings of confusion and uncertainty.

Parents such as Mary may worry that their child will persist with such behaviour into adulthood and will go on to become an adult sex offender. Media and cultural depictions of both sex offenders and of 'dangerous children' may seem incommensurate with her view of Harry, and his acting in a sexual manner may challenge inherent schema she has of childhood as a time of asexual innocence. Mary's resistance to accepting Eva's allegation may, therefore, stem from her not wanting to confront the loss of a particular idea of her child. Initial parental denial or minimisation can, therefore, be seen as a defence mechanism, which parents use to help them to cope when they hear overwhelming information about their child's actions that they cannot process and may even find traumatic (Morrison, 2004). As Chaffin puts it:

> From a trauma-processing perspective, features such as denial, unfocused anger, minimisation of the problem and ambivalence towards both the alleged victim and the abuser would be considered par for the course, rather than evidence of toxic parenting or deep-seated psychopathology (Chaffin, 1996, p. 113).

In many cases, parents will, with time, start to process experiences of anger and loss and will naturally move on from these positions of denial and minimisation, but professional approaches that are confrontational and lacking in empathy may lead to more entrenched positions being taken. It may be helpful when Jane meets Mary, for example, to underline that the allegations concerning Harry's behaviour are very serious, but incidents of this nature are not uncommon. She could reassure Mary by telling her that most children do not persist with such behaviour into adulthood, and that there are interventions shown to be effective with young people who abuse. Jane would also need to be prepared for strong feelings that Mary may have during their meeting. Mary may experience Jane's questions as intrusive, and it is likely that she will be concerned about whether the outcome of a child protection investigation will lead to the removal of her children from her care. Sensitivity and compassion as well as collaborative ways of working are needed when a parent's feelings of anger and anxiety are displaced on to professionals in these situations.

Reflective practice and staff support

Jane will need to draw on skills in relation to self-reflection when responding to this situation (Fook and Gardner, 2007). Being able to focus on aspects of the self in one's role as a practitioner and having the capacity to address the interplay of feelings, values, thoughts and actions that arise in practice situations is an essential skill in safeguarding work with children generally, and in working with this client group specifically. In particular, being able to appreciate how personal values about sex offending and childhood can link to personal anxieties and feelings we may have when working with children who have acted in abusive ways is vital. Being aware of spontaneous thoughts and feelings when working with resistance from children and/ or their parents can help frame responses that are effective and empathic.

This is also important with respect to external pressures placed upon practitioners (for example, by other professionals and society) to be 'effective' when managing risk. This involves recognising that child protection practice is not a rational-technical activity where professionals are impartial gleaners of facts, who can switch off feelings to situations involving social injustice and the emotional pain and hurt of children and their families (Munro, 2011). Cooper's (2005) analysis of the death of Victoria Climbié in 2000 concluded that the suppression of emotions by social workers compromised their decision-making and capacity to appreciate and respond effectively to risk. It is highly likely that suppression of emotions in working with this client group compromises practice in similar ways. As Morrison (2007) argues, social workers in Jane's position need to pay attention to their emotions but avoid being overwhelmed by them, and instead use their feelings as sources of information and as signals of matters requiring attention.

Practitioner well-being and effective practice generally corresponds with organisational approaches that support workers' reflectiveness. Clements *et al.* (2017) found that supervision, peer support and advice from senior colleagues all play a vital role in building the skills, knowledge and resilience required when working with this client group, with supervision being significantly associated with practitioner confidence. Practitioners in this study described being able to use supervision to reflect on the strong feelings and the processes common to work with children and young people who have sexually abused others. Unfortunately, these kinds of professional supports may be becoming increasingly rare, with a Community Care survey in 2013 finding that one-third of UK social workers were not receiving supervision; many respondents perceived that it was not regarded as an organisational priority (McGregor, 2013). However, it may be not just the availability of supervision that is important but also more specifically the kind of supervision practitioners receive. In a study of sixteen UK specialist practitioners working with this client group, a clear distinction was made by practitioners between line management supervision (addressing the needs of the organisation) and more reflective practice supervision (addressing the needs of the practitioner). Only the latter was able to assist practitioners with the feelings and associated processes that arose in the work (Almond, 2014). Knowledge of the subject matter was also noted as contributing to effective supervision.

Accordingly, Jane's reflective practice will, therefore, best be supported if she has a supervisor who can help her to:

- identify relevant information in this case and how this is to be sought;
- provide possible explanations of how the problem emerged;
- process and make sense of feelings raised by the case;
- analyse available information to formulate a clear and defendable plan to support Harry and his family and to ensure that risks are managed effectively and reduced over time (Swann, 2017, p. 37).

Conclusion

In this chapter we have considered how societal attitudes towards sex offenders and children may influence the responses of professionals, parents and children themselves, when harmful sexual behaviour is reported. These feelings and attitudes may lead to responses that are not proportionate to particular practice situations. On the one hand, unconscious processes informed by anxiety and responsibility about risk may lead to practices that are defensive, even punitive, and fail to fully appreciate the child or young person's welfare needs. On the other hand, an inclination to try to preserve a notion of childhood as a period of sexual innocence may encourage a denial or minimisation of the behaviour, its seriousness and ongoing risks. Anxiety about stigmatisation by services and professionals on the part of children and their parents may also challenge the development of therapeutic relationships.

One of the key messages for practitioners from this chapter is that they may be pulled in different directions by the child who has displayed harmful sexual behaviour, the child who has been victimised, and their respective parents and families. Paying critical attention to the attitudes, feelings and assumptions that inform everyday actions and decisions in practice is vital for professionals working in this area. Supervision allows space for reflection on practice in order to sustain a balanced and proportionate response and to ensure that core values around dignity and respect are maintained when working with these children and their families.

Additionally, advice given to children and their families, as well as the decisions made, should never be grounded in misconceptions and unhelpful attitudes. They instead must be informed by an understanding of the child in their particular circumstances and up-to-date empirical knowledge about working with this client group. The remaining chapters of this book focus on this evidence base and how it can be operationalised in policy and practice.

Chapter 2

Childhood sexualities

Introduction

When professionals receive information concerning children's sexual behaviour, there are many tasks to which they need to attend. Identifying any safeguarding issues in relation to the children involved and establishing whether a crime has been committed are priorities. However, professionals need to establish first of all whether the behaviour sits within expected parameters of healthy and safe sexual development. If not, they need a way of conceptualising this behaviour: is it inappropriate, problematic or sexually abusive? This will inform what level of further assessment is needed and what measures are immediately required to promote safety.

In Chapter 1 we argued that attitudes and values shape professional responses to situations involving harmful sexual behaviour in childhood and adolescence. In contemporary culture, the sexual behaviour of children and young people is typically considered inherently concerning. This means that prepubescent children are often regarded as asexual, while sexually active adolescents are often seen as involved in risk-taking behaviour. This can make it difficult for professionals and parents to differentiate what is normative or expected sexual behaviour at different stages of childhood from behaviour that is more problematic or abusive.

In this chapter we suggest that social and cultural context must be taken into account, along with an appreciation of the subjective experiences of participants, when understanding children's and young people's sexual behaviour. We contend that, if practitioners are to make sense of abusive sexual behaviour displayed by children and adolescents, they first need to understand how sexual behaviour naturally presents in childhood. We consider a continuum of sexual behaviour ranging from normative through to abusive and violent behaviour, and examine how this idea is both supported and complicated by research into sexual development in childhood and adolescence. Uncommon sexual behaviour and interests are not necessarily harmful, and professionals need carefully to question for whom the behaviour is problematic before it is labelled as such. We conclude by arguing that all children and young people have a right to sexual expression and sexual well-being within the boundaries of behaviour and interests that do not cause harm to themselves or others.

A continuum of childhood sexual behaviour

Consider the following scenarios:

a. A fourteen year old girl enters her six year old brother's bedroom while he is sleeping. She touches his penis and inserts her finger into his anus. She has done this on three separate occasions.

b. A nursery worker finds a four year old boy with a five year old boy's penis in his mouth in the playground tunnel. Neither seems upset when the nursery worker intervenes and speaks to them about appropriate physical contact.

c. A distressed fifteen year old girl tells her teacher that her sixteen year old boyfriend asked her to perform oral sex on him. When she refused, he got angry, took out a knife and forced her to fellate him.

d. A passenger informs a bus driver that a fourteen year old boy is masturbating at the back of the bus, touching his penis underneath his trousers. The boy has a moderate learning disability, and does not seem to understand why the behaviour is wrong. This is the first time he is known to have done this.

e. Two fifteen year old boys have anal sex. This occurs in private and in the context of a consensual relationship. One of the boys tells a friend who then informs a teacher.

f. A thirteen year old boy has accessed videos online depicting the rape of adult women. He has persisted in trying to access this material despite parental boundaries and supervision further to his mother finding out.

All of these examples raise questions about what constitutes 'normal' or 'typical' sexual behaviour at different stages of childhood. Summarising what is 'normative' for prepubescent children – i.e. '(that which) pertains to the average, as expected, behaviour patterns of a group or community' (Barker Robert, 1995, p. 64) – Johnson (2015) states that:

> Natural and healthy sexual exploration during childhood is an information-gathering process wherein children explore each other's and their own bodies by looking and touching (e.g. playing doctor), as well as exploring gender roles and behaviours (e.g. playing house). Children involved in normal sexual play are generally of similar age, size and developmental status and participate on a voluntary basis. While siblings engage in mutual sexual exploration, most sexual

play is between children who have an ongoing mutually enjoyable play and/or school friendship. The sexual behaviours are limited in type and frequency and occur in several periods of the child's life. The child's interest in sex and sexuality is balanced by curiosity about other aspects of his or her life ... The feelings of the children regarding the sexual behaviour are generally light-hearted and spontaneous (Johnson, 2015, Chapter 1).

Araji (2004) summarises normative adolescent sexual development in the following way:

> Many marked changes related to size, shape and functioning of the emotional, cognitive and interpersonal relationships occur as adolescents make the transition from pre-adolescence (Lerner and Galambos, 1998). Structural changes related to sexual development include growth of the penis and testes and lengthening of the vagina. With the onset of puberty youth experience changes related to reproduction: girls experience menstruation, boys begin to produce seminal fluids and ejaculation occurs. As physical and structural changes take place, adolescence is a time when many young men and women encounter their first interpersonal sexual experiences ... Sexual interest, sexual arousal, kissing, sexual intercourse and oral sex are also considered normal or normative for adolescents ... (sexual) interactions prior to puberty tend to be more exploratory and social. After puberty behaviours such as kissing, flirting and foreplay (touching, fondling) are more goal orientated towards intimacy, sexual arousal and orgasm (Araji, 2004, pp. 20–2).

Not all sexual behaviour displayed by children and young people is normative in nature. Chaffin *et al.* (2002) suggest that, if any or all of the following criteria are met, children's sexual behaviour may require more detailed assessment:

- occurs at a frequency greater than would be developmentally expected;
- interferes with the child's development;
- occurs with coercion, intimidation or force;
- is associated with emotional distress;
- occurs between children of divergent ages or developmental abilities;
- repeatedly recurs in secrecy after intervention by caregivers.

These are key questions that professionals need to ask when assessing children's sexual behaviour. If we consider the scenarios in light of these criteria, all of the examples would seem to require some level of further assessment with the exception of (e), involving the two fifteen year old boys. Scenario (b), involving the young boys at nursery, does not obviously meet any of the criteria, but the nature of the behaviour is sufficiently unusual to warrant further inquiry. In pursuing a more detailed assessment, rather than simply focusing on whether behaviour is harmful or not, Hackett (2010) suggests that professionals consider children's sexual behaviour as existing on a continuum stretching from normal behaviour through to abusive and violent behaviour (see Figure 2.1). Behaviour that fits into the latter three categories of the continuum can be considered to be harmful according to Hackett *et al.*'s (2016, p. 12) definition of harmful sexual behaviour, which '[is] developmentally inappropriate, may be harmful towards self or others and/or be abusive towards another child, young person or adult'.

Example (e) involves age-appropriate, consensual sexual activity between two fifteen year old boys. There are no indicators of harm to self or others, although professionals aware of this behaviour may need to rule out whether there are power differences between the participants and ascertain whether information about safer sexual practices is needed, just as would also be appropriate regarding sexual intercourse between similar-aged boys and girls. Self-touch by the learning disabled boy on a bus – example (d) – could be considered inappropriate. While it is acceptable age-appropriate behaviour in private, here it is exhibited in a public setting and there may be implications for his positive social development if he does not develop a better understanding of place-appropriate behaviour. The thirteen year old boy accessing pornography of an extreme nature – example (f) – would be considered problematic rather than abusive as no victim is involved. However, this preoccupation with non-consensual sex would be seen by many adults as concerning, and may be potentially developmentally harmful to himself. Assessment of the function of this behaviour and the compulsivity attached to it would be necessary. The sexual assault of the fifteen year old girl at knifepoint – example (c) – would fit into the 'violent category', while the anal penetration of a six year old child by his older sibling – example (a) – would be termed 'abusive'. Both are likely to lead to distress and psychological – as well as possibly physical – harm to the victim.

Normal	Inappropriate	Problematic	Abusive	Violent
• Developmentally expected	• Single instances of inappropriate behaviour	• Problematic and concerning behaviours	• Victimising intent or outcome	• Physically violentsexual abuse
• Socailly acceptable	• Socailly acceptable behaviour within peer group	• Developmentally unusual and socially unexpected	• Includes misuse of power	• Highly intrusive
• Consensual, mutual, reciprocal	• Context for behaviour may be inappropriate	• No overt elements of victimisation	• Coercion and force to ensure victim compliance	• Instrumental violence which is physiologically and / or sexually arousing to the perpetrator
• Shared decion making	• Generally consensual and reciprocal	• Consensus issues may be unclear	• Intrusive	• Sadism
		• May lack reciprocity or equal power	• Informed consent lacking, or not able to be freely given by victim	
		• May imclude levels of compulsivity	• May Include elements of expressive violence	

Figure 2.1 The continuum of sexual behaviour. Hackett, 2010. Reproduced by kind permission of the author.

Neither examples (e) or (d) would be considered to be harmful sexual behaviour according to Hackett *et al.*'s (2016) definition, although in the UK (e) could be prosecuted as a sexual offence as both boys are below the legal age of consent. Similarly, (d) could technically be prosecuted as a public order matter despite it being inappropriate rather than harmful behaviour. Serious behaviour like (a) and (c) could also be prosecuted, as could problematic behaviour like (f), which in the UK would fall under legislation regarding extreme pornography. Whether a particular behaviour constitutes a sexual offence is, therefore, often a misleading guide as to where the sexual behaviour might best be placed along the continuum, and would be a poor indicator for the appropriate allocation of scarce resources.

This leaves (b), the interaction between two boys in a playground tunnel at nursery. The behaviour here seems imitative of oral sex, which may have been seen or experienced by one or both boys and, therefore, needs to be investigated as a child protection concern. However, this could equally be two boys just exploring their bodies and doing something that feels nice to them. Further information about the children's relationship, the meaning of the behaviour for them, their development and their respective family backgrounds should be sought before a determination could be made about where the behaviour sits on the continuum. It may be hard to make such a judgement unless a pattern of behaviour were to emerge.

Problematic sexual behaviour

The notion of there being a continuum of behaviour easily arranged by age category – with normative behaviour at one end, abusive behaviour at the other, and problematic behaviour in the middle – is exemplified in a range of resources often used by practitioners, such as the 'Brook traffic light system' (Brook, 2016) and checklists developed by Cunningham and MacFarlane (1991), Ryan and Blum (1994), Johnson and Feldmeth (1993) and Johnson (2015). These resources are helpful and necessary, as only 9% of the 589 UK practitioners surveyed in Clements *et al.*'s (2017) study strongly agreed that they were confident in identifying harmful sexual behaviour in childhood or adolescence. However, there are significant challenges in locating behaviour that sits at the threshold between categories on the continuum. In one UK study, a group of experts in children's prepubescent sexual behaviour was asked to classify vignettes according to levels of concern. There were high levels of agreement with respect to normative and abusive behaviour, but high levels of disagreement with respect to behaviour deemed inappropriate or problematic (Vosmer *et al.*, 2009). Such judgements can be especially difficult around puberty in middle childhood, when children of the same age often vary in levels of physical and emotional maturity. A study of 335 US professionals' views of the acceptability of various sexual behaviours at different ages found little disagreement with respect to the behaviour of four year olds, but many differences with respect to the behaviour of twelve year olds (Haugaard, 1996).

This lack of consensus arises because sexual behaviour is not just biological but also social in nature. What constitutes normative and, indeed, problematic, sexual behaviour is socially constructed. That is to say, it is contingent upon the social conditions and culture of a particular time and place. In relation to the assessment of problematic sexual behaviour, Araji (2004) suggests that, after identifying whether behaviour violates rules or laws and establishing whether there was a lack of consent or of equality, or if coercion or force was involved, practitioners should then ask the following questions. Does the behaviour:

- put the individual or others at risk of physical harm, disease or exploitation?
- interfere with the individual's overall development, learning, or social and family relationships, or that of others?
- cause the individual, or others, feelings of discomfort, confusion, embarrassment, guilt or to feel negative about themselves?
- result in dysfunction for the development of healthy relationships or is it destructive to the family, peer group, community or society?

This contextual framing recognises that problematic behaviour is a construct used to govern children's sexual behaviour within particular social and historical norms and needs to be used cautiously. An initial assessment may necessitate moving beyond a framework that generally decontextualises behaviour and tends to ignore social and cultural factors that help shape the meanings that we bring to sexual experiences. In particular, sexual behaviour continuum frameworks often fail to differentiate according to whether the children involved are boys or girls or, indeed, if they have any form of learning disability. More thorough assessment needs to involve ascertaining the meaning placed on the behaviour not only by adults (including parents and carers) but also by all children involved, recognising that children may, at times, not always appreciate harm because of lack of developmental understanding and maturity.

When considering childhood sexual behaviour, professionals are required to make sense of multiple and often contradictory subjective experiences and the interpretations of different participants. Professionals then need to organise those meanings in an empirical and ethically grounded way. There may be disagreement between different individuals about what is considered harmful (e.g. professionals and parents, parent and child, the parents of victim and perpetrator or even between professionals). Sensitive mediation and education (both of children and adults) may be necessary in such situations. While acknowledging strong feelings of participants, practitioners need to ensure that discussions and any decisions made are guided by a focus on what actual harm was – or could have been – caused, and by proportionate estimates of future risk, as well as being grounded, as far as possible, in the empirical literature on children's sexual development.

Approaches to researching child and adolescent sexual behaviour

Over the last thirty years, empirical data on sexual behaviour in childhood has proved to be elusive. This field of childhood sexualities – described by one commentator as the 'last frontier in sex research' (Money, 1976, p. 12) – draws on a range of methodologies such as asking adults to recall their own sexual experiences in childhood (Lamb and Coakley, 1993; e.g. Lamb, 2004), adult observations of the sexual behaviour of children in their care (e.g. Friedrich *et al.*, 2000; Kaeser *et al.*, 2000) and interviewing children and young people directly about their sexual knowledge, understanding or experiences (e.g. Brilleslijper-Kater and Baartman, 2000). All have significant limitations, such as reporting bias when adults recall sexuality in childhood, and the limits to observing behaviour that takes place largely in private.

Incompatible methodologies, as well as the changing nature of what are deemed to be appropriate forms of sexual expression and interaction across different times and cultures, mean that no unified body of knowledge has emerged to date in relation to the base rates of different sexual behaviours during childhood. Nonetheless, research can assist practitioners in ascertaining the extent to which particular behaviour falls outside developmental and cultural norms. Furthermore, an understanding of the relevant literature can assist practitioners in establishing precisely what is known – and not known – empirically about children's sexual behaviour and can help us situate and contextualise our own values and attitudes when responding to practice situations. The next two sections provide an overview of this research in relation to prepuberty and adolescence.

Sexuality in prepuberty

Young children are not asexual. In-utero penile erections have been observed in boys, particularly during the third trimester and represent normal physiological activity at this stage (Jakobovits, 2001). Spontaneous erections occur post-birth (Money, 1999) and Richardson and Schuster (2004) note that girls' vaginas lubricate and clitorises swell soon after birth. Self-stimulation among children from around three months is common, involving friction, rhythmic rocking, pressing thighs together or rubbing genitals against objects. This can be self-soothing but may also be accompanied by muscle contractions, facial flushing, grunting and moaning (Martinson, 1994). Yang et al. (2005) note that such behaviour is often misinterpreted as non-sexual in nature and cites twelve cases of children under the age of one being referred to paediatricians and receiving extensive exploratory interventions, such as small bowel biopsies, before an explanation of typical infant masturbation was given.

During infancy, self-stimulating behaviour such as touching genitals and erogenous zones in public or at home is the most common sexual behaviour reported by parents (Lindblad et al., 1995; Schoentjes et al., 1999). This behaviour can have a range of functions including sexual arousal, but is often self-soothing and can increase when the child is stressed or tired. In a US general population survey examining female caregiver reports of the behaviour of 1,114 children aged between two and five, 60% of boys and 44% of girls were reported to engage in genital self-touch (Friedrich et al., 1998). The prevalence of observations of this behaviour steadily dropped with age, falling to 40% of boys and 21% of girls among 6–9 year olds, and was rarely observed among 10–12 year olds. Sexual behaviour is sensitive to social context, and children quickly learn what is appropriate and inappropriate in different settings. Genital self-touch, for example, is reported more often by parents than by staff in nurseries and primary schools (Larsson, 2000; Lopez Sanchez et al., 2002). The steady decline of observed self-touch with age may be indicative of a developing sense of social expectations and of privacy on the part of children as they get older. Children's exploration of their bodies can take other forms at this stage: toddlers and preschool children, for example, may experiment by sticking fingers or other objects inside any or all of their body openings. Insertion of objects into the anus or vagina is not unusual, but will normally result in discomfort or pain and is only a concern if the behaviour is repetitive or causes physical harm (Gil and Johnson, 1993; Doolin, 2011).

Gender role socialisation begins from the moment a child is born, with clothing colours, room decoration and toy selection among some of the many subtle stereotyping messages that teach children what behaviour is considered socially appropriate for their gender (Leaper and Friedman, 2007). By the age of two, children can usually accurately identify others as male or female (Newman and Newman, 2017). Between two and five, children gain knowledge of genital differences, gender identity, sexual body parts and (non-sexual) functions of the genitals (Brilleslijper-Kater and Baartman, 2000).

Curiosity about other people's bodies is common. Friedrich *et al.* (1998) found that 27% of 2–5 year olds regularly looked at parents or siblings while they were getting dressed or when naked, falling to 20% of 6–9 year olds and 5% of 10–12 year olds. Sexual play for children under the age of five involving looking at each other's genitals through games such as 'you show me yours, I'll show you mine' and playing 'doctors and nurses' is relatively common, particularly between children – including siblings and close family relatives – who know each other (Sandfort and Cohen-Kettenis, 2000). These activities parallel other forms of play-exploring, gender-specific roles (e.g. playing house) (Trowell, 1997). A study of Finnish children aged between two and seven (n=364) found an interest in domestic relations in games was significantly more frequent among girls than boys aged 5–7, and sexual play was also more common among girls at this stage (Sandnabba *et al.*, 2003). By the age of seven, almost 40% of girls incorporated romance or sex into their play, while boys displayed much more expressive sexual behaviour including exhibitionism, public displays of self-touch and sexualised language and banter, along with a general interest in nudity. By this stage, telling 'dirty jokes' and using sexualised language was commonplace – although four times more common in boys than girls – as was an interest in how babies are made. Growing animosity towards peers of the opposite sex was observed by age seven among both boys and girls. Behaviour such as hugging, kissing and holding hands, often imitating adults or older children, was far more common among girls than boys at this stage.

In an earlier study of gender roles in pre-adolescent sexual play, Lamb and Coakley (1993) similarly noted that between ages of five and ten children typically played mostly within their own gender group. However, when cross-gender play did take place, exploration of gender norms and stereotypes was often fore-grounded. In interviewing adults about their memories of sexual play at this stage of childhood, many participants in the study noted that force was a feature of both general cross-gender play as well as sexual play specifically. Most par-ticipants did not find these situations abusive or problematic but rather reflec-tive of social norms at the time concerning the perceived domination of men over women. Some of the behaviour described appears concerning in hind-sight – participants referred to 'sex slave' games or playing games of 'stripper and customer' – and from a present-day adult's perspective they might appear potentially harmful in nature. Notwithstanding the possibility that adults may recollect childhood abusive experiences not recognised by them as such at the time, the key factor, however, is the meaning of this behaviour for the partici-pants within their contemporaneous social context. When trying to make sense of children's sexual behaviour, this study suggests that the subjective experiences of the children involved is vital information that always needs to be gathered.

This chimes with a recent trend in research examining not just the sexual behaviour repertoires of children at different ages, but also how children reach sexual selfhood (the development of knowledge, attitudes, identity and sense of self as a sexual being) through sexual socialisation (the different social and technological contexts in which children and young people learn about and experience relationships and sexuality) (Tolman and McClelland, 2011). This shift in approaches to research reflects a trend in studying childhood sexuali-ties in ways that conceptualise sexual behaviour as a nexus where factors relat-ing to culture, psychology and biology interplay. Cultural factors are important because, although clinicians such as Johnson and Feldmeth (1993) suggest that sexual behaviour in prepubescence is generally light-hearted, playful and fun, feelings of guilt may also be present due to disapproving messages from parents, religion or culture. Shyness and embarrassment may develop as chil-dren become more aware of privacy and increasingly sensitive to social mores. Different attitudes to acceptable sexual expression, modesty and intimacy exist in families, influenced by community and cultural values, beliefs, practices and norms, as well as religion, spirituality and socio-economic status (Swisher *et al.*, 2008). Although schools, media and peer relationships are important, fami-lies (by which we mean parents, carers, siblings, grandparents and extended family members) are the primary context for most aspects of sexual socialisa-tion. The majority of what we learn about sexuality in early childhood occurs in the family home: for example, the attitudes we have about gender; how conflict is managed and resolved in intimate relations; our first experiences of nudity; the words we use for intimate parts of the body; and the sense of what is acceptable and unacceptable in relationships.

Most studies examining children's sexual behaviour involve White children growing up in principally White families, but those that have considered cultural diversity suggest that there is considerable variation between cultures in the frequency of high prevalence normative behaviour. Thigpen *et al.* (2003) found that US children brought up by African-American carers were significantly less likely than other children in large normative samples to display self-touch or to expose themselves to parents and peers. By contrast, Larsson (2000) found that Swedish children aged 3–6 displayed more behaviour in relation to nudity than US counterparts. Although there is variation in prevalence of different kinds of normative behaviour, Friedrich *et al.* (1998) found by contrast that harmful behaviour such as intrusive or aggressive sexual behaviour, or that more imitative of adult sexual behaviour (e.g. attempted intercourse, oral–genital contact, or masturbating with an object), while existing in all social and cultural groups where research has been conducted, were always reported as low-frequency behaviour.

By age ten, almost all children understand that sexual intercourse is necessary for reproduction (Gordon and Schroeder, 1995). Many children, at this stage, also know that there can be other reasons for having intercourse, such as enjoyment (more often mentioned by boys) or as an expression of love (more often mentioned by girls) (Goldman and Goldman, 1982). Behaviour that is retrospectively more frequently reported for ages 10–12 is thinking, talking and dreaming about sex; becoming interested in the opposite sex; fondling oneself and masturbation to orgasm (Larsson and Svedin, 2002; Friedrich *et al.*, 2008).

'Normative' sexual behaviour in childhood has been described by some as a 'complex and contested' term (Tolman and McClelland, 2011, p. 243) because deviation from the norm is not necessarily inappropriate in itself. Sexual attraction to a same-sex individual may place a child in a statistical minority, but this does not make the behaviour inappropriate. This is important as a range of studies have suggested that the development of sexual attraction may commence in middle childhood. Retrospective studies asking adults about their childhood memories have found that both male and female children typically become aware of sexual feelings towards others sometime around age ten with respect to both heterosexual and same-sex attraction (Boxer et al., 1993; Pattatucci and Hamer, 1995; Herdt and McClintock, 2000). This is not always the case, however, and same- or opposite-sex attraction can emerge at later stages in adolescence or even in adulthood (Savin-Williams, 2011).

One can see, therefore, that young children are not asexual; sexual socialisation begins from birth onwards, is different for boys and girls, and there is a wide range of behaviour that falls within the broad spectrum of developmentally expected behaviour. Children's sexual behaviours and identities are influenced by family and by wider culture, with significant variation across cultures and time.

Sexuality in puberty and beyond

Although all children develop at different rates, the median age in Western societies for onset of thelarche (secondary breast development) is 10.2 years, and of menarche (start of the first menstrual cycle) is 12.7 years (Rosenfield et al., 2009). The first sign of male puberty is testicular enlargement, typically at eleven years (Wolf and Long, 2016). These ages are gradually falling in most Western countries (Pierce and Hardy, 2012). Precocious puberty, defined as starting at least two years before these typical ages of onset, is thought to have a prevalence between 1 in 5,000 and 1 in 10,000, and is 5–10 times more common in girls than boys (Brämswig and Dübbers, 2009). Delayed or late onset puberty in boys involves there being no signs of testicular development by age fourteen, while in girls it generally means not having started to develop breasts by thirteen, or having developed breasts but not having started periods by the age of fifteen (Fenichel, 2012). Prevalence of late onset puberty is not known for boys and girls (Brämswig and Dübbers, 2009).

This series of biological changes associated with puberty that tend to occur between ages ten and fourteen (also involving enlargement and maturation of genitalia, breasts, and secondary sex characteristics such as growth of facial and pubic hair) are associated with increased levels of sex hormones and sexual interest, including sexual attraction and fantasies (Tanner, 1967). All of these signal to the youth and to others that she or he is becoming sexually mature. However, these physiological changes need to be considered within the context of emotional and cognitive development, as well as cultural context, if we are to fully understand adolescent sexual behaviour.

Research into adolescent sexual behaviour has been profoundly shaped by political and cultural priorities that have led to unhelpful conceptualisations of post-pubescent sexualities. Until 2000, the majority of research focused on understanding behaviour that potentially led to compromised health and social outcomes such as teenage pregnancy and sexually transmitted diseases (including HIV/AIDS). Research was undertaken mainly to answer epidemiological questions that could help improve harm-reduction strategies focusing on teenagers. Accordingly, what 'counts' as sexual behaviour for research purposes has generally been considered to be penile-vaginal penetrative acts (or occasionally penile-anal penetrative acts), often outside the context of committed romantic relationships (Tolman and McClelland, 2011). It is only relatively recently that empirical researchers have started to recognise that intimacy with a partner is an important developmental task in adolescence and young adulthood, and that sexual behaviour is not always risky but can actually be an indicator of positive development. Indeed, longitudinal studies suggest that sexual health in middle adolescence (e.g. consensual sexual interactions between peers at around age 15–17) in the context of a loving and relatively stable romantic relationship may be a factor in greater well-being in early and later adulthood, with both early and late onset of sexual intimacy being associated with poorer mental and sexual health outcomes (Boislard Pépin, 2010; Zimmer-Gembeck et al., 2012).

Moreover, researchers increasingly recognise that most adolescents follow a progressive sexual trajectory, starting with abstinence and unpartnered sex (masturbation) before moving on to partnered sex, often in a dating context (Fortenberry, 2013). This can involve non-genital behaviour (e.g. kissing, holding hands, hugging), followed by genital sexual behaviour (e.g. mutual masturbation, fellatio, cunnilingus) and, ultimately, vaginal and possibly anal intercourse (Boislard et al., 2016). Most adolescents in Western countries follow this developmental sequence (de Graaf et al., 2009; Hipwell et al., 2010), although there may be significant individual differences in timing and pacing. Lack of sexual experience is common in adolescence, but asexuality is relatively uncommon: just 2% of high school students in one study from New Zealand (Lucassen et al., 2011) and up to 3.3% of Finnish women (Höglund et al., 2014) described no sexual feelings towards peers or others.

Many males begin masturbating to orgasm between the ages of thirteen and fifteen (Pinkerton et al., 2003) although some earlier ages of onset are described in a few retrospective studies (e.g. Reynolds et al., 2003). Male ejaculation is dependent on spermarche (the beginning of development of sperm in boys' testicles at puberty), which typically occurs around age thirteen. The onset of masturbation among females is developmentally more gradual (Bancroft, 2003). An interest in erotic material, including pornography, is commonplace for both boys and girls, and this is readily available on the Internet. The most extensive UK study examining this subject with under sixteen year olds found that more boys view online pornography, through choice, than girls. By eleven, the majority of children have not seen online pornography but, by fifteen, children are more likely than not to have done so. (Martellozzo *et al.*, 2016) (see Chapter 8 for further discussion).

Baseline prevalence data about adolescent heterosexual sexual behaviour has mostly focused on vaginal intercourse, for reasons already outlined. The National Survey of Sexual Attitudes and Lifestyles in the UK found that 31% of men and 29% of women have had their first sexual intercourse by the age of sixteen. The percentages of 15–19 year olds having sex has declined significantly over the past twenty-five years (Mercer *et al.*, 2013). In 2011–2013, a US study based on data from 1,037 females and 1,088 males found that, by age fifteen, 18% of males and 13% of females had had sexual intercourse. By age seventeen, this percentage increased to 44% and 43% for males and females respectively, and by age 19 to 69% of males and 68% of females (Martinez and Abma, 2015). Internationally, sexual activity begins for most men and women in their later teenage years (ages 15–19 years), but regional variations are substantial. For women, median age at first intercourse is low in regions in which early marriage is the norm (e.g. in South Asia, central, west, and east Africa), and high in Latin America and south-east Asia (Wellings *et al.*, 2006).

Several variables influence age of onset of adolescent sexual behaviour, including self-esteem and self-efficacy (Orr *et al.*, 1989; Basen-Engquist and Parcel, 1992; Cole and Slocumb, 1995), personal values (Rozmus and Edgil, 1993; Torres and Fernández, 1995) and religion (Meier, 2003). A review of twenty-four studies found that parental monitoring may be more protective against early-onset sexual activity for boys than girls, whereas parental warmth and emotional connection may be more protective for girls (Kincaid *et al.*, 2012). Poverty, community activities and academic performance also have some influence on sexual activity in adolescence (Viner *et al.*, 2012), and peer influence is also a significant factor on age of onset of sexual activity, although there is gender variation. Boys are generally granted sexual freedoms, while stricter norms are in place in relation to expressions of female sexuality, encouraging girls to refrain from sex and to avoid accumulating multiple sexual partners (Boislard *et al.*, 2016). These social messages are communicated by peers, with girls being more likely to be discouraged from having sex, and boys receiving peer approval for, and pressure towards, sexual activity, especially from male friends (Crawford and Popp, 2003). While the variables influencing age of onset of sexual activity for adolescents are widely researched, they are under-theorised and our under-standing of how and why they have the influence they do is limited.

Despite the worldwide shift towards greater acceptance of nontraditional gender roles (Seguino, 2007), young people who do not comply to expected gender norms often report harassment and bullying from peers (McBride and Schubotz, 2017). Most children will develop a gender identity that broadly matches social expectations for their biological sex. Prevalence data about how often tensions arise between biological sex and gender role is elusive and problematic, because of varying approaches to gender socialisation within and between families and communities and because of methodological issues concerning how this is defined and measured. A Dutch normative sample of 1,200 children aged between four and eleven using a standardised tool – the Child Behaviour Checklist (CBCL) (Achenbach and Edelbrock, 1991) – found parents reported 3% of boys and 5% of girls sometimes or frequently behaved like the opposite sex (Cohen-Kettenis and Pfäfflin, 2003). Research relating to gender non-conformity in adolescence is limited to date (Diamond, 2013), although a recent study of 8,500 high school students in Tasmania found that 1.2% described themselves as transgender (Clark *et al.*, 2014). Of those who experience gender dysphoria – a sense of discomfort resulting from incongru-ence between gender identity and assigned sex – in childhood or adolescence, only a minority report continued dysphoria into adulthood and the seeking out of services for gender reassignment. Most long-term studies of gender dysphoria have also examined adolescent or adult sexual orientation, and there is an asso-ciation between the presence of childhood gender dysphoria and a heightened report of a sexual orientation directed towards the same natal sex or to both sexes (Zucker and Bradley, 1995; Wallien and Cohen-Kettenis, 2008). The relation between sexual orientation and gender identification is becoming increasingly complex, with gender identification now involving a wide spectrum of labels, e.g. 'third gender', 'pan-sexual' and 'gender fluid', that move beyond more traditional constructs of being male, female or transgender (Bockting, 2008).

The 2016 census data in the UK reveals that around 2% of the population identifies themselves as lesbian, gay or bisexual. More males (2.3%) than females (1.6%) identify themselves in this manner, and the population aged 16–24 are the age group most likely to identify (4.1%) (Office for National Statistics, 2017b). A recent large US study (n= 9,175) found that 2.8% of males and 7.8% of females aged 18–19 described themselves as gay, lesbian or bisexual (Chandra et al., 2013). However, 24% of women and 11% of men in this study noted some degree of same-sex sexual interests in this age group. Bisexual patterns of attraction are commonly considered to be the exception rather than the norm, or considered an indicator of denial about same-sex orientation. However, a number of random, representative studies conducted in numerous countries consistently show that the majority of adolescents who report any same-sex attractions also report experiencing opposite-sex attractions at various stages of adolescence (Laumann et al., 1994; Dickson et al., 2003; Mosher et al., 2005; Chandra et al., 2013). These findings suggest some fluidity in sexual interest for many in adolescence, and possibly beyond into adulthood.

Accordingly, some sexual interests and preferences that develop in adolescence may be stable over the life course, while others may be developmentally or contextually specific. This is also likely to be the case with atypical sexual interests, although research to date is underdeveloped.

Atypical sexual interests

The term 'paraphilia' – 'any powerful and persistent sexual interest other than copulatory or precopulatory behaviour with phenotypically normal consenting adult partners' (Blanchard, 2010, p. 367) – is commonly used in the clinical literature to describe atypical sexual interests, although the defining characteristic of persistence in sexual interest and the focus on consenting adult partners means that the term should be used cautiously with adolescents. Nonetheless, retrospective research suggests that adults with paraphilias (e.g. those who have an interest in particular fetishes) often describe their sexual preferences beginning in childhood and, especially, in adolescence (Lowenstein, 2002). For some, these may be optional interests that supplement a range of more typical interests while, for others, they may be a preferred sexual option or an exclusive sexual interest that precludes all others. Some non-consensual, atypical sexual behaviour that may lead to conflict with the law (e.g. voyeurism, exhibitionism, frotteurism, zoophilia) can emerge in adolescence and may be fleeting and reactive to external stimuli (e.g. exposure to particular forms of pornography online), experimental in nature or an early indicator of life course persistent preferences. A wide range of paraphilias are not in themselves problematic (e.g. infantilist behaviour such as wearing nappies or sexual arousal linked to non-sexual items such as a particular toy), but when displayed by adolescents they may cause distress and confusion for both adults and the young person themselves.

Adult responses to adolescent, atypical sexual interests raise significant issues about young people's rights to sexual choices. This may be complicated further by the presence of other issues such as learning disabilities, autistic spectrum disorders or Attention Deficit (Hyperactivity) Disorder (AD(H)D). In a Taiwanese case study, Chang and Chow (2011) describe a fourteen year old boy referred to a clinic after his mother had found nylon stockings under his pillow. When asked, he admitted to stealing the stockings and masturbating with them while putting them on or rubbing them against his genital area. In a similar Turkish study, Coskun and Ozturk (2013) describe a thirteen year-old boy who frequently stole women's shoes from people within his household and from neighbours and then used them as an aid to masturbation. Such case studies are unusual in the clinical literature, but, in both situations, professionals drew on treatment approaches typically used with adults, with extensive behavioural and pharmacological interventions being described for both boys. Such responses raise challenging questions about what proportionate interventions – if any – should be offered in such cases. The question of how inappropriate or problematic such behaviour is, and who has a right to define it in this way, also highlights issues about cultural context. Research to date suggests that certain atypical sexual interests may be less problematic in some cultures and contexts than in others (Bhugra *et al.*, 2010).

One atypical sexual interest that has particular relevance to discussions concerning adolescent harmful sexual behaviour is sexual interest in prepubescent children. This is typically described as 'paedophilia' in the clinical literature, although diagnostic criteria means that the term should not be used with anyone under sixteen (American Psychiatric Association, 2013). The equally problematic term 'deviant sexual arousal' is used in the clinical literature to describe this presentation (although the term also covers those who are sexually aroused by violence).

There is no base rate for the prevalence of sexual interest in prepubescent children among adolescents, although around 4% of the adult male population describes sexual fantasies in relation to children in some studies (Dombert *et al.*, 2016). Many adult males in retrospective studies of paedophilia recall sexual feelings towards younger children in early puberty (Seto, 2004). However, these studies may be biased by focusing only on those with stable sexual preferences from adolescence into adulthood. Prospective studies that track the developmental trajectories of young people who have sexual thoughts and feelings towards prepubescent children are lacking to date. There may be many young people with fleeting or temporary sexual feelings towards prepubescent children who grow out of these feelings with time and new developmental experiences. Some interventions are being developed for adolescents (e.g. Beier *et al.*, 2016) premised on the debatable assumption that such preferences will be stable across the life course.

Conclusion

The relevant literature on sexual development in childhood and adolescence foregrounds several points that practitioners should bear in mind when responding to concerns about sexual behaviour displayed by children and young people. Firstly, sexuality in early childhood needs to be considered on a continuum that extends into adolescence and young adulthood. Young children are not asexual, as may sometimes be supposed, but will typically engage in healthy sexual development and exploration. During an assessment of a child or young person who has displayed harmful sexual behaviour, understanding the evolution of the child's sexual behaviour, their sexual learning experiences and gathering observations made by adults of the child's sexual attitudes will ensure that any developmental chronology describing the major events that have happened in the child's life will include sexual development. The child's behaviour must be understood within the context of their sexual socialisation, including the attitudes to sex and sexuality within the family and culture.

Secondly, we need to recognise that sexual behaviour takes place within social contexts, and an understanding of cultural practice and norms is essential if we are to make sense of such behaviour. In particular, current frameworks such as the Brook traffic light system are gender neutral. This is problematic as the evidence in the relevant developmental literature conclusively shows that sexual behaviour cannot be separated from wider questions about human sexuality within a gendered society.

Thirdly, although there are some pointers in the literature regarding what is clearly normative or abusive, what is considered to be problematic is more contested. In these situations, careful assessment considering the behaviour from the viewpoint of all children involved, as well as those of parents and other adults, will be necessary. Self-reflection by professionals on personal attitudes and values will be important, as will be an understanding of where the relevant empirical literature on childhood sexualities is robust and where it is relatively weak when formulating whether behaviour is problematic.

The final message from the developmental literature is that professionals need to retain a rights-based perspective at all times. Children, and young people in particular, have a right to sexual expression and choice, as well as a right to have their needs in relation to social and sexual well-being supported. Not all adolescent sexual behaviour is inherently risky; rather, it may support the development of long-term mental health and well-being. Young people who have displayed harmful sexual behaviour may need supervision and monitoring, but the denial of sexual rights needs to be considered carefully within the context of a transparent ethical framework. When young people talk about their sexual feelings, their sexual identity or choices, professionals need to recognise and pay attention to what is being said. Adults need to respond to choices and behaviour that are harmful, but they also need to respect young people's feelings in a non-judgemental way, even when they seem confused, irrational, antisocial or elicit strong feelings for us. This is true when undertaking assessments, and is also important in interventions where professionals may be involved with teaching children about healthy sexuality. Thought needs to be given to the range of experiences that constitute healthy sexuality in childhood and adolescence when we talk to children about what is normative and what is abusive. Age-appropriate discussions with children about sexuality need to focus not just on biology and behaviour, but also on thoughts, feelings, social meanings and diversity. All of this requires sensitive support and supervision. As Dodd and Tolman (2017) note, a detailed understanding of how we support positive sexual well-being, with either adults or children and young people, is rarely a significant aspect of mainstream training in social work, psychology and allied professions.

Chapter 3

Prevalence, characteristics and backgrounds

Introduction

Understanding the nature, impact and prevalence of sexual abuse by children and young people is fundamental if we are to tackle this issue effectively through policy, legislation, multi-agency cooperation and direct practice. Although a wide range of children and young people exhibit different kinds of harmful sexual behaviour in various contexts, some commonalities emerge. Knowledge of the characteristics of this population is an essential foundation for considering many of the themes covered in later chapters of this book.

It is also important to recognise that not all children are equally at risk of displaying harmful sexual behaviour; not all are equally vulnerable to victimisation; and not all physical and social environments present the same level of risk of child sexual abuse occurring (Smallbone *et al.*, 2013). Appreciating where, when, how, by whom and to whom this abuse takes place is an important starting point in developing the kind of comprehensive and evidence-based approaches to intervention and prevention discussed in the later chapters of this book.

This chapter examines research regarding the prevalence and impact of child sexual abuse generally, before discussing the proportion of sexual abuse caused by children and young people specifically. We then summarise some of the key messages from the literature describing the characteristics and backgrounds of this client group, as well as considering the nature and context of that harm.

Nature, prevalence and impact of child sexual abuse

Article 34 of the United Nations Convention on the Rights of the Child obliges signatory states to take measures to protect children from all forms of sexual exploitation and sexual abuse including:

A. The inducement or coercion of children to engage in any unlawful sexual activity;

B. The exploitative use of children in prostitution or other unlawful sexual practices;

> C. The exploitative use of children in pornographic performances and materials (UNICEF, 1989).

The convention does not define sexual abuse or exploitation beyond this, but Article 18 of the 2007 Council of Europe Convention on the Protection of Children against Sexual Exploitation and Sexual Abuse ('Lanzarote Convention') also confers additional responsibilities on signatory states to criminalise the following activities:

- engaging in sexual activities with a child who, according to the relevant provisions of national law, has not reached the legal age for sexual activities; and
- engaging in sexual activities with a child where:
  - use is made of coercion, force or threats; or
  - abuse is made of a recognised position of trust, authority or influence over the child, including within the family; or
  - abuse is made of a particularly vulnerable situation of the child, notably because of a mental or physical disability or a situation of dependence (Council of Europe, 2007, p. 7).

Although levels of reporting vary between different jurisdictions, empirical studies show a sizeable minority of the general population have experienced sexual abuse in childhood. A meta-analysis of adult self-report studies across twenty-two countries found prevalence rates of 7.9% among men and 19.2% among women (Pereda *et al.*, 2009a). A UK victimisation survey (n= 6,198) found 11.3% of 18–24 year olds (5.1% male; 17.8% female) had by the age of eighteen experienced 'contact sexual abuse', as defined by UK law, rising to 24.1% when non-contact sexual abuse was included (Radford *et al.*, 2011).

Estimates made by the Office of the Children's Commissioner for England and Wales suggest that only around one in eight children who have been sexually abused are ever known to police and social services (Office of the Children's Commissioner, 2015). The vast majority of children who experience sexual abuse do not disclose their abuse in childhood. From a study of sixty young adults, Allnock and Miller (2013) found that typical barriers to disclosure included:

- having no one to turn to (e.g. absence of someone trusted to tell);
- perpetrator tactics, including the child's fears and anxieties being manipulated by the perpetrator;

- developmental barriers (e.g. being developmentally unable to understand that the abuse was wrong or lacking the vocabulary to describe
  their concerns);
- emotional barriers (e.g. shame and guilt);
- others' lack of recognition of abuse or signs and indicators of abuse;
- anxiety over limits of confidentiality if they told someone (Allnock
  and Miller, 2013, p. 25).

Short-term physical symptoms of child sexual abuse may be present in a small
number of children, such as sexually transmitted diseases and genital or anal
injury (World Health Organization, 2003). In the longer term, child sexual abuse
has been statistically associated with a range of issues, including:

- depression, anxiety, dissociation, low self-esteem, hyper-sexuality
  (Davidson and Omar, 2014);
- complex post-traumatic stress disorder (Kisiel et al., 2014);
- cardiovascular, immune and reproductive disorders (D'Andrea et al.,
  2011);
- unexplained chronic pain (e.g. pelvic pain, irritable bowel syndrome,
  lower back pain and fibromyalgia) (Spiegel et al., 2016).

Some survivors of child sexual abuse, however, experience few, if any, psychological effects (Bak-Klimek et al., 2014), and it has been estimated that
anything between 20% and 40% of children who have experienced sexual
abuse do not develop psychological problems (Finkelhor, 1990). Impact is
mediated by a range of factors including: nature and frequency of the abuse;
relationship between victim and abuser; individual factors such as education, interpersonal and emotional competence, coping style, optimism, and
external attribution of blame; and systemic factors such as being believed by
adults and support from family and wider social environment (Domhardt
et al., 2015).

One issue in relation to the short- and long-term impact of child sexual
abuse is that victimisation rarely occurs in isolation from other forms of
maltreatment. Some children are targeted specifically because of perceived
vulnerabilities (e.g. disability, or neglect) and research into 'poly-victimisation' (Finkelhor et al., 2007) – the impact of multiple types of victimisation from peers, family and community – points to the cumulative impact
of abuse being more detrimental to child well-being than any single experience. The 'adverse childhood experiences' (ACE) study (Felitti and Anda,

2010) also underlines the cumulative impact of various adverse childhood experiences on adult physical and mental health. Many researchers conclude that sexual abuse should be considered as one of many different equivalent forms of intra-familial and extra-familial maltreatment, and that accumulated experiences may account for poor outcomes in adulthood rather than the experience of child sexual abuse in itself.

However, there is also evidence to suggest that child sexual abuse may be particularly harmful. For example, twin studies, which control for genetic and family environment factors, have shown a causal relationship between child sexual abuse and depression, anxiety, suicide attempts and alcohol and substance misuse in adulthood (Andrews *et al.*, 2004). Subsequent re-victimisation, particularly in later adolescence and young adulthood, may also be a negative outcome characteristic of sexual abuse that distinguishes it from other forms of childhood maltreatment (Papalia *et al.*, 2017). In a US study of 195 children who had experienced sexual abuse, 95% had experienced poly-victimisation, but when compared to 573 children known to services for other non-sexual forms of maltreatment, the sexually abused group showed significantly higher levels of depression, anxiety, aggression and inappropriate sexual behaviour (Lewis *et al.*, 2016).

While the general effects of child sexual abuse are well documented, there is little research on the impact of abuse caused specifically by other children or young people. This issue has been explored in the sibling sexual abuse literature, however, and studies to date suggest that sibling sexual abuse is associated with a similar range of sequelae to those associated with child sexual abuse generally. Researchers have concluded that it has the potential to be at least as harmful as sexual abuse perpetrated by parents (Yates, 2017a). Similar findings are emerging in the literature concerning online peer-on-peer sexual abuse. A recent UK study of sixteen children who had been sexually abused online, where the majority had been victimised by peers, found self-blame, flashbacks or intrusive thoughts, depression, negative feelings about males and anxiety were common (Hamilton-Giachritsis *et al.*, 2017). While the intersubjective dynamics between perpetrator and victim may mediate the impact of child sexual abuse in individual cases (Angelides, 2004), there is no theoretical reason to suppose that child sexual abuse perpetrated by another child or young person should be any less harmful than that perpetrated by an adult.

Prevalence of harmful sexual behaviour in childhood and adolescence

A consistent finding in the research on sexual offending is that a significant proportion of sexual abuse is caused by children and young people under the age of eighteen. Information from the police on perpetrators of sexual offences against children in England and Wales gathered by the Office of the Children's Commissioner (2015) identified 34,241 perpetrators over a two-year period (April 2012–March 2014). One-third of the perpetrators were under the age of eighteen. Similarly, in the US, Finkelhor *et al.* (2009) found that 35.6% of those who committed sexual offences against children were under eighteen. Some 15% of defendants in rape cases in the court system in England and Wales in 2015/16 were young people, with 7% in sexual assault proceedings, and 2% in image-related offences. The majority of juvenile defendants were aged 15–17 (79%) (Kelly and Karsna, 2017). Sexual offences represented 3% of crimes committed by children and young people in England and Wales that year, with around one-third of cases attracting a youth caution or youth conditional caution rather than being dealt with by court proceedings (Bateman, 2017).

Evidence from victimisation studies suggests children and young people are responsible for an even higher proportion of child sexual abuse. In their study of maltreatment in the UK, Radford *et al.* (2011) found that 65.9% of contact sexual abuse reported by children and young people was perpetrated by under-eighteen year olds. A 2010 YouGov poll of 788 16–18 year old girls found that 29% had experienced unwanted sexual touch in school settings (End Violence against Women, 2010), while a study of 1,086 US high school students with a mean age of fifteen found 26% of boys and 51% of girls had experienced peer sexual assault in or outside school (Young *et al.*, 2009). This trend is emerging in international research, with a recent review of sexual abuse victimisation studies in twenty-eight low- and middle-income countries concluding that adolescent girls are at greatest risk of forced sex within the context of intimate partner relationships (UNICEF, 2017). Friends, classmates and partners were also found to be some of the most frequently cited perpetrators of sexual abuse against boys in Cambodia, Haiti, Kenya, Malawi and Nigeria (UNICEF, 2017).

Turning to investigations of male self-reported sexually aggressive behaviour, a large Norwegian study of male high school students (n= 1,933) found that 5.2% self-reported having used verbal coercion, defined as ever having talked or forced somebody into genital, oral, or anal sex (Kjellgren *et al.*, 2010). These findings parallel studies of sexual violence in young adulthood with as many as one-third of male university students self-reporting sexually coercive or aggressive behaviour towards peers (Kosson *et al.*, 1997; Wheeler *et al.*, 2002; Abbey *et al.*, 2004; DeGue and DiLillo, 2004; White and Smith, 2004). There are many definitional issues raised by these studies, and it has been argued that, when peer victimisation is included in prevalence figures for child sexual abuse, practitioners should avoid confusion by referring to 'childhood sexual abuse and assault' to make it clearer that figures include more than 'sexual abuse' in the slightly narrower child welfare sense (Finkelhor *et al.*, 2014). Nonetheless, by whatever measure, it is evident that children and young people internationally are responsible for a very significant proportion of child sexual abuse.

Descriptive studies of children and young people who have displayed harmful sexual behaviour

A range of studies over the last thirty years have described the characteristics of children and young people who have displayed harmful sexual behaviour. Most of these studies involve data sets from North America, the UK, Australia and New Zealand. However, studies are increasingly emerging from a wider range of countries in Europe (Edgardh and Ormstad, 2000; Långström and Grann, 2000; Bijleveld and Hendriks, 2003; Hosser and Bosold, 2006; Kjellgren *et al.*, 2006; Van Wijk *et al.*, 2007; Hart-Kerkhoffs *et al.*, 2009; Kjellgren *et al.*, 2010; Klein *et al.*, 2012; Lussier *et al.*, 2012; Barra *et al.*, 2017) as well as other jurisdictions including Turkey (Arslan *et al.*, 2016), Singapore (Zeng *et al.*, 2015a), Costa Rica (Ramirez, 2002), Columbia (Restrepo, 2013), Chile (Wilson and Chaud, 2013) and South Africa (Da Costa *et al.*, 2014; Wood *et al.*, 2000).

While some of these studies examine children, most focus on adolescents with some describing both. The majority are retrospective, although a few prospective studies exist (e.g. McCuish *et al.*, 2016). Most of the research involves samples of children referred to specialist harmful sexual behaviour services or young people adjudicated for sexual offences in custodial or secure settings. Consequently, it describes children at the more serious end of the continuum of sexual behaviour and may, therefore, not be generalisable to those whose behaviour may be problematic rather than abusive.

Notwithstanding these limitations, four studies stand out as being of particular value, and to which we will refer repeatedly in the remainder of this chapter:

- Finkelhor *et al.* (2009) examined data held on the US National Incident-Based Reporting System (NIBRS) regarding 13,471 cases of sexual crime reported in 2004 and perpetrated by children and young people aged between six and seventeen. The NIBRS covers 34/50 states and provides a wide range of information about victims, offenders and the circumstances of the offences, although it lacks information about the backgrounds of young people described.

- With most research involving small, clinical samples, Seto and Lalumière (2010) conducted a meta-analysis of fifty-nine independent studies. While not all studies examined the same set of factors, Seto and Lalumière statistically compared the characteristics of male adolescents who displayed harmful sexual behaviour (n=3,855) with those who committed non-sexual crimes (n=13,393).

- Hackett *et al.* (2013) examined the case files of 700 children and young people referred to nine services in the UK because of harmful sexual behaviour between 1992 and 2000. This is the largest study of its kind in the UK to date. The case records are constructed contemporaneously and from multiple sources, therefore providing information about the individual, family and abuse characteristics.

- Fox (2017) examined data extracted from a youth-offending risk assessment tool used with respect to a full population of 64,329 juveniles referred to the Florida Department of Justice between 2007 and 2012, including 4,153 involved with harmful sexual behaviour and 60,176 young people known to authorities for non-sexual offending. While the data were not originally collected for research purposes and the risk assessment tool did not ask questions specifically relevant to sexual offending, the same set of factors was examined for all of the juveniles in the study.

Below, we outline key findings from these and other studies that have been shown to be relatively consistent. More detailed discussions of girls, children under the age of twelve and children with learning disabilities, as well subgroups such as those involved with peer-on-peer sexual exploitation or sibling sexual abuse, can be found in Chapter 7.

Characteristics of children and young people who have displayed harmful sexual behaviour

Gender

The vast majority of children and young people who have displayed harmful sexual behaviour are boys. Both Finkelhor *et al.* (2009) and Fox (2017) found that just 7% of their sample were girls, while Hackett *et al.* (2013) reported 3%. Larger proportions of girls tend to be identified in cohorts of younger children who have displayed harmful sexual behaviour. Some 31% of the girls in Finkelhor *et al.*'s (2009) study were under twelve, in comparison to 14% of the boys.

Ethnicity

Research on ethnicity is relatively under-examined in the literature, with Hackett *et al.* (2013) noting that the ethnicity of the perpetrator was not recorded in 240 of the 700 case files they examined. Where it was reported, ethnic background of the young people in their sample was broadly in line with that of the UK population. Similar findings are found internationally in many studies (Ryan *et al.*, 1996; Kjellgren *et al.*, 2006). However, some research from Australia reports higher prevalence, arrest and conviction rates among minority ethnic youth (e.g. Rojas and Gretton, 2007), and Black young people are over-represented in some smaller studies of incarcerated youth convicted of sexual offences in the US (Davis and Leitenberg, 1987; Hsu and Starzynski, 1990). This is likely to mirror the over-representation of Black and minority ethnic youth in criminal justice systems in these countries.

Age at onset of behaviour

Findings about the proportion of children under twelve involved with harmful sexual behaviour are methodologically problematic as data collection typically relates to age of criminal responsibility, which varies between jurisdictions. Some 16% of the 13,471 children and young people in Finkelhor *et al.*'s (2009) research were under twelve, with a significant rise in harmful sexual behaviour from age twelve occurring and peaking at fourteen. This spike in early adolescence is well supported by other studies. The age of onset of sexual offending in Fox (2017) was between thirteen and fifteen in 51% of cases. The mean age of referral to specialist services in Ryan *et al.*'s (1996) examination of 1,616 juveniles was fourteen, and Hackett *et al.* (2013) similarly found that 54% of referrals to services were aged between fourteen and sixteen.

Cognitive abilities

Learning disability (sometimes referred to as intellectual impairment or intellectual disability outside the UK) is consistently over-represented in research describing children and young people who have displayed harmful sexual behaviour. Learning disability currently affects 2% of the general population in England (Emerson and Hatton, 2008), yet young people with diagnosed or undiagnosed learning disability represented 38% of the cases in Hackett *et al.* (2013). Seto and Lalumière (2010) similarly found that those who displayed harmful sexual behaviour had significantly more learning problems than young people involved with non-sexual criminality.

Family environment

The characteristics of families are generally less examined than those of the children and young people who have displayed harmful sexual behaviour. In a UK study of fifty-one young people who had displayed harmful sexual behaviour referred to a specialist community-based service, Manocha and Mezey (1998) found descriptions of parents as 'rejecting', 'uncaring', 'unloving' or 'disinterested' in almost one-third of cases. Marital violence was noted in 37% of families; frequent parental violence towards children in 24%; and parental criminality (including parental imprisonment) in 28%. Sibling non-sexual violence was reported in 10% of families, and in 8% of families children were reported to have been violent towards the adults in their home. A lack of sexual boundaries was described in 26% of the families, while 16% reported frequently witnessing sexual acts between parents. Substance misuse or parental mental health problems were present in one-quarter of families. Similar patterns are found in investigations of the family environments of prepubescent children (Gray *et al.*, 1997). Compromised parenting skills and strategies are noted in many studies, and a significant proportion of the parents may themselves have experienced poor parenting and childhood maltreatment (Duane and Morrison, 2004; Cherry and O'Shea, 2006). In a study of eighty families of young people who sexually abused others, for example, one-half of mothers reported having been sexually abused in childhood (New *et al.*, 1999).

Experience of maltreatment

As well as their own behaviour causing harm to their victims, research suggests that children and young people's harmful sexual behaviour should also raise questions about the extent of maltreatment to which they themselves may have been exposed and from which they may still need to be protected. Hackett *et al.* (2013) found that 66% of the young people in their sample were known to have experienced some form of maltreatment. However, there are considerable variations between studies because of different samples and lack of consistency in definition and measurement of maltreatment.

Reported levels of physical abuse experienced by children and young people who have displayed harmful sexual behaviour are consistently high. Whereas Radford *et al.*'s (2011) UK general population survey found that 8% of 18–24 year olds self-reported being physically abused at home before the age of eighteen, Hackett *et al.* (2013) and Ryan *et al.* (1996) report figures of 38% and 42%, respectively, for their samples. Seto and Lalumière (2010) conclude that young people who sexually abuse others are statistically more likely to be physically abused than young people known to youth and criminal justice services for non-sexual offending – a finding supported by Fox (2017). Witnessing physical and domestic violence is also over-represented in many studies (Skuse *et al.*, 1998; Hickey *et al.*, 2008), although levels are no higher than for young people involved with non-sexual offending behaviour (Seto and Lalumière, 2010).

Childhood sexual abuse is also over-represented among this client group. Seto and Lalumière's (2010) meta-analysis calculated that, on average, 46% of these young people had experienced sexual abuse, and it was one of only a few factors that differentiated sexual from non-sexual offending groups – the former being five times more likely to have been sexually abused than the latter. Fox (2017) also found this to be a strong predictor of juvenile sexual rather than non-sexual offending behaviour, although only 22% of young people in this study had been sexually abused. Investigations of children under twelve have generally shown even higher rates of sexual abuse victimisation (e.g. Burton, 2000; Friedrich *et al.*, 2000). Several studies have suggested that, for adolescents, their experience of sexual abuse victimisation is often at a relatively young age, with an average of 8–10 years old being identified (Brannon *et al.*, 1989; Longo, 1982; Napolitano, 1997).

There has been little research to date on poly-victimisation and the cumulative impact of different forms of maltreatment, although some studies note co-occurrence of physical and sexual abuse in the developmental histories of these children and young people (Cooper *et al.*, 1996; Fehrenbach *et al.*, 1986; Johnson and Knight, 2000; Smith *et al.*, 1987). However, a recent Swiss study examining adverse childhood experiences of 687 young people known to services because of harmful sexual behaviour (Barra *et al.*, 2017) did not find a particular set of negative experiences characteristic of this population. Instead, particular clusters of certain kinds of negative experiences were characteristic of different kinds of offence and victim characteristics. Those with neglect-only backgrounds were more likely to abuse pre-adolescent children rather than peers, as were those who had experienced bullying and social rejection among their peers. This latter group were also more likely to have been involved with a penetrative sexual act with their victim. Those who had adverse experiences in the family environment were more likely to sexually abuse others within the context of a wider range of other delinquent and non-sexual offending behaviour. Multiple experiences of adversity were linked to having multiple victims, although not statistically associated with penetrative abuse. Although these findings are promising, they would need to be replicated before they could be used by professionals in decision-making about future risk and safety planning in particular practice situations.

Victim characteristics

While the majority of children and young people who have displayed harmful sexual behaviour are male, the majority of victims are female. In Finkelhor *et al.*'s (2009) study, 79% of victims were girls, while an investigation of Swedish adolescents who sexually abused (n=199) found 77% of victims were female. This study also identified that 19.5% had male victims, and just 3.8% had both male and female victims (Kjellgren *et al.*, 2006). Other research has recorded higher levels of victim crossover, with Hackett *et al.* (2013) finding that 30% of their sample abused both males and females, while 51% abused females only and 19% males only. It is not clear as yet what may differentiate those adolescents who abuse a single sex from those who abuse both boys and girls, although harmful sexual behaviour may be influenced by social context and opportunistic access to potential victims as much as by characteristics of the perpetrators.

The victims of adolescents tend to be either peers or prepubescent children, with sexual assaults of adults being statistically uncommon. Some 59% of victims in Finkelhor *et al.*'s (2009) research were under the age of twelve. In both Kjellgren's (2006) Swedish and Finkelhor *et al.*'s (2009) US studies, male victims tended to be younger than female victims. In Finkelhor *et al.*'s

(2009) study when the victims were boys there was a marked peak reflecting 12–14 year olds targeting 4–7 year old boys. When the victims were girls, however, the peak was among 15–17 year olds targeting 13–15 year old girls. This suggests that, when adolescents target boys, they often tend to focus on much younger and sexually immature boys rather than their peers; whereas, when adolescents target girls, they tend to be older themselves and focus more on sexually mature females closer to their own age. For the 2,104 children under twelve who displayed harmful sexual behaviour in this study, 51% of the victims were under six, and there was a more even balance between male and female victims (36.6%/63.4%).

Aside from these age and gender characteristics, the majority of victims are known to the perpetrators, and the victimisation of strangers is relatively rare. Research suggests that anywhere between one-third and one-half of child sexual abuse perpetrated by children and young people is intra-familial in nature (Allardyce and Yates, 2013).

It is often assumed that children and young people who have displayed harmful sexual behaviour act on their own. However, there is evidence to suggest that group-based sexual abuse may be relatively common among adolescents. Some 24% of the children and young people in Finkelhor et al.'s (2009) study had sexually abused others alongside other perpetrators, while in an investigation of a hundred Dutch young people assessed for court purposes in relation to sexual offences (Bijleveld and Hendriks, 2003) thirty-six had committed their offence as part of a group or gang. An analysis of 340 solo and group sexual assaults perpetrated either by adults or young people in South Korea (95 of which involved three or more perpetrators, 85 of which involved double perpetrators, and 170 of which involved lone perpetrators) revealed that, the larger the group of perpetrators, the more likely they were to feature teenagers rather than adults (Park and Kim, 2016). The sexual abuse of female gang members and other victims has specifically been associated with the initiation or group-bonding processes of adolescent gangs (Beckett et al., 2013). While some peer-on-peer sexual abuse may initially appear to be an individual act, further investigation and mapping of the peer group may determine that the abuse has taken place within the context of peer relationships and pressures (Firmin et al., 2016b). This is discussed further in Chapter 7.

Place of abuse

The vast majority of sexual abuse by children and young people takes place within domestic spaces such as the family home or the homes of relatives or friends. Close family relatives or neighbours' children typically feature as victims in these settings, although abuse in foster care settings also occurs. Finkelhor *et al.* (2009) found that nearly 69% of the children and young people in their study sexually abused other children at home, while only 12% abused others in school or college settings.

There is, however, growing awareness of abuse in school settings, and data collected by the BBC in 2015 found that 5,500 sexual offences, including 600 rapes, were recorded in UK schools over a three-year period (BBC, 2015). Some studies suggest that up to half of child protection inquiries from primary schools involve concerns about children's behaviour (Carson, unpublished). Sexual abuse within schools has so far received only limited attention within the literature, as has peer-on-peer abuse in other institutional settings such as group-living residential care settings. The latter is emerging as a theme in historical inquiries into child sexual abuse in different jurisdictions (e.g. Hart *et al.*, 2017).

Sexual abuse in public spaces open and accessible to the community at large is much less prevalent than in domestic and organisational settings (McKillop *et al.*, 2012; Colombino *et al.*, 2011; Smallbone and Wortley, 2000). Stranger rape offences perpetrated by adolescents can happen in such settings but are rare; acts of public indecency or peer-on-peer sexual abuse involving girls being pressured and coerced into sexual acts by boys, often in gang or group settings, are much more common, often occurring in community spaces where youths congregate (e.g. parks, playgrounds, shopping centres, fast-food outlets, disused houses and stairwells).

Online harmful sexual behaviour – that is, behaviour that takes place exclusively online or takes place offline but is facilitated by new technology – is a focus of growing research. In an analysis of online sexual offences in Scotland between 2013 and 2016, in one-quarter of cases both the victim and perpetrator were under the age of sixteen (Justice Analytics Service, 2017). This subject is discussed in depth in Chapter 8.

Nature of behaviour

A wide range of sexually abusive behaviour is described in the research, although there is considerable diversity in how behaviour is defined and classified. In Finkelhor *et al.*'s (2009) sample, 24% of cases involved rape, 13% sodomy and 49% fondling. This compares to Hackett *et al.*'s (2013) study, in which 84% of cases involved inappropriate touching, 50% non-contact abuse, 52% penetrative abuse and 18% sexual violence. Some, but not all, children and young people who have displayed harmful sexual behaviour have been engaged in other forms of offending. Just over half of the young people in Kjellgren *et al.*'s (2006) Swedish study had previously been known to social services for antisocial behaviour.

Conclusion

Child sexual abuse is a highly prevalent form of maltreatment, with the potential for significant, long-term psychological and physical health consequences. Most sexual abuse never comes to the attention of statutory services, supporting the need for the prevention of child sexual abuse in the first place. Varying degrees of impact experienced by children who have been sexually abused underlines the importance of assessing carefully the therapeutic needs of children and adults affected by child sexual abuse – whoever the perpetrator may have been.

A substantial minority of child sexual abuse is perpetrated by children and young people themselves, and is likely to be as harmful as abuse by adults. Victims of young people can be both young children and adolescent peers, and there is a growing recognition of the level of sexual violence that occurs in the context of peer groups, school settings and intimate partner violence. These children and young people are a highly heterogeneous group, including boys and girls, younger children and older adolescents, of all ethnicities, some with learning disabilities, displaying a wide range of behaviour in different settings, perhaps on their own or as part of a group.

All of these children and young people have unique and particular needs, but a number of potential typologies emerge, which have the potential to facilitate more nuanced risk assessment and management and, therefore, the provision of healthy developmental opportunities. These typologies will be the subject of more detailed discussion in Chapter 7.

Notwithstanding the heterogeneity of these children and young people, and the limitations and biases of the research regarding their characteristics, it seems clear that the vast majority of these children and young people are likely to have experienced some form of abuse or trauma themselves. When children and young people present with harmful sexual behaviour, it is vital not only to respond by taking steps to protect their victims or potential victims, but also to consider what support and protection these children and young people need themselves in relation to their own experiences of maltreatment.

Chapter 4

Aetiology

Introduction

When a child sexually abuses another child, a number of questions are raised for practitioners about why they have acted in this way. Is it because they have been sexually victimised themselves? Are they sexually attracted to prepubescent children? Is the behaviour related to a lack of empathy, or limited knowledge about what constitutes consent? Or perhaps they just lack skills to build romantic relationships with peers and have sought another outlet for sexual experimentation?

The phrase 'children and young people who have displayed harmful sexual behaviour' describes many different kinds of children who act in many disparate ways in a range of divergent contexts. Each child or young person's developmental trajectory is unique, as are the reasons why this behaviour has emerged as an issue at this particular time. One theory is unlikely to explain all manifestations of harmful sexual behaviour. However, understanding why some individuals rather than others develop this behaviour is critically important if we are to target interventions effectively to help them desist from future sexual violence. Ultimately, if we want to tackle this issue comprehensively and prevent sexual abuse happening, we need to understand why it occurs in the first place. As Smallbone *et al.* (2013, p. 21) put it:

> Without good theory, evidence based prevention strategies may inadvertently be directed towards managing its consequences, which are more readily observable, rather than targeting its causes. A clear theoretical framework is needed that organises and makes sense of the available evidence, and provides a firm basis for making empirically defensible inferences about causal mechanisms and processes.

In this chapter we provide an overview of theories explaining why children and young people sexually abuse others, and examine research that has tested the explanatory power of these theories. We argue that current theorising generally overplays individual psychological factors and underplays social and environmental considerations when accounting for the aetiology of this behaviour.

Theories of sexual offending

Early work in the 1980s and 1990s on the causes of sexual violence focused on adult sex offenders rather than on children and adolescents who had displayed harmful sexual behaviour. It was generally accepted that there were common causal factors explaining sexually abusive behaviour that could assist professionals' understanding of why sexual behaviour was an issue for an individual rather than other kinds of behaviour. Some early theories focused on social or biological factors, such as aspects of masculinity, neurobiological dispositions or socio-biological factors (see, e.g. Ellis, 1989). Alternatively, early theorising focused on specific psychological deficits that were purported to hold the key to understanding the roots of sexual aggression: for example, sexual deviancy (McGuire *et al.*, 1964), empathy deficits (Finkelhor and Lewis, 1988) and cognitive distortions (Abel *et al.*, 1984).

Over time, it became recognised that most single-factor theories lack explanatory power and, instead, there has been a move towards considering sexual offending behaviour in adults to be multi-determined, focusing on how psychological factors interact with each other and with ecological factors (e.g. social and cultural environment, personal circumstances and the physical environment). Key theories include the four preconditions model (Finkelhor, 1984), the integrated theory of the aetiology of sexual aggression (Marshall and Barbaree, 1990), the quadripartite model of sexual aggression (Hall and Hirschman, 1996), the confluence mediational model of sexual aggression (Malamuth, 1996), the pathways model (Ward and Beech, 2006) and the new integrated theory of child sexual abuse (Smallbone *et al.*, 2013).

Theories to explain the aetiology of harmful sexual behaviour in childhood and adolescence have tended to draw on the adult sexual offending literature and have made few connections to the general literature on youth offending and juvenile delinquency. Many guides for practitioners refer only to theories of adult sexual offending and assume their applicability to children and young people. Explanations of harmful sexual behaviour are, therefore, rarely situated within a child development context (Burton and Miner, 2016; Durham, 2006)

Social learning theories

Some researchers have suggested that, because the majority of children and young people who have displayed harmful sexual behaviour have also experienced significant maltreatment in their lives, this behaviour may be a manifestation of trauma, and sexual trauma in particular (e.g. Veneziano *et al.*, 2000; Mulholland and McIntee, 1999). This idea is reflected in theories such as Rasmussen *et al.*'s (1992) trauma-processing model, which follows from the idea that sexualised behaviour can be a typical symptomatic response by young children to the experience of sexual abuse (Finkelhor and Browne, 1985). The child's abuser models and normalises the use of sexual behaviour, coercion and the manipulation of others to gain gratification and meet needs. This may be in the context of the child being confused about sexual norms because of conditioned sexual responses to non-sexual triggers and stimuli, such as grooming, where non-sexual behaviour takes on sexual overtones over time (e.g. hair stroking, eating, toileting). Sexual arousal of the child during abuse or the child taking on an 'offender' role and performing sexual acts on another child orchestrated by an adult or adolescent can also contribute to this confusion (Friedrich, 2007). Rasmussen *et al.* (1992) argue that, for children aged between four and twelve, sexually abusive behaviour can emerge from these contexts, grounded in thinking errors that normalise harm to others. They also recognise, however, that the majority of sexually abused children do not act in abusive ways, and the emergence of harmful sexual behaviour must, therefore, be related to further mediating risk factors.

There is some limited evidence supporting this model with both children and adolescents. As discussed in Chapter 3, both Seto and Lalumière (2010) and Fox (2017) found that experiencing sexual victimisation was one of the strongest predictors of sexual as opposed to non-sexual offending in adolescence. This also appears to be true for under twelves (Friedrich *et al.*, 1998; Friedrich *et al.*, 2005) – there being evidence that mediating factors such as attachment difficulties (Friedrich *et al.*, 2001) and low levels of parental support (Leifer *et al.*, 1993; Hall *et al.*, 2002) also have a role to play. Mediating factors are less researched with adolescents. However, Burton *et al.* (2002) compared a group of young people who had experienced sexual abuse and who had displayed delinquent but non-sexual offending behaviour (n=93) with a group of young people who had experienced sexual abuse and who had subsequently displayed harmful sexual behaviour (n=216). The study found that the development of sexual aggression was linked to being sexually abused by multiple perpetrators, having been sexually abused by both men and women, and experiencing more force in the abuse. Further credence to social learning theories is illustrated by a link in this study between the sexual abuse experienced by these young people and what they later did to their victims. The type of act, gender of victim, level of force and relationship often mirrored their own experiences. Likewise, Veneziano *et al.* (2000) found a relationship between the nature of the sexual abuse experienced by the child and the behaviour then perpetrated on their victim. Those who were subject to anal intercourse, for example, were fifteen times more likely to subject their victim to this form of abuse.

The key challenges to theories suggesting that there is a cycle of abuse by which victims become victimisers are that only a minority of sexually abused children and young people go on to abuse, and many who abuse have not been sexually abused. In a meta-analysis of more than fifty studies looking at an overall sample of more than 10,000 adolescents who had displayed harmful sexual behaviour, Burton and Schatz (2003) found that no more than one-half had reported histories of sexual victimisation. Seto and Lalumière (2010) and Fox (2017) found figures of 48% and 22%, respectively. Due to relatively low levels of disclosure, actual rates of sexual victimisation may be significantly higher. Nonetheless, while sexual abuse may be a key factor for many children and young people, it is neither a sufficient nor necessary precondition, even with respect to prepubescent children.

The question therefore arises as to whether other disruptive experiences to a child's sexual development may impact on social learning and are character-istic of those who sexually abuse. Large-scale studies of online pornography exposure, such as by Ybarra *et al.* (2011) and Stanley *et al.* (2016), have found significant statistical associations between pornography use and self-reported sexually coercive behaviour. Additionally, Seto and Lalumière (2010) found that adolescents who displayed harmful sexual behaviour reported slightly more exposure to pornography than those who displayed non-sexual offend-ing behaviour. There is also some evidence that significant pornography use in adolescence may adversely influence sexual scripts – how individuals are expected to interact with each other in sexual or romantic situations – and may be associated with attitudes that condone coercion in sexual relation-ships (Tomaszewska and Krahé, 2016; Metts and Spitzberg, 1996). However, as with victim to victimiser theories, most children exposed to pornography do not go on to abuse. While a child or young person's exposure to pornog-raphy should be explored in assessment work, it is not a robust-enough factor in itself to explain harmful sexual behaviour in isolation from other variables that mediate risk.

Some studies have found that sexual abuse histories are over-represented among young people with a sexual interest in prepubescent children who have displayed harmful sexual behaviour (e.g. Almond *et al.*, 2006). Such sexual interests may be socially learnt through victimisation experiences, although the majority of young people who sexually abuse are not motivated by such sexual interests. Worling (2006) found that only 30% of a sample of 136 adolescent boys who had displayed harmful sexual behaviour were reported by clinicians as having sexual interests in prepubescent children – a proportion broadly in line with other studies (e.g. Seto *et al.*, 2000; Seto *et al.*, 2003). However, Seto and Lalumière (2010) found that, ranked by effect size, the largest group difference among those who committed sexual offences compared to those who committed non-sexual offences was in relation to atypical sexual interests such as attraction to prepubescent children. It is, therefore, likely to be a causal factor in the offending of some adolescents, but the relationship that this has to an experience of childhood sexual abuse is arguable.

Early research into adult paedophilia suggested that sexual victimisation in childhood is a common causal factor (Freund *et al*, 1990), but more recent research has found that this is not well supported (Seto, 2008), with neurobiological factors such as impairment of the frontal or temporal lobe of the brain having better explanatory power (Tenbergen *et al.*, 2015). Furthermore, although a sexual interest in prepubescent children may be an aetiological risk factor in some cases, it is likely that other aggravating factors such as poor emotional regulation skills and victim availability are necessary for abuse to occur.

In conclusion, there is some evidence of harmful sexual behaviour being a learnt social behaviour for some individuals, but this theory – which tends to foreground single-factor explanations of sexual aggression – has poor explanatory power in itself when accounting for the aetiology of this behaviour for many children and adolescents.

Integrative theories

Specific multifactorial theories integrating physiological, psychological and emotional elements to explain the emergence of harmful sexual behaviour in the context of child and adolescent development have been slow to develop. Friedrich's (2007) integrative model, developed to explain problematic sexual behaviour in children under the age of twelve, is an exception and borrows from Greenberg *et al.*'s (1993) theory, which accounts for why some young children persevere with aggressive behaviour in childhood and others do not. It explains how normative sexual behaviour can develop into inappropriate and harmful sexual behaviour in pre-adolescence through complex interactions within four domains of risk:

- cumulative stress in the child's life;
- parental modelling of coercion (relating to the quality of early attachment and modelling of respectful boundaries shown by the parents);
- a tendency towards externalised behaviour (including bullying and treating others cruelly);
- disruptions in the child's psychosexual development (e.g. experience of sexual abuse; living in a home environment with inappropriate adult sexual behaviour or exposure to pornography) (Friedrich, 2007).

Friedrich argues that the second and fourth domains are closely connected as some children with impaired attachment are vulnerable to sexual abuse (Friedrich, 2007; Zeanah *et al.*, 2002; O'Connor and Rutter, 2000) and an experience of sexual abuse – or any form of maltreatment – potentially predisposes a child to insecure attachment (Cicchetti and Toth, 1995). This model considers psychological factors within the context of the child's circumstances and environment and incorporates parenting styles and attachment patterns as determining factors in the aetiology of harmful sexual behaviour. A recent Canadian study found some empirical support for Freidrich's theory in an analysis of 117 cases involving children aged 6–12 who had displayed problematic sexual behaviour (Boisvert *et al.*, 2015).

A further example of a multifactorial explanation can be found in Marshall and Barbaree's (1990) integrated theory, originally developed as a general theory to explain both adolescent and adult sexual offending. As with Friedrich's (2007) integrative model, Marshall and Barbaree argue that attachment difficulties are central to the aetiology of sexual violence. They propose that abusive or neglectful early environments distort internal working models of relationships and influence children's expectations about the emotional availability of significant others. Having limited opportunities to co-regulate feelings with a primary caregiver disrupts the child's capacity to develop positive self-regulation skills, which then impacts on their ability to control both aggression and sexual urges in later childhood and adolescence. Experiences of sexual abuse may compromise the acquisition of healthy interpersonal and sexual scripts, while coercive forms of parental control and exposure to domestic abuse may model the use of control and force in intimate relationships. This leads to the child having a diminished capacity to build positive relationships with peers in childhood and adolescence and to learn appropriate ways of showing intimacy. Marshall and Barbaree (1990) conclude that, while these issues can have an impact on individuals at any point in childhood, early adolescence is a critical period in any child's sexual development – it being a stage when sexual drives may be at their most urgent but least controlled, and when sexual experimentation can go wrong for even the most well-adjusted of young people. Put simply, if a young child has learnt to meet their needs through coercive means and has few, if any, healthy relationships with peers, it would follow that when they reach adolescence they may impulsively try to meet their sexual needs in a coercive manner or may seek to do so with younger or more vulnerable children.

Barbaree and Marshall's (1990) theory focuses on the impact of adverse childhood experiences on social skills and sexual regulation skills. It provides a way of understanding harmful sexual behaviour within the context of adolescent development – and sexual and romantic development in particular (Burton and Miner, 2016). The theory has been particularly influential in shaping contemporary intervention approaches with adolescents by suggesting that intimacy deficits may be a more important intervention goal than a focus on sexual fantasy or sexual deviance. The combination of factors described in the theory resonates with some research findings. For example, a recent Icelandic study of a non-clinical sample of 10,515 students (mean age 17.7 years) in further education (Sigurdsson et al., 2010) identified a subgroup of young people who self-reported using sexual violence towards another in childhood (n=334). They were differentiated from non-abusive contemporaries by factors such as (in order of statistical significance): having a history of sexual abuse; experiencing violence at home; disinhibited sexual behaviour (including frequent pornography use); and having delinquent peers.

Seto and Lalumière's (2010) meta-analysis and Fox's (2017) study comparing sex offending and non-sex offending adolescents offer less support to Barbaree and Marshall's (1990) theory. Seto and Lalumière (2010) found that attachment difficulties were not significantly over-represented among young people with harmful sexual behaviour in comparison to those involved with non-sexual offending, although they caution that only two of the studies examined attachment specifically. Social isolation rather than poor social skills differentiated the sex offending from the non-sex offending group. Neither the meta-analysis nor Fox's (2017) study found differences in impulsivity across the two groups, although in both studies impulsivity was generally high. Household violence in both studies was lower among the sex offending groups. Particular attitudes and beliefs about women or sexual offending did not help to explain the commission of sexual offences, as these attitudes were as common in the non-sexual offending group. Accordingly, Seto and Lalumiere (2010) suggest that arguments about problematic sexual scripts in relation to consent and coercion have poor explanatory power and could not explain why some young people with similar backgrounds display harmful sexual behaviour while others engage in non-sexual offending behaviour.

However, just because a factor is common to both young people who have displayed harmful sexual behaviour and those involved in non-sexual offending behaviour does not necessarily mean that it is irrelevant to the aetiology of harmful sexual behaviour or should not be targeted in the course of interventions. While these factors may not differentiate these two particular groups, they may still hold explanatory power for why a young person has become involved in some kind of offending behaviour. They might also help to explain sexual offending in particular through interaction with other factors. Accordingly, Seto and Lalumière (2010) suggest that theories that include factors that do not differentiate sex offending from non-sex offending groups should drop those factors or specify their complex causal relationship with other variables.

Seto and Lalumière (2010) argue that young people who have displayed harmful sexual behaviour share a lot of commonalities and characteristics with young people who have been involved with delinquent behaviour. However, they suggest general delinquency theories insufficiently explain harmful sexual behaviour, because several variables distinguish sex offending and non-sex offending groups, such as atypical sexual interests and experiencing sexual abuse. A simpler and more straightforward theory of adolescent sex offending might be provided by a combination of general delinquency risk factors and factors that have negatively impacted on sexual development in childhood. This theory may be particularly relevant with respect to those young people involved with both sex and non-sexual offending (Butler and Seto, 2002) but may be less useful in explaining why some young people commit only sexual offences. In short, although the empirical research literature highlights common influencing risk factors, attempts to knit these together in a psychological theory that causally explains the emergence of harmful sexual behaviour in some children and young people rather than others have so far been unsuccessful.

Sociological explanations

In a critical review of empirical evidence relating to the aetiology of child sexual abuse over the last fifteen years, Clayton *et al.* (2018, in press) conclude that:

> The causes and conditions leading to the perpetration of child sexual abuse are numerous, varied, and operate at different levels of influence. Child sexual abuse is related to static factors such as victim disability; dynamic factors such as offence location; proximal factors such as perpetrator psychology; and distal factors such as perpetrator childhood experiences.

Smallbone (2016) expands on this point by drawing on situational crime theory to argue that child sexual abuse results from the relationship between three elements – a place, a perpetrator and a victim. Just as not all children and young people are equally disposed to act in sexually abusive ways, and not all children are equally at risk of being victimised, not all settings are equally likely to be scenes of abuse. Thinking about sexual abuse as an incident occurring in a specific time and place involving more than one participant encourages a shift from viewing harmful sexual behaviour as inherent to an individual with certain dispositional traits, and instead to seeing risk of abuse as involving an interplay between self and environment. At present, risk is generally assessed by focusing on a young person's psychological profile without considering the impact of environment, even though 'high risk' young people are not at high risk all the time and other proximal or distal factors must moderate or amplify risk. While acknowledging the role of human agency in sexual abuse, Smallbone (2016) suggests that we may need to think a little less about risky people and a little more about risky contexts.

Consideration of contextual factors has also been highlighted in recent research by Firmin (2017) in an analysis of nine cases of adolescent peer-on-peer violence. Three of the cases involved murder, and six involved multiple-perpetrator rape. Through case file reviews of 145 individuals connected to these incidents as victims, perpetrators, family members or peer group members, an explanation of the behaviour that moves beyond individual characteristics of the perpetrators and victims emerges. Firmin argues that experiences in the home, in conjunction with experiences in peer groups and school environments that reinforce hegemonic masculine relations between adolescent boys, provide a more contextual narrative explanation of abuse. This deepens and extends our understanding of this behaviour beyond the analysis of individual psychological factors that are insufficient in helping us to understand why, in a group of children with similar backgrounds, some emerge as victims and others as perpetrators. Firmin challenges us to consider whether what appears to be the behaviour of a single individual might be better understood within a wider context of social networks and social spaces. She concludes:

> While police investigations drew evidence from peer groups, schools and neighbourhoods to build a case about the murders and rapes in question, the assessments of young people involved failed to recognise the significance of their relationships with these same social spaces ... In failing to assess the interplay between agency and context in the cases under consideration, professionals were left with the impression that risk was solely the product of young people's behaviours, and not the relationship between contexts and the behaviours that occurred within them (Firmin, 2017).

Firmin (2017) highlights how social contexts are gendered, and how other people within these contexts may reinforce or challenge harmful gender norms. This theme also emerges in research undertaken by Messerschmidt (2012) involving a series of detailed life history interviews with thirty White, US, working-class girls and boys aged 15–18. Ten had displayed harmful sexual behaviour, ten had engaged in violent non-sexual offending behaviour and ten had shown no signs of sexual or non-sexual violence. Messerschmidt (2011, p. 207) found these interviews to represent 'detailed accounts of embodied gender interactions in three distinct "sites": the family, the school and the peer group'. He sees harmful sexual behaviour as a situated dynamic involving the performing of gender as a form of social control over others. When aged fifteen, one of the boys in the study sexually abused two girls aged between six and eight, for whom he was babysitting. Messerschmidt argues that one way of understanding this behaviour is within the context of a set of socially constructed assumptions about male sexuality, which legitimised the boy's belief in his 'entitlement' to apply pressure on girls to have sex. The boy experienced bullying at school and felt unable to connect with female peers to whom he was sexually attracted, all within a context of a male peer discourse that sexually objectivised girls and valued public boasting about heterosexual sexual exploits and experiences. Messerchsmidt concludes that this boy:

> decided to attempt to overcome his lack of masculine resources and thereby diminish the negative masculine feelings and situations through controlling and manipulating behaviour ... expressing control and power over younger girls through sexuality (Messerschmidt, 2012, p. 101).

This contrasts with Seto and Lalumière's (2010) finding that problematic sexual scripts concerning consent and coercion did not differentiate adolescent boys who had displayed harmful sexual behaviour from those who had engaged in non-sexual offending, and their conclusion that such problematic sexual scripts held poor explanatory power. Messerschmidt (2012), drawing on qualitative rather than quantitative methodologies, suggests that the concept of hegemonic masculinities allows us to see the interaction between social isolation, problematic sexual scripts and a particular male peer discourse that are the social factors in which this particular boy's abusive behaviour is rooted.

Both Firmin (2017) and Messerschmidt (2012) argue that questions about gender have been strikingly absent from aetiological theories of harmful sexual behaviour. It is indeed the case that more sexual violence is perpetrated by boys in comparison to girls, just as it is that more girls are sexually victimised than boys. As Clayton *et al.* (2018, in press) put it in their discussion of the aetiology of child sexual abuse generally:

> Noticeably absent from the research is evidence pertaining to community and sociocultural factors. It is important to question critically how different factors interact. For instance, the evidence indicates that girls are more at risk of child sexual abuse, however we do not know what mechanisms are operating to produce this increased risk for girls. Feminist theory hypothesises that culture enforces an unequal social structure that disadvantages women and girls. In addition, patriarchal structures may discourage boys from reporting or recognising their experiences as abusive. However, we found no studies exploring the intersections between gender identities and sociocultural constructs.

Durham (2006) also examines, from a theoretical perspective, why boys are over-represented among those who sexually abuse and why girls are over-represented as victims. He explores elements that often cluster together when harmful sexual behaviour emerges and links this to power relationships operating at different but inter-related levels of social interaction in the context of widespread oppressive social and political influences. At the heart of the model is the young person as an agent of choice and action, with particular wishes, desires and beliefs. However, the young person is impacted by experiences at different levels of social ecology (see Figure 4.1). Interactions with family, peer group and society provide sites of learning and influence.

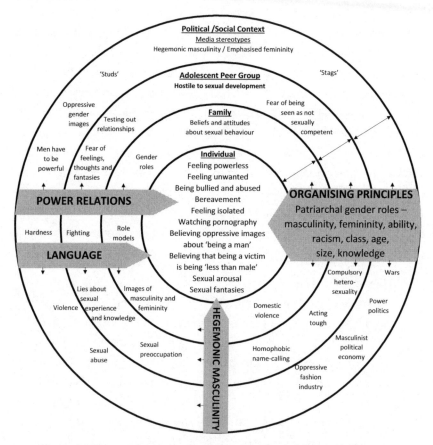

Figure 4.1 The social context of young people's harmful sexual behaviour.
(Durham, 2006, p. 32).

Durham (2006) argues that this model encourages practitioners to think about the wider social and cultural influences on the abusing child's actions. By considering the wider social messages a young person receives about how they should feel and behave, we find clues about how a diverse range of factors have intersected and accumulated to precipitate the circumstances, thoughts, feelings and beliefs that underpin harmful sexual behaviour. Furthermore, the model allows the practitioner to address their power relationship with the child or young person through understanding these power relationships with which the young person has grown up. This is critical to any reflective practice involving children who have abused, children who have experienced abuse, and children who have both abused and been abused. Durham's argument helps us to develop ways of framing ethical approaches to working with people who have caused suffering to others, but who have experienced many injustices themselves, and who may now find themselves in a criminal justice system that could cause them developmental and/or psychological harm. This model suggests ways in which we 'respectfully address young people's experiences of disadvantage and victimisation, without sacrificing the priority of responsibility and accountability for their abusive actions' (Jenkins, 2004b, p. 99). This could, for example, involve using young people's experience of maltreatment and injustice in order to help construct a 'moral compass' that allows them to appreciate the impact of their own behaviour upon others more successfully than they could prior to exploring their own victimisation (Jenkins, 2004a).

Sociological theories are ultimately difficult to test, but they do highlight significant gaps in our understanding of why harmful sexual behaviour occurs, as well as presenting some account of its gendered nature. They highlight the need to consider why a particular young person abused a particular victim at a particular time and place instead of analysing a set of characteristics that construct the young person as 'other'. Rather than asking us to consider what is wrong with the young person who has abused, they ask us to find out what experiences and contexts have contributed to shaping the individual and the behaviour that cause harm to others and themselves.

Conclusion

Harmful sexual behaviour displayed by children and young people is unlikely to be explained by one single theory. Contradictions remain between the theories that are currently available, and the challenge for theorists set out by

Seto and Lalumière (2010) is to be able to specify and demonstrate the causal relationships of factors in interaction with each other, where those factors on their own do not differentiate between groups of children and young people who have engaged in harmful sexual behaviour, non-sexual offending or no offending behaviour at all.

In the meantime, practitioners are likely to be in the position of using available theories judiciously, in considering which of the theories or combinations of theories might help to provide the most plausible explanation for the harmful sexual behaviour displayed by a particular young person. In general terms, however, it is important to consider not only the individual histories and psychological factors that may have contributed to the behaviour, but also the wider social networks and environments that set the context for the behaviour. Individualist theories may overplay psychological factors and unnecessarily pathologise individual children and young people involved in harmful sexual behaviour, which might be better understood as a social problem taking place in particular social spaces and contexts.

The analysis of the meaning of gender norms – and masculinity in particular – for both the young person, their family context and their peer group, needs to be a focus for both assessment and intervention work. Such assessment and intervention work should be trauma-informed, cognisant not only of sexual victimisation but also of multiple forms of adverse experiences that many children and young people who have displayed harmful sexual behaviour are likely to have experienced. It is possible that, in some circumstances, the abusive behaviour displayed by the child could provide some insight into the kind of trauma that they have suffered. Harmful sexual behaviour can, sometimes, be the first indicator to professionals of child protection concerns and/or unmet needs in relation to a child's welfare and emotional well-being.

Chapter 5

Assessment

Introduction

> In 1989, we assessed an adolescent male who had offended sexually, and we concluded that he was a high risk to reoffend – based on our unstructured clinical judgment. In 1989, there was virtually no guidance from published research regarding risk assessments for this population, and most professionals relied on unstructured clinical judgment. Ten years later – in 1999 – this young man was a father of a young boy. A child protection worker came across the ten year old risk assessment and subsequently removed the young boy from his parents (Worling, 2017).

This quote illustrates the degree of responsibility that sits with professionals when assessing children and young people who have displayed harmful sexual behaviour. Overestimation of risk, on the one hand, can lead to disproportionate measures to protect public safety, the stifled social development of children and adolescents, anguish and distress for families and even breaches of basic human rights. Underestimation of risk, on the other hand, can lead to inadequate public protection and further abuse and harm to victims. The stakes in assessment work are high.

In this chapter we consider contemporary approaches to the assessment of this client group. We argue that a broad understanding of behaviour within the context of the child's development and social ecology is necessary if we are to reduce risk, promote community safety and improve outcomes. Assessments need to inform defendable plans to prevent harm rather than predict risk, and particular attention needs to be paid to the promotion of welfare needs.

This chapter is not a practical guide to undertaking assessments with children and young people who have displayed harmful sexual behaviour; rather, it sets out the key principles and debates within this field. For a more comprehensive introduction to interviewing young people and their families and to report writing, the reader is advised to consult guides such as Prescott (2009), Rich (2009), O'Reilly and Carr (2004), Brady and McCarlie (2014) and Worling and Langton (2016).

A tiered approach to assessment

Assessment has been described as the cornerstone of good practice with children and young people who have displayed harmful sexual behaviour (Rich, 2017a). Assessments can be undertaken for different purposes in diverse contexts, such as child welfare or child protection decision-making, as part of youth and criminal justice processes or when clinical assessments are requested in child and adolescent mental-health settings. They can also take place at different stages: to inform early interventions and responses immediately after concerns are raised; prior to sentencing if a young person has been charged with a serious sexual offence; or even after interventions have been completed to evaluate progress and identify whether ongoing risk management measures are needed in the community.

There are a wide range of behaviour and contexts leading to children and young people getting into trouble because of their sexual behaviour, and the level and intrusiveness of assessment needs to match the seriousness of the behaviour and legal context. Initial assessment or screening will be necessary to appraise whether the sexual behaviour is normative or harmful. If screening suggests that the behaviour is inappropriate or problematic rather than abusive or violent, a brief assessment would be appropriate, involving an interview with parents, limited engagement with the child, and a review of collateral sources of information (e.g. statements from children interviewed by professionals, a developmental chronology, a full summary of behavioural concerns and reports from education, police, health and social services). Behaviour of this nature is often an expression of a range of problems or underlying vulnerabilities. Detailed and lengthy assessments are likely to be stigmatising, result in avoidable upset for the child and their family and are unlikely to lead to positive outcomes.

Where behaviour has been abusive or violent, a more comprehensive assessment is required to consider risk within the context of the child's broader welfare needs. The analysis of the behaviour and its context to help estimate the likelihood of future harm – the component of the comprehensive assessment typically described as the 'risk assessment' – will be used to inform decision-making about proportionate measures to protect future potential victims; to identify risk factors to be addressed through interventions in order to reduce the level of risk presented; and to lay the foundations for supporting the child or young person's ongoing social development in safe and healthy ways. In short, comprehensive assessments need to answer the following questions:

- Why has the young person behaved in a harmful sexual manner?
- How likely are they to do so again, to whom and in what particular circumstances?
- What needs to be done in the short term to manage risks?
- What are the indicators of risk increasing or decreasing?
- What needs to be done in the longer term to reduce risks and to support prosocial development?
- How will progress be measured?

All comprehensive assessments tend to follow a similar process:

- collecting data, and identifying historical and current factors about the child, their life circumstances, family, peer group and environment as well as the context of the behaviour that supports further harmful sexual behaviour (risk factors) or desistance (strengths);
- applying professional knowledge to interpret the meaning of risk factors and strengths to consider the pattern, seriousness, nature and likelihood of future harmful behaviour to produce an understanding of risk;
- making judgements about relationships, risks, safety and potential for change for the child, family and environment;
- recommending the measures required to facilitate safety and change. This will typically include type and intensity of intervention tailored to individual, family and community characteristics and consideration of how progress will be measured;
- ensuring meaningful communication of the assessment to those who need to act upon it (Milner *et al.*, 2015).

Accordingly, a tiered approach to assessment would involve initial screening of concerns, brief assessment for the majority of cases involving children and young people who have displayed harmful sexual behaviour, and more comprehensive and detailed assessments for the critical few where behaviour is abusive or violent and/or there is a high level of complexity (see Figure 5.1).

Factors related to sexual recidivism

It is widely assumed by the public that most young people are at high risk of persisting with harmful sexual behaviour and will go on to become adult sexual

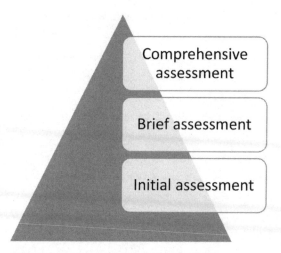

Figure 5.1: A tiered approach to assessment.

offenders (Rich, 2017a). The overwhelming empirical evidence does not substantiate this, and the majority of children and young people grow out of this behaviour before they reach adulthood. Counterintuitively, past behaviour is not the best predictor of future behaviour when we consider young people who sexually abuse others. Reitzel and Carbonell's (2006) meta-analysis of relevant studies found sexual recidivism rates of 19% for young people who had not participated in interventions and 7% for those who had. A more recent meta-analysis of 106 studies involving 33,783 adolescents adjudicated for a sexual offence between 1938 and 2014 reported even lower sexual recidivism figures of 4.9% over an average follow-up period of nearly five years (Caldwell, 2016). Low recidivism rates are also reported in studies with relatively long follow-up periods. Worling *et al.* (2010), for example, in a study of 148 Canadian young people who completed intervention work in relation to harmful sexual behaviour, found a sexual recidivism rate of 5% after ten years and 9% after twenty years.

While encouraging, the low recidivism figures are specific to sexual recidivism only. Non-sexual recidivism has been found to be six times more likely than sexual recidivism in samples of these young people (Caldwell, 2002). It is important that risk assessments and interventions, therefore, address risk of possible future non-sexual offending as well as sexual offending. Furthermore, these figures underestimate genuine rates of reoffending as they are based on reported crime only; child sexual abuse is significantly under-reported by victims, and many cases involving recidivism will never be known to statutory authorities.

Finally, even though the numbers of young people who persist with abusive sexual behaviour into adulthood are low, these young people often cause very significant harm to further victims. Risk assessment is crucial, therefore, if professionals are to target scarce resources at the minority who are most in need and present the highest levels of risk to others.

Recidivism studies highlight specific psychological and contextual factors statistically associated with reoffending, which may be different from aetiological factors because the reasons why an individual persists with a behaviour may be very different from the reasons relating to the emergence of the behaviour. Findings in relation to risk factors that are empirically associated with recidivism have, to date, been equivocal and often contradictory. Worling and Långström (2006) examined twenty-one of the most commonly cited risk factors identified in the literature and tested which were supported by research (see Figure 5.2).

Empirically supported risk factors	Promising risk factors
Supported in at least two published, independent research studies • sexual interest in prepubescent children and/or sexual interest in violence; • prior convictions for sexual offences; • multiple victims; • social isolation; • failure in completing an intervention programme in relation to harmful sexual behaviour.	*Supported by at least one study* • problematic parent–child relationships; • attitudes supportive of sexually abusive behaviour.
Possible risk factors	**Unlikely risk factors**
Clinical support only • impulsivity; • anti-social orientation; • aggression; • negative peer group association; • sexual pre-occupation; • harmful sexual behaviour towards a male victim; • harmful sexual behaviour towards a prepubescent child; • use of violence, force, threats or weapons in sexual offence; • environmental support for re-offending (e.g. unsupervised access to potential victims).	*Contradicted by empirical evidence* • history of sexual victimisation; • history of non-sexual offending; • sexual offences involving penetration; • denial of sexual offending; • low victim empathy.

Figure 5.2: Typology of risk factors for adolescent sexual recidivism (adapted from Worling and Långström, 2006).

This typology has not been replicated to date, although a more recent meta-analysis by McCann and Lussier (2008) found most empirically supported factors were consistent with Worling and Långström's (2006) review. However, they also found that several factors, which had been considered unlikely or empirically unsupported by Worling and Långström, were predictive of future sexual offending, including previous non-sexual offending, use of threats or weapons, having a male victim and having a prepubescent victim. Other empirically supported factors that have emerged in recidivism studies include having a victim who is a stranger, onset of harmful sexual behaviour in prepubescence, and impaired social functioning (Richardson, 2009). It is likely that low base rates of recidivism and the heterogeneity of this population combined with small sample sizes in studies have contributed to the inconsistency of these findings.

A criticism of recidivism studies is that they typically focus on deficits and negative experiences in the life of the child and their family to the exclusion of strengths and protective factors that may moderate risk in some way. Some structured methods for measuring strengths have emerged: for example, the Protective Factors Scale (Bremer, 1998), DASH-13 (Worling, 2013) and the SAPROF-YV (de Vries Robbé et al., 2015). Further research is required before strengths can contribute consistently and successfully to risk assessment. However, assessing for strengths remains important in order to identify factors that may promote prosocial development and to establish approach-orientated goals in intervention (Spice et al., 2013; Langton and Worling, 2015; Zeng et al., 2015b). Recent guidance from the Association for the Treatment of Sexual Abusers (ATSA) has suggested that factors which warrant consideration as potential protective factors include:

- personal responsibility and self-efficacy;
- emotion regulation skills and coping strategies;
- self-control and impulse management;
- problem-solving skills;
- a close relationship with at least one competent, caring, prosocial adult;
- positive caregiver and family relationships;
- caregiver monitoring and positive discipline;
- friendships and/or romantic attachments with prosocial peers;
- prosocial investments such as school engagement (ATSA, 2017).

Risk assessment tools

Approaches to risk assessment have evolved considerably over the last thirty years. As the quote at the beginning of this chapter illustrates, until the 1990s risk assessments were undertaken by professionals using 'unstructured clinical judgement' – professional discretion based on experience rather than an understanding of empirical risk factors and how they are associated with risk. There is considerable evidence that unstructured clinical judgement is generally poor at predicting risk (Hanson and Thornton, 2000; Grove and Meehl, 1996; Harris *et al.*, 1998). The abusive nature of a young person's behaviour can raise professional anxieties, leading potentially to assumptions about the inherent 'dangerousness' of the child and overestimation of risk (see Chapter 1).

Despite poor, limited and contradictory evidence about risk and protective factors, a range of structured risk assessment instruments or tools have been developed by researchers to guide professionals in the task of empirically based estimation of risk. Most focus on adolescence, although assessment manuals and protocols have been developed for use with children (e.g. Friedrich, 2007). Guidance for practitioners in relation to the assessment of adolescent harmful sexual behaviour typically recommends the use of these tools (e.g. Youth Justice Board, 2008; Hackett *et al.*, 2016; NICE, 2016; ATSA, 2017; CYCJ, 2017) and they are increasingly adopted by practitioners and agencies. Indeed, in the US, they were used by more than 50% of adolescent community-based programmes in 2009 in comparison to only 20% of programmes in 2002 (McGrath *et al.*, 2009). The most commonly deployed are listed in Figure 5.3, although there is some geographical variation in relation to their use, with AIM2 being popular in the UK and J-SOAP II and ERASOR being widely adopted in other jurisdictions.

As with structured assessment tools in the child protection field (Gold *et al.*, 2001), predictive validity of risk assessment tools with adolescents who have displayed harmful sexual behaviour have been highly inconsistent to date. A meta-analysis of published and unpublished validation studies found only moderate predictive validity among all risk assessment tools examined (Viljoen *et al.*, 2012). At the time of writing, robust and independent empirical validation of tools is lacking.

It may be that inconsistent findings from small studies of risk factors have contributed to adolescent risk assessment tools having poor predictive accuracy, and less accuracy than those in the adult sexual offending field. Some

Risk-assessment tool	Age/gender applicability	Description
Assessment, intervention and moving on (AIM2) (Print et al., 2007)	12–18 males	• 75-item assessment framework designed to help practitioners consider relevant intervention goals in addition to quantifying risk and level of supervision; • assesses both strengths and concerns in 4 domains.
Estimate of risk of adolescent sexual offence recidivism (ERASOR) (Worling and Curwen, 2001)	12–18 males	• 25-item structured assessment tool with 4 subscales; • based on structured professional judgement approach and does not apply cut-off scores in determining level of risk.
Juvenile sex offender assessment protocol (Prentky and Righthand, 2003)	12–18 males	• 28-item checklist of static and dynamic risk factors with 4 subscales; • no cut-off scores and authors recommend judgement of risk of reoffending not made exclusively on J-SOAP-II scores (Righthand et al., 2005)
Juvenile risk assessment tool (J-RAT, v4) (Rich, 2017b)	12–18 males	• 97-item structured clinical assessment tool designed to assess risk with individuals who have displayed – or are alleged to have displayed – harmful sexual behaviour; • features 12 risk domains, 3 scales and 24 protective factors.
Juvenile risk assessment scale (JRAS) (New Jersey Attorney General's Office, 2006)	under age of 18 males and females	• 14-item actuarial tool designed to assess the risk of future sexual harm among males and females; • rates offender characteristics as 'low', 'medium' or 'high' risk.
Sexually harmful adolescent risk assessment protocol (SHARP) (Richardson, 2009)	13–18 males	• 62-item structured assessment tool that evaluates risk of future harmful sexual behaviour; • clusters items in 12 domains; • based on structured professional judgement approach.
Juvenile sex offending recidivism risk assessment tool (J-SORRAT- II) (Epperson et al., unpublished)	12–18 males	• 12-item actuarial tool designed to assess risk of sexual recidivism among males who have displayed harmful sexual behaviour; • comprised solely of static items.
Multiplex guided inventory of ecological aggregates for assessing sexually abusive adolescents and children (MEGA) (Miccio-Fonseca, 2006)	4–19 males and females	• 76-item structured assessment protocol designed to assess risk of 'coarse improprieties or sexually abusive behaviour' (author's terms); • features 4 scales and includes both protective and risk factors; • classifies youth as 'low', 'moderate', 'high' and 'very high' risk.
Assessing risk to repeat sexual behaviour problems (AR-RSPB Version 2.1) (Curwen, 2011)	under 12 males and females	• 34-item assessment tool designed to assist in assessment of children's risk of continued 'sexual behaviour problems' (author's term); • clusters items into 6 categories; • modelled on ERASOR.
Protective and risk observations for eliminating sexual offense recidivism (PROFESOR) (Worling, 2017)	12–25 males and females	• structured checklist to assist professionals to identify and summarise protective and risk factors for adolescents and emerging adults who have offended sexually; • 20 risk/protective factors; • intended to assist with planning interventions that can help individuals to enhance their capacity for sexual and relationship health and, thus, eliminate sexual recidivism.

Figure 5.3: Child and adolescent sexual recidivism risk assessment tools

(adapted from RMA, n.d.).

authors argue that more precise and focused risk prediction and decision-making in the forensic risk assessment field generally may in the future flow from better algorithmic modelling of risk through the use of larger data sets (Duwe and Kim, 2015). However, plasticity of developmental traits in childhood may make accurate prediction of this kind impossible. For example, there is evidence to suggest that the relevance of different factors changes at different stages in childhood. Van der Put *et al.* (2011) note that peer influence increases with age, while the impact of parental supervision decreases. They conclude that the meaning of risk and protective factors are not fixed and accordingly need to be considered within the context of the age and stage of a particular child's development. Undertaking a risk assessment without a comprehensive history of the child's development, an understanding of family and peer dynamics, and knowledge about typical social and psychological maturation processes in adolescence and young adulthood will lead to a limited appraisal of risk and a potentially ineffective intervention plan (Rich, 2017a).

Myers (2007) argues that risk assessment tools meet a need for certainty among professionals when dealing with anxiety in relation to risk. In fulfilling that need, professionals often pay too little attention to the context of research findings, their limitations and the level of disagreement between studies. Myers goes on to suggest that tools often ask practitioners to assess fluid and contextual factors, such as antisocial attitudes and sexual interests, with no baseline data about the nature and prevalence of these factors in the general population and without an understanding of the specific mechanisms through which they develop and impact on the behaviour of children and adolescents.

Other authors have similarly noted that the construct of 'risk factor' purports to be scientific, but often masks significant definitional and conceptual issues about how they causally relate to recidivism. Heffernan and Ward (2017) argue, for example, that 'social isolation' as a risk factor raises questions about what causes that social isolation: over-sensitivity to interpersonal threat; shyness; a lack of social skills; harassment and stigmatisation in the community; or any combination of these or other influences. Different contexts for social isolation may mean that the factor will have a variety of meanings in relation to risk and desistance for different young people and will need to be addressed in alternative ways. Turning risk factors into intervention goals requires an understanding of what that factor means in the context of the child's life and social ecology.

A further danger with the uncritical use of risk assessment tools is that they can lead to overly simplistic constructions of risk. Consider the challenges the practitioner faces when undertaking an assessment. Decisions dependent on risk assessments may include whether a child can remain at home or whether an alternative placement should be sought; whether a child can stay at a particular school or whether a move to a more restrictive educational environment is needed; whether a child can continue living with a sibling they have abused, and if separated whether they should maintain contact, or at what point they could return to live at home. In such situations, practitioners need to consider risk management measures such as levels of supervision required, monitoring, victim safety planning and information-sharing including the need for community notification. Tools that simply band young people into high, medium and low risk provide little guidance for making judgements about such complex issues, and qualitative studies have suggested that practitioners find it difficult to interpret the scoring of assessment tools for these purposes (Deacon, 2015).

The overall consensus is that risk assessment tools should be used to guide plans to reduce risk and prevent relapse rather than predict risk in an actuarial or statistical fashion (Rich, 2017a). It may be impossible to predict with certainty what an individual will do in the future, but it is possible to use the evidence in an individual case, in the context of what is known about similar individuals from the research literature, in order to identify risk and protective factors of relevance to understanding previous harmful sexual behaviour and the potential for future similar behaviour. Evidence is uneven about the value of specific tools, but the overwhelming evidence is that risk assessment tools are a better guide to identifying young people who require targeted resources and specific support in relation to this behaviour than unstructured clinical judgement. Tools should not be used uncritically. Assessment approaches are needed that not only consider the likelihood of risk, but also consider in a more narrative way what the individual is likely to do, whom they are most likely to harm and in what particular circumstances or contexts.

Moving beyond the risk assessment paradigm

It is further argued that current assessment approaches significantly misunderstand key challenges posed by children and young people who have displayed harmful sexual behaviour. A primary concern with risk in assessments, for example, potentially diverts attention away from evaluation of the more general welfare needs of the developing child. This issue is underlined in research into the life course trajectories of young people who have displayed harmful sexual behaviour. One UK study followed up sixty-nine young people as adults at least ten years after the end of interventions (Hackett *et al.* 2012; Hackett and Masson, 2012). A small proportion had reoffended sexually (6%), with a limited number having been reconvicted for serious offences of physical assault, violence and – in one case – murder. However, when welfare outcomes were examined, only about one-quarter reported positive outcomes in terms of employment, health, housing, lifestyle, romantic relationships and family contact. Stable partner relationships or enduring carer and professional relationships were a feature of most adults who had managed to progress in terms of quality of life. Relationship failure, chaotic or unstable living conditions and drug and alcohol misuse were common among those with the worst outcomes.

A similar smaller Swedish study followed up twenty young people who had displayed harmful sexual behaviour ten years after they had completed interventions and found that most had significant difficulties with intimacy, which then limited their capacity to develop romantic relationships and friendships (Ingevaldson *et al.*, 2016). Furthermore, a Dutch study using longitudinal data concerning a group of young adults who had committed sexual offences in their adolescence (n=496) found that employment was associated with desistance, but many young people faced considerable barriers in securing and maintaining stable employment (Van den Berg *et al.*, 2014).

If risk of sexual recidivism in adulthood is generally low for young people who have sexually abused, but outcomes in relation to emotional well-being and social capital are generally poor, assessments need to consider risk within a broader appraisal of the wider welfare needs of these children and young people. Assessments, therefore, should make recommendations about how both criminogenic and welfare needs are targeted holistically during the intervention phase of the work, including therapeutic needs relating to experience of trauma in childhood. Hackett and Masson's (2012) research, in particular, suggests that assisting young people with the support and resources required to become more socially anchored within their communities as they move into young adulthood should be a key focus of interventions, and assessments should identify how this is best achieved.

Furthermore, a primary concern with psychological factors in assessing risk potentially ignores situational and contextual factors that may need to be addressed if sexual abuse is to be prevented in similar settings in the future. With peer-on-peer sexual abuse, data will need to be collected and analysed in order to inform future situational prevention (Firmin *et al.*, 2016b). A local authority manager in a recent study illustrated how this could be done:

> Our borough has seen a big increase in online exploitation in the last year, this in part due to peer exploitation online. This has led to a profile specifically around peer exploitation and online exploitation and what it looks like in our borough. Specific schools have been identified where a high volume of 'sexting' reports have been received and additional training/awareness-raising has been rolled out. We have also been able to look at the most common social media sites/ apps that are being used for online exploitation and have started a dialogue with one of these pages around what steps we can take to address these issues (Firmin *et al.*, 2016a, p. 109).

Requesting a multi-agency review of factors relating to safety in a particular setting or context may be an appropriate assessment recommendation in order to help safeguard potential future victims. Frameworks for considering risk in institutional and community settings may be relevant (Johnstone and Cooke, 2008; Firmin *et al.*, 2016a). Managerial oversight of assessments linked to strategic multi-agency governance and coordination is important in detecting emerging local patterns, which can then inform strategic decision-making that avoids a fragmented and non-systemic approach to risk reduction.

An evidence-based approach to assessment

Several findings drawn from relevant research and the general practice literature can inform the comprehensive assessment of children and young people who have displayed harmful sexual behaviour.

Context of assessment

Clarification of the legal context (criminal proceedings, care proceedings, parental responsibility, child protection context etc.) is necessary before beginning an assessment (Vizard, 2002). Legal processes vary between jurisdictions, but there is a common view that assessment should occur only after any legal processes are completed if the young person is charged with a sexual offence (Worling and Langton, 2016). However, such processes can create delays – sometimes taking years rather than months – and significant decisions often need to be made in the meantime about where a child can live, where they go to school and what activities they can participate in. An interim pre-adjudication evaluation akin to the brief assessment process described at the start of this chapter can ensure that decisions are made in a transparent, ethical and evidence-based way, rather than relying on unstructured judgements that are likely significantly to underestimate or overestimate risk (Allardyce and McAfee, 2016).

Confidentiality, privacy and consent to assess

Rapport building and the development of a trusting, therapeutic relationship in a safe environment will be necessary when working with children and young people who are likely to be experiencing shame, embarrassment and distress. A recent evidence review of research regarding assessments suggests sensitivity to cultural perspective and specific family supports is necessary (Campbell et al., 2016a). Assessment approaches should be motivational, and model hope and the potential for positive change. Partnership and collaboration are fundamental to working with children and their families who may already have been affected by abuse and maltreatment, and who may also feel disempowered and stigmatised by child protection and legal processes. The child and their parents or carers will need to make an informed decision based on clear information about whether they wish to be involved in an assessment. Some will feel pressurised to attend, and particular care will be necessary when obtaining consent from individuals such as children and young people with learning disabilities (Worling and Langton, 2016). Professionals will need to explain to the child and their parents:

- the nature and purpose of the assessment, outlining potential benefits, risks and limitations of the assessment procedures that will be used;
- the potential implications of participating or declining to participate in the assessment;
- the limits of confidentiality, such as persons or agencies to whom the findings will be provided and under what circumstances information will be shared with other agencies (ATSA, 2017).

Process of assessment

The goal of assessment is to build a holistic understanding of the child's life and their therapeutic needs to inform future prosocial development in a safe manner (O'Reilly and Carr, 2004). Information will be drawn from multiple sources and use multiple evaluation methods (such as interviews, psychological and educational testing and observation). Physiological testing is common in some countries (e.g. polygraphy and plethysmography) but there is limited evidence to ethically justify the use of intrusive techniques with children who are already likely to have experienced abuse in their lives (Worling and Langton, 2016). Professionals should read all relevant reports and recordings, but be aware that they may be incomplete or incorrect. Interviews should be used to gather data as well as to critically appraise, supplement, question, review and clarify information (Rich, 2009). Family members, teachers and other professionals who have information or experience of the child should be interviewed, as well as the child themselves. Professionals should recognise that feelings of shame, embarrassment and fear may mean that self-reports about the behaviour are often inaccurate, and access to victim statements will, therefore, be important (Worling and Langton, 2016).

Content

Comprehensive assessments will generally cover: developmental history; experiences of abuse and neglect; history of harmful sexual behaviour; other behavioural issues; family background; current home environment; social history; educational history; cognitive functioning; mental health and well-being; community factors and amenability to intervention on the part of parent and child (Worling and Langton, 2016). Sensitive issues such as maltreatment experiences, sexual knowledge, sexual history and sexual functioning (e.g. precocious or delayed sexual development, atypical sexual interests, sexual behaviour meeting non-sexual needs) should be addressed in the context of a safe and supportive relationship (Richardson, 2009).

Problem formulation

The task for professionals is to evaluate how the child and their family can best rebuild their lives and move on from harm in safe ways. This will involve drawing on aetiological theories to formulate a defendable hypothesis about why the behaviour developed and why it has persisted over time (if there is evidence it has). Use of assessment tools (to assess both sexual and non-sexual risk) can anchor judgements in relation to risk, but they should be integrated into a more comprehensive assessment of how the child's welfare needs are supported, and how interventions to help reduce risk are linked to the achievement of welfare goals. Activities that facilitate prosocial development, such as school engagement, prosocial peers and associations and positive mentoring relationships, can foster attitudes, skills and behaviour incompatible with sexual and non-sexual offending. Although risk management measures and interventions may be needed, it is important that they do not detract unnecessarily from prosocial activities and normative development. Assessments should consider the child's rights, and specifically how the child:

- is protected from abuse, neglect or harm at home, at school and in the community;
- learns to make healthy, safe choices;
- is supported and guided in the development of skills, confidence and self-esteem;
- has a nurturing place to live;
- has opportunities to participate safely in activities such as play, recreation and sport, which contribute to healthy growth and development, at home, in school and in the community;
- has the opportunity to be heard and involved in decisions that affect them;
- has opportunities and encouragement to play active and responsible roles at home, in school and in the community, including help to overcome social, educational, physical and economic inequalities;
- is supported to be part of the community in which they live (Scottish Government, n.d.).

Recommendations

Practitioners should recommend content, sequencing, duration and intensity of interventions that can occur in the least restrictive setting possible, while maintaining community safety and involving family or other caregivers (unless contraindicated). Indicators of how progress will be measured should be established, drawing on multiple methods: for example, behavioural information;

formal reassessment; self-reports; and reports from family and other adults in the young person's life (Mercer *et al.*, 2013). Some tools for measurement of intervention progress are available, such as the Treatment Progress Inventory for Adolescents who Sexually Abuse (TPI-ASA) (Oneal *et al.*, 2008), although they are under-evaluated. The rapid changes in physical, cognitive, emotional and social development that occur in adolescence also mean that evaluation of progress and reassessment will be necessary on a regular basis. Estimations of risk should be short-term only, and reports should note the time period for which they are valid (Fanniff and Letourneau, 2012; Worling *et al.*, 2012). Feedback regarding recommendations should be provided to the child and family in ways that they can easily understand. Situational or environmental risks should be highlighted to senior managers so that contextual risk can be strategically addressed.

Conclusion

There is a great deal at stake in assessment work, with the potential for far-reaching and long-term consequences for both public safety and for children or young people who have displayed harmful sexual behaviour. Unstructured clinical judgement is poor at predicting risk, and low rates of sexual recidivism mean that tools perform inconsistently, and provide limited assistance with respect to the complex decisions that may need to be made in response to harmful sexual behaviour. Professionals undertaking assessments should use them with a critical mindset, to guide and structure their professional judgement and problem formulation, cognisant of base rates of recidivism, the strengths and weaknesses of risk assessment tools generally, and the merits and demerits of the specific tools they use.

Assessments need to incorporate a situational perspective and should record both risk and protective factors, indicating why the practitioner thinks they are relevant to risk. Risk assessments should be used to guide short-term plans only, must be reviewed regularly, and the risks of both sexual and non-sexual recidivism need to be considered. They should also be undertaken as part of a much broader assessment task, which is concerned with intervention decisions and the wider welfare and developmental needs of the child or young person. Thought should be given to factors that build resilience and contribute to desistence, that support positive life-course trajectories, helping children to remain anchored as part of their community and ensuring that stigma and labelling are kept to a minimum.

Chapter 6

Interventions

Introduction

In previous chapters we have discussed a gradual shift away from aetiological theories and assessment approaches based on adult and individualist psychological models, towards developmentally orientated perspectives, which recognise harmful sexual behaviour displayed by children and young people as situational and multi-determined. In this chapter we discuss how this shift is reflected in changing approaches to intervention. We outline some core principles regarding tailoring of intervention to individual needs and consider the evidence as to the overall effectiveness of intervention with this client group, before going on to explore some developments and debates in relation to specific theoretical approaches.

We conclude that non-sexual recidivism studies and research regarding the life-course trajectories of these children and young people support responses that are ecologically orientated and individualised, addressing not only sexual behaviour specifically but also experiences of trauma, wider welfare and relationship needs, and the nature of their environments. We finish by discussing how current approaches to risk management may run against the grain of the ecological and developmentally sensitive intervention approaches currently advocated.

The changing nature of interventions

A survey of specialist services in the US found the number of agencies offering interventions with children and young people who had displayed harmful sexual behaviour increased fourfold between 1986 and 2002 (McGrath *et al.*, 2010). This, in part, resulted from a range of different specialised intervention manuals, workbooks and programmes for both adolescents and younger children becoming available during this period.

However, most of these programmes were modelled on manualised approaches to working with adult sex offenders and advocated a number of methods more suitable for adults. For instance, most of these programmes were delivered in groupwork contexts. This approach was considered appropriate for young people on the grounds that it was a cost-effective way to work with adult sex offenders and was assumed to be suitable for interventions with young people, who were seen as 'mini-adult sex offenders'. Over the last twenty years, there has been a gradual shift towards more developmentally orientated, systemic, holistic and – in particular – individualised approaches with children and young people. This results from the growing recognition that, although group-work may add value to certain aspects of interventions, identity formation and individuation are key tasks in adolescence. Approaches where young people in a group are treated in exactly the same way are unlikely to be dynamic enough to respond to the varying individual needs of children and young people who sexually abuse. Similarly, asking adolescents in a group context to share details of their offences and sexual thoughts and feelings at a developmental stage where they are particularly suggestible to peer influence and susceptible to bullying is likely to be counterproductive.

Core intervention principles

Interventions may take place in community, residential or custodial settings. Studies comparing interventions in community and institutional settings have found little difference in outcomes (Kahn and Chambers, 1991; Winokur *et al.*, 2006). However, guidance from ATSA concludes that interventions targeted at young people:

> ... are best offered and provided along a continuum of care – from community-based (outpatient) interventions to secure residential or correctional-based treatment programs ... Most adolescents can be safely treated in community settings. Residential and correctional settings should be reserved for the minority of youth who present with significant risk factors for recidivism or other treatment needs that cannot be met in community settings (ATSA, 2017, p. 42).

If only a minority of these children and young people are at high risk of causing further harm through sexual abuse, the majority will be suitable for interventions in the community.

This conclusion is drawn from a recognition that the nature and intensity of intervention needs to match assessed levels of risk, in line with the principles of risk, need and responsivity. These three principles have been shown to be central to effective rehabilitation services for adults and adolescents who offend (Andrews *et al.*, 1990) and have subsequently been influential in shaping practice with adolescents who sexually abuse.

The first principle – risk – requires delivery of services to focus on higher-risk cases, and is consistent with the ethics of children's legislation whereby services provide the minimum necessary level of intrusiveness to achieve a desired outcome. This means that intensive interventions and restrictions put in place to promote public protection should be reserved only for those who present the highest risks.

The second principle – criminogenic need – involves targeting interventions at factors that sustain and support criminal behaviour. As noted in the previous chapter, a developmentally orientated approach requires attention to be paid to the child or young person's wider welfare needs, but, if interventions are to foster healthy development in a safe way, it will be necessary to target factors empirically associated with harmful sexual behaviour relevant for the particular individual. This, then, creates opportunities for safe and positive prosocial experiences, which, in turn, contribute further to desistance.

The third principle – responsivity – requires the delivery of intervention programmes to be matched to the characteristics and learning styles of the child and their family to maximise positive engagement. Sensitivity to gender, along with consideration of cultural diversity and anti-oppressive practices, also relate to this principle. This may require specific knowledge and experience, such as highlighted in work with Maori youth, where practitioners found that the sexual content of questions asked of parents was considered too explicit in some communities and could lead to disengagement (Geary *et al.*, 2006; Geary *et al.*, 2011). This requires self-reflective skills in practice, such as recognising the power imbalance that exists when a practitioner is White, and the young person is from a non-White community (Mir and Okotie, 2002).

The role of the practitioner and agency

Although the 'what works' literature in relation to practice with children and young people who have displayed harmful sexual behaviour has focused on content and theoretical orientation of intervention programmes, a range of other factors may be as important in risk reduction and helping young people live more prosocial lives. One such factor is the nature of the relationship between practitioner and child.

The quality of the relationship between practitioner and client has been found to be a core condition of change in counselling, psychotherapy, and work with both adults and adolescents who offend (Dowden and Andrews, 2004; Whyte, 2008; Zuroff *et al.*, 2010; Falkenström *et al.*, 2013). Research regarding children and young people who have displayed harmful sexual behaviour has similarly found that how you work with a young person may be as important as what you do with them. In a study of adults and adolescents who completed a UK custodial sex-offending programme, between 30% and 60% of variance in beneficial effects of intervention programmes was associated with therapist style and the client's perception of the therapist (Marshall *et al.*, 2002). In a study of twenty-four young people at three community-based intervention programmes in New Zealand (Geary *et al.*, 2011), they and their parents valued practitioners who were caring, encouraging, challenging, respectful and non-judgemental. Being available outside session times, having a sense of humour and showing genuine and personal interest in the young person were qualities that were particularly appreciated. A clear continuity from assessment to intervention phase was also noted as optimum. Such qualities take on special significance in light of the shame and mistrust that many young people feel as a result of their own behaviour and the maltreatment they may have previously experienced, which leave them untrusting of new adults in their life. Sensitivity and careful pacing are required in relation to rapport building and responding to issues around denial and minimisation. Recognising that dropout from intervention programmes may elevate risk, a focus on motivation and engagement is critical (Jenkins, 1990; Jenkins, 2009).

Practitioner qualities such as empathy, respect and understanding are necessary, but they are insufficient conditions for effective work with this client group. A recent Scottish Government publication suggests that practitioners working with these children and young people will also typically require:

- an understanding of child protection and the legislative and policy context of working with children;
- training in communicating with children at all ages and stages of development, including children with special needs and/or disabilities;
- an understanding of child development and the impact of trauma;
- an ability to self-evaluate;
- skills in working with service users who do not comply with services (Scottish Government, 2014, p. 16).

To achieve this, good recruitment practices, adequate training and reflective supervision are essential, in addition to the personal characteristics of practitioners. Agency and organisational processes are vital, but under-appreciated, core constituents of effective practice. Clarity about the philosophy or theory underpinning interventions, clear programme aims, programme integrity, agreed referral pathways, consistent and proportionate responses matching interventions to those who would most benefit from them, processes for measuring outcomes, pre-prepared session plans, high-quality case recording and effective policies and procedures may all be as important as rolling out the 'best evidenced' programme locally. All of these are organisational features as much as they are the responsibility of individuals (Morrison, 2004).

Our capacity to change behaviour through a skilled and carefully planned relationship with children and young people is also inextricable from interagency context, and lead professionals will need to collaborate with other professionals, carers and family members in order to facilitate appropriate information-sharing and further the goals of intervention (Morrison, 2000). High-quality interagency work is likely to be based on:

- a shared understanding of the tasks, processes, principles, and roles and responsibilities outlined in guidance and local arrangements for protecting children and meeting their needs;
- clear communication between practitioners, including a common understanding of key terms, definitions and thresholds for action;
- effective working relationships, including an ability to work in multidisciplinary groups or teams;
- sound decision-making, based on information-sharing, thorough assessment, critical analysis and professional judgement (Scottish Government, 2014).

Frameworks and guidance are emerging to assist multi-agency partnerships to audit local service provision and working arrangements in relation to identification, assessment, intervention and risk management of this client group (e.g. Hackett et al., 2016). These can help ensure that practice is effective, consistent and sustainable over time. This is particularly important as the UK children's service managers, who participated in Clements et al.'s (2017) study, found leading multi-agency partnerships, and the design and commissioning of services in relation to harmful sexual behaviour, particularly challenging and an area in which most lacked confidence. A rapid review found that good practice in the commissioning of services in relation to harmful sexual behaviour in England was rare, and a reliance on youth justice services solely responding to this issue inhibited the amount of prevention work undertaken, as well as the timeliness of support when a child or young person is under criminal investigation or prosecution (Kaur and Christie, 2018).

Evidence of effectiveness

There is some general evidence to suggest that interventions for working with children and young people who have displayed harmful sexual behaviour may be making an increasingly significant contribution to public safety. In an overview of 106 studies of adolescent recidivism, Caldwell (2016) notes that studies conducted between 2000 and 2015 reported a sexual recidivism rate of 2.75% compared to 10.3% in the period prior to the widespread use of programmes between 1980 and 1995. In a meta-analysis of nine adolescent programmes, Reitzel and Carbonell (2006) found an average sexual recidivism rate of 7.4% for those who had completed programmes compared to 18.9% for those who had not, after an average follow-up of five years. Similarly, in a review of eleven studies of interventions for children aged 3–12, St Amand et al. (2008) found that both sexual behaviour-focused and trauma-focused interventions, particularly when linked to targeting of parenting management skills, were effective at reducing children's sexual behaviour problems.

While this all appears promising and we can have confidence that some progress has been made in the effectiveness of interventions, study designs have been insufficiently sophisticated to identify precisely what it is in these programmes that is effective. High dropout rates in studies are often reported with little analysis of the characteristics of those who did not engage, and it is not yet clear why some children and young people respond poorly to intervention and which contexts may compromise positive outcomes. Interventions with specific subgroups of young people are under-researched: for example, girls; young people with learning disabilities; and those who have abused siblings. These research gaps make it difficult to draw on empirical evidence to match specific interventions to the particular needs of specific children and young people. Furthermore, the base rate for sexual recidivism is generally low with or without intervention, making it hard to draw statistically significant conclusions from small studies. There are few large-scale collaborations between researchers to develop larger data sets; replication of studies is rare, and evaluations are often undertaken by authors of programmes themselves, with inevitable risk of bias. Most studies also focus exclusively on sexual recidivism as the key measurement of effectiveness. Quite apart from the under-reporting of sexual abuse making this a significantly flawed outcome measure, the wider welfare outcomes for these children and young people have been largely ignored, despite their being generally poor (Hackett and Masson, 2012). All of these issues have led the UK-based National Institute of Health and Care Excellence (NICE) to conclude from an overview of the intervention literature that 'the strength of the evidence is weak' (Campbell et al., 2016b, p. 118).

Traditional interventions

Notwithstanding the growing recognition among practitioners of the importance of individualised and responsive approaches, many programmes continue to share similar components, and there is considerable consensus about certain aspects of programme content. In a survey of more than 500 agencies working for adolescents and children, the following were cited as the most common elements (McGrath et al., 2010):

- victim awareness and empathy;
- social skills training/developing intimacy and related skills;
- reducing offence supportive attitudes;
- problem-solving;
- arousal control;
- emotional regulation/self-monitoring;
- increasing effectiveness of family support networks.

The majority of services providing interventions in North America and the UK are based on a cognitive behavioural therapy (CBT) model, with 80% of the services in McGrath et al. (2010) describing themselves this way. This is the theoretical approach that underpins most interventions with adult sexual offenders. Cognitive behavioural programmes encourage individuals to consider how thoughts such as attitudes to children, sex, power within relationships and the impact of their behaviour on others have justified and supported their behaviour. The focus of intervention is on changing these thought patterns, so that further harmful behaviour is avoided.

Many programmes also have a relapse-prevention component, encouraging individuals to practise relevant skills to help lead offence-free lives in the community. Increasingly, there is an emphasis in programmes focusing on skills. CBT interventions targeted at sexual thoughts and feelings in relation to younger children, for example, typically now concentrate on the skills necessary to manage and control those feelings – with some clinicians, particularly in the US, somewhat controversially suggesting these skills be bolstered by anti-libidinal pharmacological interventions (see Thibaut *et al.*, 2016 for a discussion) – rather than on the replacement of these feelings with more prosocial sexual thoughts.

Meta-analysis of programmes using CBT methodologies have found it to be moderately effective at reducing risk (Reitzel and Carbonell, 2006), although an overview of intervention effectiveness studies found that, after controlling for publication bias, a significant intervention effect was no longer found (Ter Beek *et al.*, 2017). Some have argued that studies of effectiveness of CBT programmes have been methodologically weak (Dopp *et al.*, 2017). Attrition is often an issue with these approaches, with a 28% dropout noted in a study of a UK-based, CBT-orientated programme run by the National Society for the Prevention of Cruelty to Children (NSPCC) for adolescents who had displayed harmful sexual behaviour (Belton, 2017). Some studies describe art therapy, meditation and yoga or social skills training as adjuncts to mainstream CBT approaches (Gerber, 1994; Derezotes, 2000; Graves *et al.*, 1992), and promising results are emerging from integration of CBT approaches with adventure-based programmes (Somervell and Lambie, 2009; Norton *et al.*, 2014). Although these additions have a number of different functions, they may help engage and maintain motivation among young people who struggle with the cognitive element of these programmes.

Ecologically orientated Approaches

A major criticism of CBT approaches is that they situate the problem of harmful sexual behaviour within the individual psychological profile of the child or young person rather than in the interaction between individual and their environment. This is often reinforced by the delivery of CBT interventions in settings such as clinics and institutions that provide little consideration as to how learning might be applied in real-world contexts (Letourneau *et al.*, 2009). A more developmentally nuanced approach would require practitioners to move beyond a focus on the individual to address the wider systems in which the child or young person is embedded.

Multisystemic Therapies (MST) were developed to address some of these shortcomings of CBT programmes with respect to juvenile delinquency, and an adaptation of the programme (known as MST-PSB) is used with young people who have displayed harmful sexual behaviour (Borduin *et al.*, 2011). Grounded in theories of socio-ecology (Bronfenbrenner, 1986) and family systems (Minuchin, 1985), MST proposes that behaviour is multi-determined and linked to the characteristics of the individual and their wider family, peer group, school and community contexts. MST does include some cognitive behavioural elements, but also incorporates aspects of family therapy, parent/carer training and schools-based interventions.

Four randomised clinical trials have evaluated the effects of MST-PSB to date. Two of these studies (Borduin *et al.*, 1990; Borduin *et al.*, 2009) found that MST-PSB produced significant reductions in sexual recidivism when compared to individual therapy (including CBT). A third trial (Letourneau *et al.*, 2009) compared MST-PSB to treatment-as-usual (i.e. community-based group CBT) and found that those in the MST group displayed fewer sexual and delinquent behaviour problems, less substance abuse, were less likely to externalise symptoms and had fewer out-of-home placements. A UK-based randomised clinical trial was compromised by low take-up. Although it was well evaluated by young people and their families, some staff questioned whether the model was applicable to the heterogeneity of young people who have displayed harmful sexual behaviour, and doubted whether it would be possible adequately to attend to the trauma experienced by children and their families within the programme's general 5–7-month time frame, and the limited training therapists had in working with trauma (Fonagy *et al.*, 2017).

Multimodal approaches are not unique to MST. Although there have been evaluations of other multimodal models with this client group – for example, the Wraparound Milwaukee Programme (Hunter *et al.*, 2004) – the most significant evidence of the shift to more ecologically orientated approaches is the general increased use of focused support for parents as an important adjunct to individualised CBT. In an Australian study examining the families of thirty-eight adolescents who had sexually abused in intra-familial contexts and who then attended a community-based treatment program, reported improvements were more likely when at least one parent was engaged in treatment (Thornton *et al.*, 2008). In another Australian study,

85% of twenty-four adolescents and twenty-four caregivers thought that the success of programmes was attributable to family and caregiver involvement and the young person's involvement in school, work, sports teams, church youth groups and other community activities (Geary *et al.*, 2011).

Duane and Morrison (2004, p. 123) suggest that family-focused interventions typically involve engaging parents in longer-term work to:

- increase openness and emotional expressiveness within the family;
- clarify, consolidate or restore appropriate parental and child roles;
- identify family strengths and needs;
- acknowledge and interrupt abusive family patterns;
- increase parental skills, confidence and competence in promoting accountable behaviour within the family and in handling negotiation and conflict;
- enhance the parents' protective capacity, especially in relation to boundary-setting;
- assist the parents to structure the young person's time and social activities;
- and, where it is not possible for the young person to return home, to renegotiate family relationships in order to clarify, maintain or improve contact with the family and enable the family to be a source of continuing support and significance.

Allan (2004) notes the different roles of mothers and fathers, suggesting that practitioners may need to make particular efforts in engaging with fathers. This view is supported in the wider child protection literature (e.g. Scourfield *et al.*, 2016).

School-based interventions are an important component of multimodal approaches, but are under-evaluated, reflecting a more general gap in research into schools-based programmes in non-sexual adolescent offending (Whyte, 2008). One study of 107 teachers in Australia found that 40% had taught children who had displayed problematic or harmful sexual behaviour, but most lacked confidence in such cases (Ey *et al.*, 2017). This finding is replicated in several studies of primary school teachers (Lindblad *et al.*, 1995; Larsson and Svedin, 2002). Some forms of guidance for working with children and young people who have displayed harmful sexual behaviour in educational settings have been developed in different jurisdictions, although remain under-evaluated with no data on the level of implementation (British Columbia Ministry of Education, 1999; South Australia Department for Education and Child Development, 2013; Carson, 2017).

Another promising multimodal development is the adolescent adaptation of the Good Lives Model developed by the UK-based G-Map service (Print, 2013). This model is widely used with adult sexual and non-sexual offenders (Ward and Gannon, 2006). While it is not in itself an ecologically based intervention, the G-Map adaptation (GLM-A) opens out the principles of the model so that it engages with strengths and areas for growth for both the child and adults around the child. The basic tenet of the model is that any activities people engage in involve an implicit motivation of meeting fundamental human needs, such as for safety, a sense of belonging or a sense of achievement. Children and young people who engage in harmful sexual behaviour try to meet basic needs in inappropriate ways. The goal of assessment is to identify what those needs may have been, and the intervention is then framed around the acquisition of necessary knowledge and skills in order to work towards the young person's engagement in alternative activities to meet those needs in more socially appropriate ways. The model is, therefore, not an intervention in itself; rather, it is a positive and holistic framework within which to situate an intervention plan. As Ward *et al.* put it:

> we have been so busy thinking about how to reduce ... crimes that we have overlooked a basic truth: recidivism may be further reduced through helping offenders to live better lives, not simply targeting isolated risk factors (Ward *et al.*, 2006, p. 391).

The Good Lives Model helps facilitate an ecological approach by providing clear and practical ways in which parents, carers and others can be involved in supporting the intervention plan and helping the child meet basic needs in more prosocial ways. This adaptation of the model recognises that children and young people will rarely have the skills, knowledge and authority to make significant changes in how they live their lives; they need the positive support of adults around them to make these changes. The Good Lives Model allows an element of co-construction, with goals being set in partnership between practitioner and child. Early evaluative data is positive (Print, 2013), and practitioners have reported finding it useful for ensuring that interventions are holistic, socially orientated and encourage social development within the context of natural maturation (Vaswani and Simpson, 2015).

Trauma- and attachment-based approaches

The degree of maltreatment experienced by many children and young people who have displayed harmful sexual behaviour has led to increased recognition of the relevance of trauma-related approaches to intervention. With the arrival of new techniques such as brain imaging technology (e.g. MRI scans), more is becoming known about how the brain develops and the impact of neglect and complex trauma on child and adolescent neurological, affective and cognitive development. This is still a new area of research, and sometimes stronger claims have been made than the evidence warrants (Wastell and White, 2012). Nonetheless, there is broad agreement that, during childhood, each stage of development of the brain's functions builds on the previous development, progressing from lower to higher degrees of complexity (Creeden, 2011; Perry, 2009; Painter and Scannapieco, 2013). Our ability to plan ahead, to take into account the feelings of others and to make good social choices rests on our ability to think and to reason, which builds on our ability to regulate our emotions.

Early experiences of abuse are associated with changes in both the structure and functioning of the child's brain (McCrory *et al.*, 2012; Glaser, 2014), which may not become apparent until later years (Glaser, 2014). These neurobiological changes are adaptive to the abusive environment, such as devoting the brain's resources to being constantly on the lookout for danger, but this may be at a cost to the development of more complex functions and the child's ability to cope in their wider world, in school and in their relationships with teachers and friends. In particular, without the necessary building blocks in place within the limbic system to regulate emotions, and within the cortex to think and to reason, the growing child's 'executive functions' (the ability to plan ahead and to make decisions, to control impulses, to take into account the feelings of others), which are controlled primarily by the pre-frontal cortex, remain underdeveloped.

Such an understanding of the impact of abuse and trauma on how the brain develops may assist in providing the child and their family with appropriate help and support that can aid the child's recovery from experiences of trauma. Perry (2009), for example, argues that traditional CBT-style therapies for abused children have tended to focus on activities abused children find challenging, such as reflecting on and talking through their problems, taking part in social-skills groups, or being given star charts, which reward good behaviour. The impact of trauma makes it difficult for the child to think, talk and control their impulses in this way. Instead, Perry (2009) argues, 'building blocks' need to be established prior to CBT interventions, to calm down the overactive brain stem and limbic system, to help the child become more emotionally regulated, less anxious and less vigilant for danger. Repetitive and patterned movement, music and rhythm, therapeutic massage and yoga may all be helpful for the child in therapy, in order for them to build networks within the lower brain and to provide the platform on which the more complex brain functions develop.

Creeden (2011) provides a useful outline of how harmful sexual behaviour intervention programmes in both community and residential settings can be adapted to be more effective with children and young people who have experienced trauma in their lives. This intervention model uses as its framework a trauma-informed developmental model. The ordering or priority of the intervention is based on developmental needs (safety, attachment, competencies) and also reflects typical neurodevelopmental sequencing of learning and integration (body-based, sensory-based, motor-based, language-based, abstract thinking) that mirrors normal brain development. The approach focuses on four key areas.

(1) Overcoming emotional dysregulation:
- understanding physical sensations (including use of biofeedback);
- understanding triggers for personal emotional distress;
- teaching structured skills in self-regulation through, for example, breathing, yoga and mindfulness;
- learning to become attuned to others and experiencing being valued and 'attuned to' by caring and engaged adults.

(2) Understanding behaviour:
- increasing self-awareness and sensory integration through mindfulness, yoga exercises and kinaesthetic responsivity work;
- understanding the dynamics of physical, emotional and sexually abusive relationships.

(3) Resolution of trauma:
- dealing with memories with as little shame as possible;
- making sense of past losses through detailed autobiographical work;
- addressing experiences of trauma: through stabilisation; recognising how trauma is 'stored' or 'contained in' our bodies; and using techniques such as Eye Movement Desensitisation and Reprocessing (EMDR) to help process and integrate experiences;

- having present and future focus to trauma treatment that highlights current safety, improves decision-making, the development of trust and supports, and identifies future goals.

(4) Developing relationships:

- reconnecting to peers safely and appropriately;
- learning about healthy sexuality, including acceptance and comfort with your body, examination of assumptions and beliefs regarding gender roles, clear and appropriate sex education, consideration of the sexual messages conveyed by media including pornography;
- learning about and clarifying the role of being a man.

Each of these areas involves hands-on activities and regular practice outside weekly sessions. Caregivers are actively involved in sessions, with fathers having an important role in relation to work regarding positive masculinity. Arousal control and regulation are addressed in non-cognitive ways, and general arousal control may be a more effective intervention goal than control of problematic sexual arousal specifically. Building skills in general affect regulation can assist in building skills concerning sexual regulation (Creeden, 2009).

Approaches such as these are at present under-evaluated but are congruent with research regarding both the neurological and developmental impact of trauma on young people, and levels of traumatisation often experienced by children and young people who have displayed harmful sexual behaviour. These approaches raise an interesting question as to whether (and for whom) specific harmful sexual behaviour work is needed, or whether more general, trauma-informed emotion regulation and impulse control work would be sufficient to alleviate harmful sexual behaviour problems in most children and young people.

Risk management approaches

Whatever the approach taken, any intervention must be offered within the context of a safety plan to manage risk. Risk management is the professional task of applying a range of activities with the aim of reducing the risk of serious harm to others. Intervention work is, of course, one of these activities for managing and reducing risk but other measures include:

- monitoring;
- supervision (reducing risk by restricting a child or young person's freedom or requiring some form of external oversight, including

activities and relationships that need to be restricted, or which can take place only with supervision and support);

- community disclosure (reducing risk by sharing information with individuals, agencies or organisations);
- victim safety planning (where risks may be presented to specific known individuals) (Scottish Government, 2014).

In contrast to the emergence of more developmentally orientated approaches to intervention, use of risk management processes with young people over the last few years has become more common, paralleling a growing trend towards higher levels of monitoring of adult sexual offenders, particularly in the US and the UK. These risk management plans and processes can support the overall task of the rehabilitation of the child or young person, but they can also undermine it. In a Scottish study of the use of adult-focused, multi-agency, public-protection arrangements (MAPPA) with twenty-one under-eighteen year olds convicted of sexual offences, there was little evidence of engagement with families, and professionals found MAPPA to be too narrowly risk-focused for work with young people, who were still developing socially. As one practitioner put it:

> MAPPA increases the risk management because there is multi-agency accountability, but it is very much set up for adult sex offenders. This boy committed his offence when he was 15 and I believe there is an element of MAPPA not giving him the opportunity to mature (Rigby et al., 2013a, p. 24).

In another case, youth justice workers saw themselves as minor partners in decision-making:

> We facilitated a training placement, but the transport issue became sticky. MAPPA would not agree on him using public transport … We felt planned use of public transport would work towards better socialisation, but we ended up paying for a taxi for him. The police and the social work service manager from justice both felt it was too risky (Rigby et al., 2013a, p. 24).

It may be that such approaches protect the public, but, if they dispropor-tionately hamper prosocial development, they may perpetuate risk without creating opportunities for young people to develop in positive ways. They may also violate international statutes such as Article 6 of the United Nations Convention on the Rights of the Child (UNCRC), which states that children and young people should be able to grow up in conditions that do not impact negatively on their physical and mental well-being (UNICEF, 1989).

One consequence of these critiques of adult-orientated, risk management processes has been an increased number of multi-agency protocols specific to children and young people who have displayed harmful sexual behaviour. Allardyce (unpublished) found that most local authorities in Scotland have protocols, albeit of mixed quality and with limited evidence of how they are being used. Although more child-centred protocols have started to emerge in some jurisdictions, risk management and its implications for young people remains under-researched.

In some jurisdictions, sex-offender registration and community disclosure measures are common with young people who have displayed harmful sexual behaviour. In a survey of professionals in the US working in this field, 52% of 492 practitioners suggested sex-offender registration made no difference to community safety, and 26% thought it made it worse (Harris *et al.*, 2016). Furthermore, comparisons between states that employ registration of young people and those who do not show no evidence of them contributing to lower rates of sexual recidivism (Sandler *et al.*, 2017). Human Rights Watch found that many young people placed on the registry in the US experienced severe psychological harm and described feeling stigmatised, isolated and depressed (Pittman, 2013). Some individuals and their families experienced harassment, physical violence and public shaming. For example, some had to post signs in their windows stating 'sex offender lives here' and others had to carry driving licenses with 'sex offender' printed in bright orange letters. There were examples of young registrants being denied access to education, employment and housing because of residency restriction laws and of families being unable to live together because of prohibitions about living with other children.

It may be that such measures breach fundamental international human rights protocols, which prohibit inhumane or degrading treatment or punishment, and which recognise the right to private and family life. Risk management approaches, therefore, raise many challenges in terms of proportionate responses to protect the public from harm, while recognising that children and young people who have displayed harmful sexual behaviour also have rights to basic human needs and opportunities for development if they are to move on into adulthood and become responsible members of our communities. None of these tensions is easy to resolve, nor should they be in light of the complexity of this issue. As Burman *et al.* (2007) affirm in their conclusion to a literature review on juvenile risk management, such debates are:

> ... rooted not just in complex technical questions about scientific accuracy and reliability but in moral, social and political questions about child protection and public protection, security and insecurity, and tolerance and intolerance (Burman *et al.*, 2007, p. 90).

Conclusion

In keeping with the changing understanding of the aetiology of harmful sexual behaviour in childhood and adolescence, we have seen a gradual, though not uniformly implemented, shift towards more ecological, developmentally sensitive and individualised approaches to intervention. While effective interventions are likely to require a CBT component, it is increasingly recognised that CBT is unlikely to be sufficient on its own to effect sustainable behavioural change. Interventions need to flow from a high-quality assessment and will usually require a multimodal and multi-agency approach, involving parents and potentially the wider family and community. The sequencing of intervention components also needs to be thought about carefully, in recognition of the possible impact of trauma on a child or young person's ability to think, reflect and plan ahead. That said, the evidence for the effectiveness of interventions remains weak. There is clearly a need for further research on a much larger scale, and with more sophisticated studies, to understand more precisely what works and for whom. Outcome measures need to broaden in scope beyond recidivism to incorporate wider indicators of well-being. At the same time, the research regarding effective interventions for children and young people who have displayed harmful sexual behaviour needs to be communicated to policymakers so that risk management strategies do not pull in the opposite direction. However, this is not likely to be a simple matter of presenting evidence. How to strike a balance between the rights of these children and young people and the rights of the wider community will entail not just a scientific debate about what works, but also a more fundamental and political debate about values and the kind of world we want to live in.

Chapter 7

Special populations

Introduction

Although a range of assessment tools, intervention manuals and workbooks are now available, most adopt a 'one size fits all approach' and are designed to meet the generic needs of adolescent boys who have committed a sexual offence against another child in the community. Although traditionally discussed as a homogenous population, there is increasing recognition of the heterogeneity of children and young people who engage in different kinds of harmful sexual behaviour across widely divergent contexts.

Over the last few years, a number of studies of special populations or subgroups of children who have displayed harmful sexual behaviour have been published. In this chapter, we examine some of these subgroups based on gender, age, victim type and developmental background, in order to explore the extent to which they can assist practitioners and agencies in developing effective responses to this issue.

Thinking about subgroups

Subgroups can be useful in work with children and young people who have displayed harmful sexual behaviour as they provide professionals with signposts to help them analyse complex situations. Furthermore, they can assist practitioners in attuning to the specific needs of individual children and young people referred to services. Knowledge of the general characteristics of particular special populations can aid assessments and the development of relevant interventions.

However, there are limitations to applying research regarding special populations in practice. Any attempt to move away from homogenising generalisations about children and young people by the use of typologies ironically risks encouraging further generalisations to be made. 'Special populations' describe groups rather than individuals, and a particular child may not necessarily exhibit all the characteristics of the subgroup to which they are assigned.

For example, although girls who have displayed harmful sexual behaviour are more likely to have been sexually abused than boys (Van der Put, 2015), this insight is of limited use when working with a girl who has not been sexually abused. Furthermore, a child might fit the criteria for a number of different subgroups concurrently. A boy aged ten with a learning disability who has sexually abused his brother crosscuts at least three of the subgroups outlined in this chapter.

Caution is also needed because subgroups prioritise certain ways of bringing meaning to complexity, and in so doing they limit other ways of creating meaning. They emphasise differences between special populations rather than emphasising commonalities, and they may also obscure more detailed special populations: categorising boys as either sexual abusers of family members or of children in the community may obscure the possibility of a third category, of boys who abuse in both settings. What follows is a list of subgroups that we have found helpful in our practice. Other subgroups, such as those based on personal and family variables (O'Brien and Bera, 1986), pathways into abuse (Hackett, 2016) or personality type (Worling, 2001; Richardson *et al.*, 2004; Oxnam and Vess, 2006) could have been described, but we have chosen the subgroups below as they avoid defining special populations by particular psychological traits. The descriptions of special populations below should, therefore, be read critically, recognising that typologies simply provide a shortcut to assist our understanding of a child, but practitioners must always remain aware of particular and unique needs.

Girls who have displayed harmful sexual behaviour

As noted in Chapter 3, the vast majority of children who have displayed harmful sexual behaviour are boys. As a result, most studies comparing boys and girls draw on small samples of girls, although there are exceptions (e.g. Finkelhor *et al.*, 2009; Fox and DeLisi, 2017). The research consistently shows some clear differences between boys and girls, suggesting that the aetiology, social context and nature of girls' harmful sexual behaviour are often different from those of boys.

The age of onset of harmful sexual behaviour is often significantly younger for girls. Finkelhor *et al.* (2009) in their US sample of 971 girls who came to the attention of the police because of allegations of harmful sexual behaviour, found that 31% were under twelve, compared with only 14% of the sample of 12,450 boys. Girls were more likely to have sexually abused in a domestic setting and to have abused in caretaking roles (e.g. babysitting), and were less likely to have offended in a school setting. More girls had victims under the age of eleven than boys (60% versus 43%) and were more likely than boys to have male victims (37% versus 21%). However, this latter finding has been contradicted by smaller studies (e.g. Schmidt, 2008). A range of other research has noted that girls are less likely to have penetrated their victim, are less likely to use coercion and more likely to have been involved with sexual touch of their victim (Ray and English, 1995; Bumby and Bumby, 1997; Miccio-Fonseca, 2000; Kubik et al., 2003; Vandiver and Teske Jr, 2006).

Girls are significantly less likely to have been charged in relation to their behaviour (Hutton and Whyte, 2006; Vandiver and Teske Jr, 2006; Hickey et al., 2008). They are also more likely to be dealt with through children's welfare systems and, for those girls who deny allegations, the details about what actually happened may never be tested in law, which can create challenges for both engagement and assessment. Multiple factors may account for this finding. Girls may be younger than boys and, therefore, some will be below the age of criminal responsibility; the behaviour may be less intrusive in comparison to those displayed by boys; and victims may be younger and less able to give clear accounts of what they have experienced.

A further possible explanation is provided by Robinson (2005), who suggests that girls tend to be referred for services as victims rather than as perpetrators because of a traditional belief that females are protectors and nurturers rather than abusers. Their behaviour is, therefore, explained as an exosomatic response to their own victimisation experiences, which may then minimise the seriousness of the behaviour and the level of risk presented. On the other hand, when charged with offences, girls may be subject to harsher sentences as they have not only abused their victim but also transgressed traditional female roles.

This latter argument about professionals foregrounding the victimisation experiences of girls is congruent with the evidence that girls who have displayed harmful sexual behaviour are more likely than boys to have experienced sexual victimisation. Mathews et al. (1997), in a comparison of sixty-seven girls and seventy boys who had displayed harmful sexual behaviour, found that girls were twice as likely to have a history of childhood sexual abuse. Furthermore, they tended to have been sexually abused at an earlier age than boys (64% before the age of five) and were more likely to have been abused by several different abusers at various stages in their childhood. Such findings have been replicated in other studies (Hickey *et al.*, 2008; Hunter *et al.*, 1993; Hutton and Whyte, 2006). In research comparing forty adolescent girls with 743 adolescent boys, van der Put (2015) found sexual abuse or exploitation outside the family home was a key characteristic among girls who had sexually abused others. This finding could relate to girls who were re-victimised in adolescence after being sexually abused in their earlier years. Sexual harassment by peers and teenage relationship abuse are also over-represented in girls who have displayed harmful sexual behaviour (Taith, 2016).

However, there are divergent findings emerging from studies concerning girls' maltreatment backgrounds. Fox and DeLisi (2017) analysed the characteristics of 286 girls and young women who came to the attention of law enforcement because of harmful sexual behaviour. They proposed that the sample could be broken down into two distinctive groups. In the first one, 85% had experienced sexual abuse and were characterised by early onset of harmful sexual behaviour (before age twelve), high levels of impulsivity, mental health issues and low levels of empathy towards their victims. In the second group, there was a lower sexual abuse rate (although still relatively high at 35%), lower levels of impulsivity and mental health issues, later age of criminal onset and higher rates of empathy towards their victims. This study implies that there may be further subgroups of girls within this special population that describe distinctive pathways into, and out of, harmful sexual behaviour.

Higher levels of sexual victimisation reported by girls, and their experiences of betrayal and exploitation by adults (often men), may make it particularly difficult to build a trusting therapeutic relationship within which to address their harmful sexual behaviour. While it is an issue not unique to girls, consideration should be given to the appropriate gender of worker(s), weighing the relative merits of facilitating engagement and the value of positive male role models. In any event, professionals working with girls often need to work hard to model respect, compassion and empowerment, which should begin from the outset of the assessment stage. The high rate of reported sexual abuse also means that related health concerns (e.g. sexually transmitted diseases, reproductive concerns, abortions, unwanted pregnancies) (Miccio-Fonseca, 2016) and potential psychological factors relating to trauma need to be robustly assessed, including depression, suicide attempts, dissociation, post-traumatic stress disorder, substance misuse, association with violent men, relational problems, and poor self-image and self-confidence (Bumby and Bumby, 1997; Willis and Levenson, 2016). Although individualised intervention goals are likely to be similar to those used with boys, trauma-informed approaches to intervention – such as Creeden (2011) described in the previous chapter – is indicated, with a particular focus on making sense of past and present relational patterns. The impact of abuse on family relationships will need to be analysed, some authors noting significant family issues including a relatively high prevalence of disrupted mother–daughter relationships, which may relate to issues around attachment and trauma within family systems (Robinson, 2009; Taith, 2016).

There may be key differences in aetiology of harmful sexual behaviour between girls and boys. They have divergent experiences of socialisation because of social scripts regarding relationships and gender roles. From an early age, boys are rewarded for being independent, separate and autonomous, while girls are often encouraged to be more interpersonally orientated (Robinson, 2009). Girls internalise feelings far more than boys (Harris *et al.*, 1991), and in social circumstances 'relational aggression' (Simmons, 2002) – rumour spreading, name-calling, giving people 'the silent treatment' and manipulation – is cited as more common among adolescent girls than boys. Some authors have suggested that, in certain situations, sexualised aggression may be a form of relational aggression for girls where anger is generally denied or cannot be openly expressed (Robinson, 2009).

With respect to previous experiences of sexual abuse and exploitation, careful attention needs to be given to the context of the harmful sexual behaviour, including an understanding of previous experiences of grooming, the normalisation of sexual abuse or exploitation, and the ways that abusers limit life choices in concerted ways to make abuse possible. In some circumstances, particularly in peer and gang settings, sexual exploitation will be contemporaneous with and causally linked to the girl's harmful sexual behaviour. As Firmin *et al.* (2016b, p. 2,327) note: 'Young people may be coerced or manipulated into abusing others and, in this regard, groomed choices overlap with …. survivalist behaviours.' This resonates with Finkelhor *et al.*'s (2009) study, which found that one-third of girls abused with at least one other individual in comparison to one-fifth of boys.

Smaller and more qualitative studies have examined the dynamics of these situations. In a Dutch study of sexual offending involving at least one adolescent female adjudicated for a sexual offence (n=35), 63% of girls described their actions as resulting from group influences, and 31% cited instrumental motives such as revenge against the victim (Wijkman *et al.*, 2015). Power dynamics and leadership varied in different situations involving group sexual offending. In some cases, males involved female co-offenders to gain access to girls, and, in other instances, adolescent girls used males to humiliate chosen victims. Sexual gratification was less often a factor for girls than boys in this study. Mapping peer friendships and associations is a vital part of the assessment of such situations, as is a clear understanding of group power dynamics and the role of leadership and coercion, which can be achieved through interviews with all participants and understanding the details of the incidents.

Small study sample size means that sexual recidivism rates for girls are unknown. Studies of risk assessment tools in relation to adolescent non-sexual offending have found that they are generally useful in predicting risk of reoffending for girls but are likely to overestimate risk (Onifade *et al.*, 2009). In a study comparing 953 boys and 102 girls, Miccio-Fonseca (2016) found a similar bias with a risk assessment tool designed for children and young people who have displayed harmful sexual behaviour. This may mean that risk assessment tools encourage unnecessary intervention and excessive supervisory measures for girls in some situations. Professional judgement and an understanding of issues in relation to girls who have displayed harmful sexual behaviour would be necessary in contextualising the results of any risk assessment tool in a particular practice situation.

Prepubescent children who have displayed harmful sexual behaviour

Prevalence data concerning harmful sexual behaviour exhibited by prepubescent boys and girls is elusive. Finkelhor *et al.* (2009) found that 16% of their sample of 13,471 children and young people who had displayed harmful sexual behaviour were under the age of twelve, but as the study included only children reported to the police, it is likely to underestimate the proportion of younger prepubescent children engaging in this behaviour. There is some evidence of a rise in referrals to specialist services for children under twelve, although this may indicate growing recognition rather than increased prevalence (Smith *et al.*, 2013).

Another key challenge relates to aetiology. There is some empirical support for the view that problematic and abusive sexual behaviour in early childhood is linked to sexual abuse experienced by the child in many cases. A general population survey of the sexual behaviour of more than 2,000 children under the age of twelve found that contact sexual abuse was the factor most frequently associated with elevated levels of inappropriate, problematic or abusive sexual behaviour. Exposure to adult nudity, sexual materials and sexual activities, often in home situations, were also strongly associated (Friedrich et al., 1997; Friedrich et al., 1998; Friedrich et al., 2005). However, experiencing sexual abuse or a sexualised environment is not always present in the histories of prepubescent children who have displayed problematic or harmful sexual behaviour. Friedrich et al. (1998) identified a small group of children who exhibited precocious sexual knowledge and/or behaviour beyond developmental norms but who had no known histories of sexual abuse or sexual exposure. Sexual abuse may have gone undetected, but family stress, domestic violence and physical abuse were common in this group. It may also be that excessive parental responses to normative sexual behaviour, such as disgust, anger or distress, sometimes reinforce this behaviour and lead to an escalation in frequency and seriousness. Practitioners need to be open to the possibility that, in some cases involving pre-adolescent harmful sexual behaviour, sexual abuse or exposure to family sexuality may not feature and that other dynamics may be at play.

Providing a proportionate response that avoids underreacting or overreacting is one of the key challenges in working with prepubescent children. When behaviour is self-directed or involves mutual sexual behaviour without coercion, clear boundaries, redirection and input about healthy relationships will often be sufficient to ensure that the child is nudged on to a more positive developmental pathway (Friedrich, 2007). Guidance for nursery and primary schools suggests that low-level problematic sexual behaviour should be responded to in line with other challenging behaviour, requiring adults to be specific about naming and describing the behaviour, pointing out to the child the impact on others, setting clear boundaries and developing individualised strategies to reduce the likelihood of repetition (British Columbia Ministry of Education, 1999). In home settings, explaining why the behaviour is inappropriate in a way that does not increase shame, setting boundaries, encouraging strategies around self-control and positive emotional expression, and establishing a plan to increase safety, are often measures sufficient to modify behaviour (Bateman and Milner, 2014).

More unusual presentations, which occur but are relatively rare, are clearly abusive or sexually violent in nature, where distress or physical discomfort is experienced by the victim, and may involve force, intimidation, coercion and/ or an obvious age or power difference between participants (Araji, 1997; Hall *et al.*, 1998). Gil and Johnson (1993) noted that these presentations typically represent less than 5% of referrals to specialist child sexual behaviour clinical settings.

Accordingly, significant evidence is needed before professionals can conclude that prepubescent behaviour is sexually abusive in nature (Friedrich *et al.*, 2005). Such children need, first of all, to be provided with a safe environment and should be allocated higher levels of support and targeted interventions. The question of intervention intensity is, however, controversial. Although many children will naturally grow out of such behaviour through maturation and consistent redirection by adults, sexual behaviour problems for some children can persist into adolescence or sometimes re-emerge as harmful sexual behaviour in their teenage years. A retrospective study of 263 adolescents found that 43% had displayed problematic sexual behaviour before the age of twelve, and it may be that harm in adolescence could have been avoided if effective responses had been provided in earlier childhood (Burton, 2000). This conclusion is supported by findings from a multi-agency inspection of twenty-five youth justice cases involving harmful sexual behaviour in England and Wales, which reported that eight of the adolescents had displayed behaviour in pre-adolescence that had not been adequately addressed (Criminal Justice Joint Inspection, 2013). Pithers *et al.* (1998) suggest that the frequency of incidents rather than seriousness of the behaviour may be a critical factor in risk of persistence into adolescence, and this should then guide intensity of intervention. However, while this may be important, thorough assessment is needed when such issues emerge in childhood.

This assessment needs to start with gauging whether the behaviour is age appropriate and, if not, in what way is it concerning, to whom and why. Where behaviour is persistent and/or beyond developmental norms, a comprehensive assessment involving detailed analysis of concerns and strengths will be required. As with adolescents, this assessment needs to be systemic and ecologically orientated, with particular attention given to safeguarding needs and to the child's family and living environment. Intervention is unlikely to be successful within a context of discontinuity of care, or persisting physical abuse, domestic violence or other such significant adversity. Practitioners will need to employ clinical judgement, although some risk assessment frameworks such as AR-RSBP under twelve (Curwen and Costin, 2007), AIM for under twelves (Carson, 2007), MEGA (Rasmussen and Miccio-Fonseca, 2007) and MARR (Brady and McCarlie, 2014) as well as that found in Friedrich (2007) may be helpful in appraising risk and identifying intervention goals.

Sexual victimisation and other forms of maltreatment experienced by many of these children suggest that intervention should be trauma-informed (Hackett, 2014). The evidence to date suggests, however, that expressive therapies (e.g. play therapy and creative therapies) may be relatively ineffective. Cohen *et al.* (2005) found no change in sexual behaviour problems for children who received non-directive therapy, in a study of eighty-two children randomly assigned to non-directive or trauma focused cognitive behavioural therapy (TF-CBT). In another study, Bonner *et al.* (2001) randomly assigned sixty-nine children with sexual behaviour problems either to a twelve-session, psycho-educational, CBT groupwork programme or to a twelve-session play therapy group. In a ten-year follow-up of these groups, sex-offence arrest and child-welfare, sexual-abuse-perpetration report outcomes were significantly higher among children who received non-directive therapies (Carpentier *et al.*, 2006). Positive findings have been replicated in relation to later iterations of this CBT approach, which place emphasis on parent/child sessions (Swisher *et al.*, 2008). However, Carpentier *et al.* (2006) found that, although CBT programmes seemed to be most effective with non-symptomatic, abuse reactive and highly traumatised groups, both approaches were relatively ineffective with children who were assessed as sexually aggressive. It may be that, as with adolescents, more intense, multisystemic approaches are necessary to support children with more complex needs who present higher levels of risk.

Overviews of intervention approaches suggest that a focus on recognising, understanding and expressing feelings; promoting prosocial behaviour and coping skills; teaching methods of relaxation, rules about understanding and maintaining interpersonal boundaries; addressing cognitions such as maladaptive beliefs about appropriate touch; and educating children about sexuality may all be vital intervention goals (St Amand *et al.*, 2008). Developmentally appropriate activities to facilitate learning (e.g. singing, drawing, use of puppetry, playing games) and practising skills are important

(Silovsky *et al.*, 2007). Approaches that either involve parents directly (including dyadic work) or provide parallel sessions with both children and parents are recommended (Friedrich, 2007).

Peer-on-peer sexual abuse

Peer-on-peer abuse can include: sexual bullying or harassment; peer sexual assaults; intimate partner violence; being coerced into sending sexual images; and grooming by peers. Some of this behaviour overlaps with the concept of child sexual exploitation, which has been statutorily defined in England and Wales as occurring:

> where an individual or group takes advantage of an imbalance of power to coerce, manipulate or deceive a child or young person under the age of 18 into sexual activity (a) in exchange for something the victim needs or wants, and/or (b) for the financial advantage or increased status of the perpetrator or facilitator. The victim may have been sexually exploited even if the sexual activity appears consensual (Department of Education, 2017, p. 5).

A significant literature comparing adolescent boys who sexually abuse peers with those who abuse prepubescent children has developed over the last twenty years, paralleling the literature comparing profiles of adult rapists with those who sexually abuse children. Although there are definitional problems with what constitutes a 'peer' as opposed to a 'child' victim, a systematic review of twenty-one studies comparing data on these two groups of adolescents found key differences as well as similarities (Keelan and Fremouw, 2013). Most studies found that those who abused peers were more likely to abuse girls, and that acquaintances were the most likely victims, followed by strangers. Those who abused prepubescent children were as likely to abuse boys as girls and were most likely to abuse an acquaintance followed by a family member. Peer abusers were more likely to use force and coercion. Those who abused prepubescent children were significantly more likely to have been sexually abused themselves, especially if they had a male victim. Otherwise, the groups could not be differentiated by family background, although some studies suggested that peer offenders generally came from families with higher levels of domestic abuse, less supervision and higher levels of general criminality. Age of onset and rates of sexual recidivism were similar for both groups.

To date, there is no strong evidence of different aetiological pathways into harmful sexual behaviour for individuals who sexually abuse these different victim types. However, in an exploratory study of 14 police investigations of child sexual exploitation where the perpetrator was under the age of eighteen, Hackett and Smith (2018) found that 12 of the perpetrators had extensive and pervasive histories of non-sexual offending. A lower rate of victimisation reported than in other studies of young people who had displayed harmful sexual behaviour and a later typical age of onset (16 and above) led the authors to speculate that this group had a propensity to anti-social and disinhibited behaviour that became sexualised during puberty. In contrast with other studies looking at recidivism, they also noted that several had been involved in multiple and in some cases escalating harmful sexual behaviour over time.

Some caution is necessary with the construct of 'peer-on-peer abuse', as some studies have noted that a minority of adolescents abuse both prepubescent children and peers. It is unclear whether those in this crossover group are more likely to sexually reoffend than other young people, although one study found that, compared to adolescents who have abused multiple peer victims or multiple child victims, the crossover group generally had a higher number of victims (Kemper and Kistner, 2007). Until there is more robust evidence differentiating single victim-type groups from victim crossover groups, the utility of these typologies for risk assessment and intervention is unclear. Another under-researched area concerning victim type is relatively rare situations where adolescents sexually abuse adults (Keelan and Fremouw, 2013).

Research into peer-on-peer sexual abuse in intimate partner relationships is also underdeveloped. An NSPCC survey of 1,353 seventeen year olds in England, Scotland and Wales found that one in three girls and one in six boys aged 13–17 reported experiencing some form of sexual partner violence, but dynamics have been little studied (Barter *et al.*, 2009). By contrast, research into gang-based sexual violence has started to emerge. Several studies have suggested that multiple-perpetrator offences are more likely to occur among young people than adults (Bijleveld and Hendriks, 2003; Park and Kim, 2016). These offences tend to be associated with higher degrees of violence and to occur with other types of crime, such as robbery (Wright and West, 1981; Ullman, 2007; Hazelwood and Burgess, 2016). Porter and Alison (2006) reported that, in approximately one in four multiple-perpetrator rapes, the perpetrators stole personal items from the victim.

These kinds of sexual assaults often involve 'leaders' and 'followers', with (usually) older perpetrators ordering younger ones to offend, or in some group situations members instigating abuse in which the rest of the group then takes part. Research commissioned for an inquiry undertaken by the Office of the Children's Commissioner in England and Wales focusing on gang-based sexual violence showed that, while it has much in common with sexual violence outside of gangs, it also has several characteristics of its own (Beckett *et al.* 2013). For example, rape may be used as a punishment or as a weapon within gang conflict. Younger girls may offer sex, particularly to a gang leader, to achieve some kind of status within the gang, to gain protection against sexual violence by other gang members or as an act of initiation into the gang. Sexual relationships might be used to 'set up' rival members or associates to be attacked. Within gangs, therefore, sexual violence and exploitation may perform very specific functions (Berelowitz, 2013).

Our understanding of how to respond to sexual violence and exploitation in these contexts is at an early stage, and there is little evidence to date generally regarding effective practice with young people involved with gang-based violence (O'Connor and Waddell, 2015). Following interviews with seventy-six professionals on this subject, Beckett *et al.* concluded that:

> a lot of participants' discourse about potential responses to young men (many of whom were identified as perpetrating sexual violence within the gang environment; some of whom were identified as being victimised through it) focused more on helping them to exit that environment, than it did on responding to the sexual offending (Beckett *et al.*, 2012, p. 49).

Worling (2001) suggests that, when working with young men who are involved with harmful sexual behaviour within the context of other offending behaviour, interventions need to include core social-skills categories such as 'alternatives to aggression', 'using self-control' and 'avoiding trouble with others', and should be integrated with broader interventions focusing on desistance from general offending. Both sexual and non-sexual offending behaviour can be addressed concurrently, and it may be that more mainstream intervention programmes focusing on non-sexual offending provide a framework, within which specific factors around sexual violence can be approached. Skills-based programmes, which focus on helping young people control behaviour and develop prosocial skills, and family-based interventions aimed at improving home circumstances and building on protective factors, are robustly evidenced in relation to general delinquency (Whyte, 2008).

Assessments and interventions in the harmful sexual behaviour field generally focus on behaviour as a manifestation of psychological factors, so professionals need to be careful to consider contextual factors, peer influences, antisocial peer networks and possible involvement of other participants as abusers when working with young people who have sexually harmed peers. Firmin *et al.* (2016a) describe a multi-agency assessment model profiling peer-on-peer sexual abuse locally, founded on the idea of contextual safeguarding circles (see Figure 7.1).

A multi-agency meeting then involves considering the following factors, paying particular attention to where each sits in relation to contextual dimensions:

- each young person's current situation;
- harmful sexual behaviour;

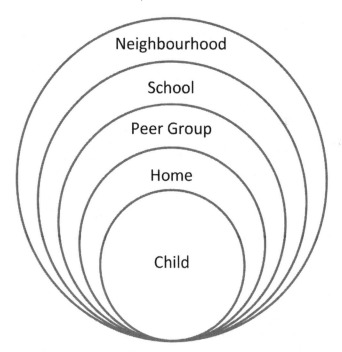

Figure 7.1: Contextual safeguarding circles (Firmin *et al.*, 2016a, p. 150). Reproduced by kind permission of the author.

- vulnerabilities and risks;
- resilience and strengths;
- professional involvement to date and planned actions/interventions;
- challenges/barriers to interventions.

Peer group mapping can sit alongside this process. Meetings focused on exploring harmful sexual behaviour in such ecological ways can lead to multi-agency plans to prevent peer-on-peer sexual abuse targeting themes at different levels. This may involve, for example, directing educational measures at a particular school year-group, focusing detached youthwork on particular places where abuse has been reported, and specific supports and interventions for those identified as perpetrators or victims. Such approaches can be particularly useful when sexual abuse within peer groups has been raised as a concern but a lack of disclosure (or withdrawal of disclosures because of peer pressure) means that there is no specific legal mandate to assess and intervene at a statutory level (Firmin et al., 2016a).

Intra-familial sexual abuse

Somewhere between one-third and one-half of the sexual abuse perpetrated by children and young people involves siblings or close family relatives such as cousins, nephews and nieces as victims (Hackett et al., 1998; Shaw et al., 2000; Worling, 2001; Beckett, 2006). Several studies suggest that the backgrounds and developmental trajectories of children who sexually abuse in family settings may be different from those who abuse in the community (O'Brien, 1991; Worling, 1995; Tidefors et al., 2010; Yates et al., 2012). All of these studies find higher rates of sexual victimisation experienced by boys who abused siblings compared to those who abused in the community. Latzman et al. (2011), for example, examining a sample of 166 boys referred for residential treatment, reported that 58% of those who sexually abused siblings had been sexually abused themselves, compared with 35% of those who sexually abused other victim types. They also identified higher rates of witnessing domestic violence and exposure to pornography (58% versus 20%, and 58% versus 24%, respectively). In smaller studies, both Worling (1995) and Tidefors et al. (2010) observed that those who displayed harmful sexual behaviour towards siblings had experienced higher levels of family dysfunction, including marital discord, parental rejection and physical discipline, in comparison to those who offended in the community.

Worling (1995) found that the key differences between those who had abused a sibling and those who had abused in community settings were related to family rather than individual factors. Some caution is needed here, as some young people abuse in both family and non-family settings. Indeed, in a study of 372 adolescents in custodial settings who had been convicted of sexual offences, Beckett (2006) identified that 35% had abused within the family, 50% in the community and 15% in both settings. Nonetheless, Bass *et al.* (2006) criticise the sibling sexual abuse literature for focusing on the individual characteristics of the victim or the perpetrator to the detriment of exploring the potential significance of the relationship between the siblings. This oversight in the literature is, to some extent, addressed by a study of thirty-four boys referred to a specialist service for children who had displayed harmful sexual behaviour (Allardyce and Yates, 2009; Yates *et al.*, 2012). Boys who abused siblings, boys who abused only children in the community, and a crossover group of boys who abused in both settings, were identified. Boys in the sibling-only group were more likely to have been motivated to abuse by intense feelings of jealousy and anger and to have begun abusing during adolescence. The crossover group were more likely to have experienced multiple traumas and to have begun their sexually abusive behaviour in pre-adolescence. This suggests that there may be two possible pathways into sibling sexual abuse: a trauma-related, early-onset route and a later-onset route related to power dynamics and sibling rivalry. The study reminds us to be cautious about binary either/or typologies when considering special populations defined by victim type.

Risk assessment tools may provide a general indication of the level of risk a young person may present to others in the community, but they do not consider the nature and levels of risk to specific possible victims in certain settings. In particular, they do not help to determine the levels of risk to siblings or other close family members at home. Allardyce and Yates (2013) recommend that risk assessment tools be contextualised within a broader assessment of the dynamics of victim selection. Practitioners should reflect upon why a particular victim was targeted and the nature of the relationship between perpetrator and victim, both to consider the risks of that same victim being re-victimised and to extrapolate to other possible specific victims. A consideration of typologies can also assist assessment. They conclude, for example, that a child who has suffered significant trauma themselves, who lives with younger siblings at home and whose abusive behaviour within the community started in pre-adolescence, may present a risk to the siblings they live with, and careful thought should be given as to whether an assessment should be undertaken to ascertain if the siblings have already been abused.

When the victim is a close family member such as a sibling, particular decisions often need to be made, sometimes immediately, as to whether they can continue to live together, if they should have any contact with each other, or at what point they can resume contact or shared living arrangements. There is some degree of variation within the practice literature as to how these decisions are best made (see Fahy, 2011, for a discussion regarding prepubescent children), but Yates (2015) recommends that, in cases involving adolescents, such decision-making should include exploration and consideration of the emotional impact of the behaviour on the children; the views of the children; the risks of future sibling sexual behaviour taking place; the quality of the sibling relationship; and the protective abilities and capacities of the parents. While some authors suggest that a child should not be removed from the family home unless this is the only way to prevent recurrence (e.g. Keane *et al.*, 2013), most writers suggest that, in cases involving adolescents, the siblings should be accommodated separately, at least in the first instance, while assessment is undertaken, to help manage risk and to allow the victim an opportunity to make sense of their situation without ongoing contact with their abuser.

In such situations, family reunification may be a presumed goal of intervention, although short of full family reunification there is a whole continuum of possible outcomes depending on how the intervention and ongoing assessment progress. Some authors emphasise the critical importance of the clarification stage, involving the siblings coming together for the first time in a safe environment to acknowledge the sexually abusive behaviour (Hodges, 2002; Rich, 2003; Thomas and Viar, 2005). Different authors vary slightly on what is required within this stage but there is some agreement that the well-being of the victim should be the primary concern and their needs should define the pace of progress. Hodges (2002) argues that the child who has abused must demonstrate genuine remorse, and the victim must acknowledge that the abuse was not their fault, if further steps are to be taken towards family reunification. Thomas and Viar (2005) promote the need for the child who has abused to accept responsibility and answer questions the victim may have. Both children may require considerable individual intervention to reach this stage. This process has been seen by some authors as akin to those described in restorative justice processes, which bring parties affected by crime together to appreciate and understand the harm caused, in a more constructive way than is typically possible in legal processes premised on the idea of punishment (O'Neill and Heaney, 2000; Rich, 2003). While to date unevaluated, family therapy and restorative justice approaches appear particularly well-suited to supporting the complex and multiple roles that exist in families where sibling sexual abuse occurs. They may offer the opportunity for family members to articulate, perhaps for the first time, their conflict of roles and avoid having to reject one child and protect the other. They provide an opportunity and a process for repairing relationships and processing emotional hurt. Put simply, the key tasks in working with families affected by intra-familial abuse are the prevention of further harm and helping all family members to heal and move on from trauma.

Children and young people with learning disabilities who have displayed harmful sexual behaviour

We noted in Chapter 2 that young people with learning disabilities are over-represented in cohorts of adolescents who have displayed harmful sexual behaviour – a finding that has been replicated in many studies (Bagley, 1992; James and Neil, 1996; Hackett, 2013; Manocha and Mezey, 1998). Learning disability is defined in the UK as:

- a significantly reduced ability to understand new or complex information, to learn new skills (impaired intelligence);
- a reduced ability to cope independently (impaired social functioning);
- which started before adulthood, with a lasting effect on development (DOH, 2001).

One of the problems with the literature regarding young people with learning disabilities who have displayed harmful sexual behaviour is that this kind of clear definition is rarely used to identify a particular and discrete group of children and young people. Instead, a whole array of different terms and definitions are deployed, including 'intellectual impairments', 'learning difficulties', 'educational difficulties' and 'special needs', so synthesis of the literature difficult.

In addition, more general academic discussion of learning disability rarely reflects the heterogeneity of children's disabilities, which may be mild, moderate or severe, and may be co-morbid with other physical disabilities and complex needs. Notwithstanding these limitations in the literature, some general points can be made.

Inappropriate and problematic, rather than abusive or violent, sexual behaviour may be relatively common among young people with learning disabilities. In a survey of forty schools for children with 'special needs', Fyson (2007) found that 88% had experienced pupils behaving in sexually inappropriate ways, with 19% reporting incidents on a weekly basis. Reported behaviour included public masturbation (reported by 58% of schools) and inappropriate touch (85%). However, some behaviour was clearly of a more harmful nature and included actual or attempted penetration (15%). It is important to be careful about minimising the seriousness and impact of behaviour displayed by children with learning disabilities and simply discounting them as manifestations of the child's disability and social difficulties. Young people with learning disabilities are, indeed, less likely to be charged (Gilby et al., 1989), and parents or carers may be less likely to report their concerns to professionals (Tudiver and Griffin, 1992; Lindsay, 2002; Fyson, 2007). Swanson and Garwick (1990) noted that young people involved with problematic sexual behaviour that is minimised by family members and other adults can often be confused when, at later stages in their development, they are charged in relation to behaviour that had previously not been deemed as serious.

Fyson (2007) found that young people with learning disabilities are more likely to abuse younger children than peers and tend to be less discriminating in terms of gender of victim, a finding supported by other studies (Tudiver and Griffin, 1992; Balogh et al., 2001). Other studies have found that adult sex offenders with learning disabilities are more likely to sexually reoffend than sex offenders with no learning disability (Craig and Hutchinson, 2005), although research in relation to adolescent recidivism is underdeveloped. High impulsivity and poor social skills may be factors in relation to harmful sexual behaviour among this population (Tudiver and Griffin, 1992; Stermac and Sheridan, 1993; O'Callaghan, 1998; Timms and Goreczny, 2002).

A prevalence study that examined 50,000 case files in the US (Sullivan and Knutson, 2000) found that disabled children generally were twice as likely to be sexually abused as other children, and four times more likely to be physically abused. These factors may have a bearing on the aetiology of harmful behaviour in some contexts. Assessment and intervention will need to consider the child's experiences of trauma and adversity, and how they have been able to process these experiences, if these have been features in their life. In addition, a lack of sexual knowledge (sometimes caused by limited education in healthy sexuality), limited opportunities for appropriate sexual expression, and having parents and carers who discourage sexual expression or see their child as inherently asexual, are common (Tudiver and Griffin, 1992; O'Callaghan, 1998; Murphy, 2003). Educational inputs about healthy sexuality and relationships may be particularly important to include in intervention programmes, and it should not be assumed that these children and young people have even basic knowledge. Through environments such as schools for children with special needs, children with learning disabilities may be frequently and regularly in contact with other vulnerable children and young people and, therefore, have considerable opportunity to engage in harmful sexual behaviour. However, it may also be that the high level of adult supervision of this group means that sexual behaviour is more likely to be observed and problematised than for children without such impairments.

Assessment tools designed for non-impaired young people may be useful in assessing risk with children and young people with learning disabilities (Griffin and Vettor, 2012); however, some specific tools have been developed that recognise the potentially different aetiology of such behaviour and the significance of environment in the maintenance of behaviour for children and young people with learning disabilities: for example, J-Rat (LD) (Rich, 2009). Understanding the function of the behaviour for the young person is key, and will involve an understanding of antecedents, behaviour (duration, frequency, intensity) and consequences (including how the behaviour was responded to) (Wilson and Burns, 2011).

Working in partnership with parents and schools is always necessary with young people who have displayed harmful sexual behaviour, and it is especially important to work with systems around the child where the individual has a learning disability. Learning may need to be constantly reinforced across different settings, as retaining key messages and generalising from one situation to another may be challenging for some children. Promoting prosocial development safely is crucial, but this can be challenging for parents, and professionals need to appreciate the additional stresses of caring for a child with social impairments, as well as the anxieties that exist for many parents as their child moves towards young adulthood.

Engaging the child in the assessment – and intervention work – may raise particular challenges, and, although changes to content may be minimal, practitioners may need to adapt their approaches. Visual, experiential learning styles are often necessary; however, most practitioners typically use cognitively orientated rather than kinaesthetic approaches. Understanding how the child communicates, makes sense of the world and processes information will be fundamental to the assessment. Giving the child time to process information is important, without rushing to reword and repeat questions. Using the child's signs and words, avoiding jargon and understanding for how long the child can concentrate will all assist with engagement. Care must be taken not to provide too much information in meetings, and recapping at the end and at the beginning of the next meeting may help reinforce learning and develop continuity. The goal is to build a predictable and safe relationship, but there will also be a need to consider the role of creativity and fun in the work. Making use of different resources – video, drawing, puppets, role-play, sculpting – and using visuals for illustrating everything – pictures, photos, symbols, maps, timetables, timelines – are often vital when working with children and young people with learning disabilities.

Some specific programmes for young people with learning disabilities have been developed, such as the Good Ways model (Ayland and West, 2006) and Keep Safe (Wiggins *et al.*, 2013). Successful aspects of the latter approach include the use of visual resources and multisensory activities, which have been shown to lead to improvements in sexual knowledge and social and emotional skills (Wiggins *et al.*, 2013). Social stories that take the form of social scripting or comic-style cartoon stories (Gray *et al.*, 2002) may be effective in communicating key messages about safety.

While they by no means necessarily have a learning disability, and may indeed have above-average intelligence, it is important to note that children and young people with autistic spectrum disorders/condition (ASD/C) – social and communication deficits and restricted interests (American Psychiatric Association, 2013) – are increasingly being referred to specialist services for children and young people who have displayed harmful sexual behaviour (Smith *et al.*, 2013). It is unclear whether this is because of increasing numbers of young people being diagnosed with this condition within the general population or whether this group is over-represented among young people who abuse. Many people with autism may experience some form of sensory sensitivity or under-sensitivity: for example, to sounds, touch, tastes, smells, light or colours. People with autism often prefer to have a fixed routine and can find change extremely difficult to cope with. There is some limited evidence that inappropriate and problematic sexual behaviour occurs relatively more frequently among this population, and Ray *et al.* (2004) suggest that obsessional interests, dismissal of social conventions, a poor ability to decode social gestures and language, and a limited repertoire of appropriate behaviour may be aetiologically related to inappropriate and harmful sexual behaviour. Behaviour commonly described includes misunderstandings of social situations, inappropriate seeking of physical contact, repetitive behaviour, fetishistic preoccupations and systematically collecting sexual images (including illegal sexual images) (Hellemans *et al.*, 2007). To date, there has been little research regarding young people with ASD/C who have displayed harmful sexual behaviour and almost no empirical support for specific intervention programmes; however, positive outcomes in case studies using structured behavioural interventions have been described (Pritchard *et al.*, 2016).

Conclusion

We have suggested in this chapter that research regarding subgroups of children and young people who have displayed harmful sexual behaviour may assist professionals in attuning to the specific needs of individual children and in identifying and tailoring appropriate interventions. We have cautioned, however, that it is important not to make assumptions about any particular child fulfilling all of the characteristics of the subgroup to which they have been assigned. We should be equally careful of lazy stereotyping. All children are unique, and individualised assessment is always required.

Throughout the chapter, we have noted areas where there is scope for further research. There is clearly potential to develop further and more specific subgroups, to evaluate the effectiveness of tailored interventions and, in particular, to explore what might be the specific needs of children who cross over different subgroups. In this chapter we have explored a number of different typologies of children and young people who have displayed harmful sexual behaviour, organised by gender, age, victim type and intellectual and social ability. One typology that we have not considered is children and young people's harmful sexual behaviour organised according to the particular type of sexual behaviour that they have engaged in. In recent years, there has been particular concern regarding harmful sexual behaviour perpetrated online, and this will be the subject of the next chapter.

Chapter 8

Harmful sexual behaviour online

Introduction

This chapter provides an overview of current research regarding harmful sexual behaviour displayed by children and young people online. This is a relatively new and contested subject, where empirical evidence is limited by a number of methodological, conceptual and definitional issues. Throughout this chapter, we use the term 'online' broadly to refer to activities involving use of new technologies, most of which involve access to the Internet, although some – e.g. sending texts – may not. For convenience, we will refer to sexual behaviour that takes place 'in person' as occurring 'offline', although a key theme in the emerging literature is the concept of 'cyber-enabled' harmful behaviour that blurs the distinction between online and offline behaviour.

The chapter starts by outlining the context of children and young people's use of new technologies and the ways in which adolescents, in particular, may access the Internet to explore their developing sexuality. We then go on to examine some particular aspects of online harmful sexual behaviour, including the use of pornography, 'sexting', and the viewing and downloading of child sexual exploitation material. We argue that, as children and young people's offline and online social lives become increasingly enmeshed, practitioners need to consider technology-mediated activites when assessing and intervening with individuals who have displayed any form of harmful sexual behaviour. We conclude by summarising some of the emerging approaches to assessment and intervention.

Young people and new technologies

In 2017, the Internet was used by 58% of the world's population, and by 80% and 88% of the populations of Europe and North America, respectively (Miniwatts Marketing Group, 2017). The Internet has impacted the social landscape significantly over the last twenty-five years, and has revolutionised many aspects of young people's lives in particular. Learning, entertainment, relationships and creativity all look radically different from even a generation ago. A survey in 2017 of 1,936 UK children aged 5–16 found that 91% of 5–10 year olds and 98% of 11–16 year olds reported using the Internet (Childwise, 2017). The amount of time children and young people spend online continues to increase each year (Livingstone *et al.*, 2017), with a survey of parents and children in the UK finding that weekly hours online have risen from nine hours in 2007 to around fifteen hours in 2016 for 5–15 year olds (Ofcom, 2016). Children and young people in the UK increasingly go online using mobile technology such as tablets and smartphones. In 2016, 39% of UK children aged 5–10 and 94% of children aged 11–16 owned a mobile phone, with around three-quarters using their phones to access the Internet (Childwise, 2017). For many, if not most children, mobile technologies mean that online experiences are inextricably woven into the fabric of everyday offline experiences.

Children and young people access the Internet for a variety of different reasons that tend to vary with age. Older children use it more broadly (e.g. for social networking, uploading photos and homework), whereas younger children go online for more specific reasons (e.g. watching videos and playing games) (Livingstone *et al.*, 2017). Although the Internet affords a myriad of positive opportunities for children and young people, most research has tended to emphasise online risk rather than its potential to enrich children's lives. This tension is central to how we think about the Internet generally:

> Popular discussions of the internet … veer between celebration and paranoia: on the one hand, the technology is seen to create new forms of community and civic life and to offer immense resources for personal liberation and empowerment; on the other, it is seen to pose dangers to privacy, to create new forms of inequality and commercial exploitation, as well as leaving the individual prey to addiction and pornography (Buckingham, 2013, p. 31).

Clearly, this is a false dichotomy. The Internet affords both opportunity and risk, with risk needing to be contextualised and seen as inseparable from opportunity and development in childhood. Learning how to ride a bicycle or how to swim are life-enhancing opportunities that necessarily entail some risk if children are to gain mastery of these skills. Children require help from adults to develop these skills, and to be able to identify and manage, or avoid, situations that are unsafe. In this regard, learning to use the Internet is the same as these more traditional experiences.

Harmful sexual behaviour online

Given that adolescence is a key period in sexual development and is also a time when technologies such as smartphones and tablets are critically important, it is unsurprising that young people use the Internet and social media as a place to explore, experience and express their sexuality. This includes using the Internet as a source of information about healthy and safer sex, relationships and intimacy, as well as for flirting, dating, online sexual interactions and to facilitate offline sexual interactions. The privacy and anonymity afforded by the Internet, along with a growing availability of online pornography and other adult material, are also factors in explaining why young people increasingly use the Internet to make sense of their sexuality. Mobile technology means that young people are now more able to go online in unsupervised spaces, in contrast to when access could be monitored by keeping computers in communal parts of the home. Privacy modes in web browsers, apps that facilitate self-deleting content and higher levels of encryption in online communication have all contributed to the Internet becoming a space for adolescents that is ever more removed from adult supervision (Denner, 2016).

As with offline sexual behaviour, child and adolescent online sexual behaviour can be conceptualised as existing on a continuum ranging from normative through to inappropriate, problematic and, ultimately, abusive behaviour. Problematic presentations could include, for example, sending an explicit photograph of oneself to express sexual interest in someone, compulsive use of online pornography, or the viewing of pornography by young children. Abusive presentations could include, for example, coercing another person online to perform sexual acts or the viewing and trading of child sexual abuse material.

There is no clear agreement in relation to where thresholds are drawn between what constitutes normative, inappropriate, problematic and abusive sexual behaviour online, and there is no common terminology that is universally agreed among professionals. The NSPCC has recently adopted the term *technology assisted harmful sexual behaviour*, which it defines as:

> One or more children engaging in sexual discussions or acts – using the internet and/or any image-creating/sharing or communication device – which is considered inappropriate and/or harmful given their age or stage of development. This behaviour falls on a continuum

of severity from the use of pornography to online child sexual abuse (Hollis *et al.*, 2017, p. 11).

However, as with definitions of harmful sexual behaviour generally, this definition raises the question of who considers the behaviour to be inappropriate or harmful: the child who has displayed the behaviour; the 'victim' (who may not define themselves as a victim); or the adults, in this case. As with offline sexual behaviour, some adolescent sexual activities may be normative and result in no obvious harm to self or others, but they may technically break the law and be perceived as inappropriate or problematic by many adults. As we discuss below, incidents involving adolescents exchanging or circulating sexual images of themselves with others via social media in consensual contexts may be an example of this.

In Chapter 1 we discussed how our attitudes and values can shape our responses to children's sexual behaviour, and this may be particularly the case when adults encounter sexual interactions involving children online. A UK study compared a group of young people who had displayed harmful sexual behaviour online (n=21), a group of young people who had displayed harmful behaviour offline (n=35) and a group who had abused others in both settings (n=35) (Hollis *et al.*, 2017). More criminal justice involvement and a more punitive response was reported towards the young people in the online-only group. There may be different reasons that account for this finding, including online behaviour leaving electronic traces than provide clearer indictable evidence of criminality than is often found in cases involving offline behaviour. However, it may also be that online transgressions are responded to more seriously because online adolescent harmful sexual behaviour raises adult fears and anxieties about a range of issues relating to technology, childhood and sexuality.

Online pornography use and harmful sexual behaviour

Children and young people are exposed to an unprecedented range of media content, and the proportion of that content that is sexual or even pornographic is increasing at a dramatic rate (Papadopoulos, 2010). There is no universally agreed definition of 'pornographic', but one study examining adolescent exposure to pornography defined it in the following way:

> ... images and films of people having sex or behaving sexually online. This includes semi-naked and naked images and films of people

that you may have viewed or downloaded from the internet, or that someone else shared with you directly, or showed to you on their phone or computer (Martellozzo *et al.*, 2016, p. 16).

While prevalence rates vary greatly from study to study (Peter and Valkenburg, 2016), a UK survey of 1,001 11–16 year olds found that 47% had viewed online pornography by the age of sixteen, with the likelihood of exposure increasing with age. Boys were more likely than girls to have viewed online pornography at an earlier age, as well as being more likely to have seen more images, seen more extreme images, viewed images more often and actively sought out those images rather than being inadvertently exposed to them. The line between intentional and accidental exposure was sometimes blurred – accidental exposure sometimes also leading to individuals intentionally seeking out images (Martellozzo *et al.*, 2016). Young people who actively seek out pornography online do so out of curiosity, as an aid to masturbation, for educational purposes and to explore what may sexually interest them (Häggström-Nordin *et al.*, 2009; Horvath *et al.*, 2013). There are also key gender differences in attitudes to pornography and its social acceptability. In a UK survey of 500 eighteen year olds (Parker, 2014), more young men (45%) than women (29%) agreed that 'pornography helps young people learn about sex', and half as many men (18%) as women (37%) strongly agreed that 'pornography encourages society to view women as sex objects'.

The degree to which viewing pornography online is harmful will be mediated by the child's age and stage of development, the nature of the material viewed, and frequency and context of the exposure, as well as other factors relating to the child's experiences of sexual socialisation. Peter and Valkenburg's (2016) systematic review of research published between 1995 and 2015 suggests that pornography use is generally associated with more permissive sexual attitudes, stronger gender-stereotypical sexual beliefs and distortion of young people's sexual knowledge by portraying sex in unrealistic ways. This may be exacerbated by the nature of material that can readily be found online. There is some evidence that themes of aggression, power and control, and the blurring of lines between consent, pleasure and violence are common in contemporary mainstream pornography (Ringrose, 2010; Papadopoulos, 2010).

Peter and Valkenburg (2016) also found a correlation between pornography exposure and sexual behaviour, in that pornography use among adolescents was related to larger numbers of self-reported instances of sexual intercourse and greater experience of casual sex. There is some evidence that it is also associated with sexual aggression, in terms of both risk of perpetration and victimisation. Two large studies have shown a relationship between self-reported adolescent sexual coercion and exposure to certain forms of pornography. In the first of these, a large school survey of 4,564 young people aged 14–17 in five European countries found a statistical association between self-reported regular viewing of online pornography and self-reported sexual coercion and abuse (Stanley et al., 2016). The second study involved six waves of data collected nationally online, between 2006 and 2012, from 1,586 US children and young people aged between ten and twenty-one years of age. An average of 23% of boys surveyed reported perpetrating sexual harassment either online or via technology, 10% self-reported perpetrating a sexual assault and 3.6% self-reported committing an act of rape. Average age of perpetration was between fifteen and sixteen dependent on type of sexual aggression. The authors found that exposure to violent (but not non-violent) pornography was associated with a fourfold increased odds or higher, depending on the type of sexual aggression (Ybarra et al. 2017). Causation cannot be inferred from association, of course, and it is quite possible that the viewing of violent pornography and harmful sexual behaviour both indicate underlying adverse childhood experiences. Nonetheless, the viewing of violent pornography may be a factor linked to the potential for the perpetration of harmful sexual behaviour.

Self-produced sexual images

The issue of young people engaging in the sharing of private, naked pictures of themselves or others, sometimes without the owner's permission, has been a source of considerable social anxiety over the last few years. The term 'sexting' has commonly been used by the media to describe these self-produced images, although the term is inherently problematic as it is rarely used by adolescents themselves (Ringrose et al., 2012).

Wood et al. (2015) examined this behaviour in romantic and dating contexts among 724 children and young people aged 14–17 in England. Some 38% of the sample had sent sexual images to a partner during or after a relationship, and 49% had received them. The proportion sending and receiving such images increased with age (26% aged fourteen compared with 48% aged sixteen). Some 20% of the participants who reported sending sexual images indicated that they had been pressured into doing so. Girls were more likely to report pressure (27% compared to 7% of boys), and 98% of the girls who reported feeling pressured experienced negative impacts as a result. Some 32% of the sample reported that their partner subsequently shared images more widely without their consent – this being much more frequently reported by girls (41% compared with 13% of boys). It is clear, therefore, that, while the sharing of images within the context of dating relationships may be common and often initially consensual, it may sometimes involve coercion or become non-consensual (Cooper *et al.*, 2016).

The consequences for adolescents of these self-produced sexual images have largely been seen as negative (Houck *et al.*, 2014; Lunceford, 2011), but some researchers argue that assumptions about coercion and harm do not reflect the experiences of the majority of girls who engage in such behaviour, and pleasure and desire may be motivating factors (Lee and Crofts, 2015). Research increasingly suggests that a more nuanced understanding of sexting, distinguishing between the 'consensual' and 'non-consensual' creation and distribution of sexual images, is needed to inform policy and educational resources (Powell and Henry, 2014).

Self-produced sexual imagery does not always take place within the context of dating relationships, and from an analysis of more than 500 US cases that were referred to law-enforcement agencies, Wolak and Finkelhor (2011) developed an empirically grounded typology of this behaviour (see Figure 8.1). They highlighted a range of 'aggravated' incidents involving youth-produced sexual images that entailed criminal or abusive elements, involving either – or both – adult perpetrators and peers. This latter category included behaviour with 'intent to harm', such as extortion, threats or malicious conduct that arose from interpersonal conflict, and behaviour arising out of 'reckless misuse', such as involving someone who was pictured in an image who did not willingly or knowingly participate in the taking or sending of the picture. The authors also highlighted a range of 'experimental' incidents, typically involving 'romantic' situations where consenting peers under the age of eighteen shared images with each other in the context of intimacy, or 'sexual attention seeking' situations where individuals sought out positive sexual responses from peers with whom they were not romantically involved. An 'other' category was applied to cover cases involving

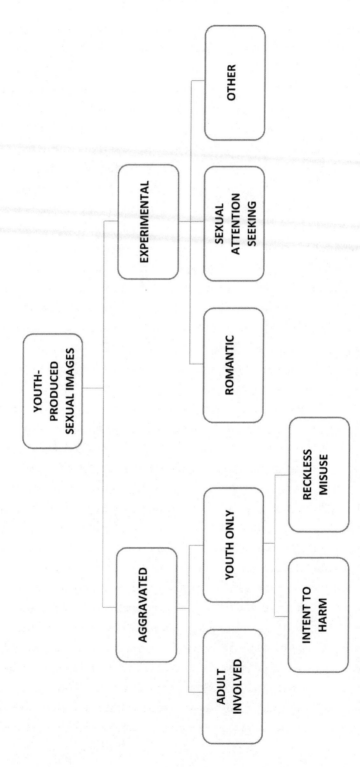

Figure 8.1 Wolak and Finkelhor's 'sexting' typology (Wolak and Finkelhor, 2011, p. 1). Reproduced with kind permission of the authors.

non-sexual presentations, such as boys sharing photographs of their genitals with male peers to embarrass or amuse others.

A recurrent issue in different countries is how legal systems respond to issues related to the sending of self-produced sexual images by adolescents. Even when shared in 'experimental' situations, these images can technically be prosecuted as crimes in relation to the viewing and sharing of sexual images of children (termed 'indecent images of children' or 'child pornography' in different countries). A Freedom of Information request in Tayside, Scotland, revealed that, between 2013 and 2016, 166 individuals were charged with downloading child sexual exploitation material, of whom fifty-five were under the age of nineteen and thirty-three were aged between thirteen and fifteen. The majority were charged with sexual offences resulting from their sending private, self-produced images (*Evening Telegraph*, 2017). Leukfeldt *et al.* (2014) arrived at similar findings in an analysis of 159 Dutch police files. There are strong arguments for diversion or decriminalisation of such cases, particularly when images are shared in consensual contexts, and since January 2016 in England and Wales, the police have had discretion to record that a crime has been committed but not take further action when responding to complaints of this nature when there is no evidence of abuse or harm. However, establishing whether the behaviour has involved coercion may be challenging, particularly when there may be power differences in relationships that young people misread or misunderstand because of developmental immaturity.

This latter point about coercion means that, in some contexts, the use of youth-produced sexual images may have stronger parallels with intimate partner violence or online sexual harassment than with offences involving downloading child sexual exploitation material. Indeed, using data from a survey of 4,564 young people aged 14–17 across five European countries, Wood *et al.* (2015) found that girls who had experienced intimate partner violence were approximately twice as likely to have sent their partner a sexual image compared to those who had not experienced intimate partner violence. Similarly a US study of 1,385 young people and young adults (572 aged under 18) who had experienced what the authors described as 'sextortion' (threats to expose sexual images to provide additional pictures, sex, or other favours), found that most perpetrators were known to the victims, were typically romantic partners and victimisation often occurred within the context of teen dating violence (Wolak *et al.* 2018). These findings needs to be seen in a wider culture of offline and online sexual harassment and gender norms. A focus group study of eighty-three Belgian adolescents aged 12–18, for example, found that personally targeted, gender-harassment online was viewed as relatively normalised (Van Royen *et al.*, 2015). Furthermore, a survey of a representative sample of 3,503 Swedish children aged 16–22 (Jonsson *et al.*, 2014) found a significant association between voluntary sexual exposure online and the numbers of different forms of online harassment individuals had experienced. This is particularly relevant in terms of future trends, as US survey data suggests that young people's self-reporting of online sexual harassment is significantly on the increase (Jones *et al.*, 2013).

Downloading child sexual exploitation material

Prevalence data suggests that the downloading and viewing of images of the sexual exploitation of children by adolescents is uncommon. Wolak *et al.* (2011) report that, in 2006 in the USA, just 5% of those arrested for possessing such images were under eighteen years old. Higher figures have been identified in some other jurisdictions and, in New Zealand, Wilson and Andrews (2004) found that one-quarter of all offenders were under twenty years old. This, however, raises the question as to what is meant by the term 'child sexual exploitation material'. As is clear from the discussion above, two fifteen year olds sharing self-produced sexual images of themselves could technically be defined in law in this way in many countries, although relevant legislation was not designed to criminalise such cases. This picture is further complicated in practice. Hollis *et al.* (2017) found that a minority of young people who downloaded child sexual exploitation material had traded sexual images of themselves for those of others. Most of these images were of children in erotic poses and, in some cases, could be considered as the age-appropriate, albeit illegal, seeking out of sexual images of similar-aged peers.

Definitional issues aside, some studies report that the age of onset of young people who have downloaded child sexual exploitation material tends to be a couple of years younger than adolescents who have displayed offline harmful sexual behaviour (Aebi *et al.*, 2014; Hollis *et al.*, 2017; Stevens *et al.*, 2013) and are significantly less likely to be from a lower socio-economic group (Aebi *et al.*, 2014). In terms of education, they are more likely to be of average or above-average intelligence, doing well academically and to be in full-time education or employment (Moultrie, 2006; Stevens *et al.*, 2013). Adverse childhood experiences seem to feature less often, and most come from relatively stable family backgrounds with positive parenting experiences (Moultrie, 2006; Stevens *et al.*, 2013; Aebi *et al.*, 2014; Hollis *et al.*, 2017). These findings suggest that the developmental pathways towards the downloading of child sexual exploitation material may be different from those leading to offline harmful sexual behaviour.

However, caution is needed with these findings, as two of these studies are of very small, UK clinical samples involving just six and seven young people (Moultrie, 2006; Stevens *et al.*, 2013). In one study, two young people had received the images from another individual, perhaps through being groomed, and the question of whether they were a 'victim' or 'perpetrator' is unclear (Moultrie, 2006). This finding also emerged in Hollis *et al.*'s (2017) UK study of twenty-one young people involved with online-only offending and thirty-five young people engaged with both online and offline harmful sexual behaviour. A quarter of the online-only group reported that they themselves were sexually groomed or abused online. Some 44% of the online-only group and 57% of the dual harmful sexual behaviour group actively sought out images of child sexual exploitation, highlighting how some intentionally viewed and collected these images for their own use and to trade with others. One-third of all of those with online-only behaviour were involved in distributing these images.

In Hollis *et al.*'s (2017) study, one-third of the young people in the online-only group had accessed the most serious types of images of child sexual abuse and exploitation, and almost one-third had viewed images of younger children. This may be indicative of a sexual interest in younger children, and the authors concluded that children who are found to possess such images may benefit from targeted interventions focused on dysfunctional Internet use and problematic sexual arousal. These findings are supported by a survey of a representative sample of 1,978 Swedish males aged 17–20 years (Seto *et al.*, 2015), which found that a total of eighty-four (4.2 %) young men reported that they had ever viewed 'child pornography' (the term used in this study). Self-reported sexual interest in children was strongly associated with self-reported viewing of this material. Frequent mainstream pornography use and viewing violent pornography were strongly associated with viewing child sexual exploitation material, which reflects the findings of other studies that have noted that frequent (daily) adolescent use of pornography increases the risk of accessing illegal material, including material involving children (Svedin *et al.*, 2011; Štulhofer *et al.*, 2010). Some viewers of child sexual exploitation material may engage in this behaviour because they are risk-takers and curious about taboo-breaking and transgressive illegal content. Some, however, may be motivated by a sexual interest in children and may gravitate towards more illegal materials over time as they become bored with mainstream pornographic materials.

One of the key questions for practitioners is the nature of the link between offline harmful sexual behaviour towards children and online viewing of child sexual exploitation material. This remains understudied. Hollis *et al.* (2017) found that young males with dual presentations shared a number of background characteristics with those involved with exclusively offline harmful sexual behaviour. This finding replicates those in relation to adult offenders, where the background characteristics of Internet offenders involved with contact sexual offending include higher rates of unemployment, greater access to children, greater childhood difficulties and experiences of sexual abuse, more previous convictions and greater substance misuse problems (McManus *et al.*, 2015; Babchishin *et al.*, 2011). Those involved with dual offending are more likely to have a sexual interest in children than contact-only offenders. The adult literature also suggests that those who sexually abuse children offline may be at higher risk of downloading images of child sexual abuse online than vice versa. This literature implies that the majority of those who offend online are not subsequently engaged with offline offending against children, with around one in six involved with both downloading images of child sexual abuse online and sexually abusing children offline (Wolak *et al.*, 2011). The sample sizes in studies such as Aebi *et al.* (2014) and Stevens *et al.* (2013) are as yet too small to establish whether similar characteristics and dynamics are present in relation to adolescents.

Online solicitation and grooming

Unwanted sexual solicitation has been defined by Ybarra *et al.* (2007, p. S32) as:

> the act of encouraging someone to talk about sex, to do something sexual, or to share personal sexual information even when that person does not want to.

Grooming has been defined by McAlinden (2012, p. 11) as:

> the use of a variety of manipulative and controlling techniques (2) with a vulnerable subject (3) in a range of inter-personal and social settings (4) in order to establish trust or normalise sexually-harmful behaviour (5) with the overall aim of facilitating exploitation and prohibiting exposure.

It is likely that a significant proportion of online solicitation and grooming of children and adolescents involves adolescents and young adults as perpetrators. Wolak and Finkelhor (2013) report that, in 2009 in the US, 8% of arrests for sexual crimes involving online sexual communication with children, where the offender met the victim online and brought up sex or sex-related topics during online interactions, involved a perpetrator under the age of eighteen. They go on to state that 43% of perpetrators were aged 18–25. In a study of sexual offending in Sweden, Shannon (2008) found that 21% of grooming offences involving online-only contact were by people under the age of eighteen, while 10% of offenders who met the victim online and then sexually abused them offline were under eighteen. In addition, the US-based Youth Internet Survey in 2010 of 1,500 young people aged 10–17, found that 9% reported unwanted requests from other young people to engage in sexual activities or sexual talk, or to give personal sexual information. Some 43% of incidents involved perpetrators under the age of eighteen, and 24% were aged 18–25, with the majority of sexual solicitations taking place on social networking sites (Mitchell et al., 2014).

However, without wishing to undermine altogether the evidence that a significant proportion of these offences are committed by young people, the lines between clumsy, awkward and unwanted online sexual advances on the one hand, and solicitation and grooming on the other, are often far from clear in interactions between adolescent peers, where there may be high levels of disinhibition in behaviour occurring far from adult oversight. Retrospectively interpreting the intentions behind communication that builds relationships and trust as 'grooming' may be especially problematic when involving similar-aged peers. McAlinden (2014) points out that the concept of grooming defines a linear and one-dimensional relationship between victims and offenders, implying that the victim is always the 'innocent' and 'unsuspecting target' of the abuser. This may be the case in many situations, but it is also an over-simplistic formulation, particularly when describing the behaviour of young people similar in age where both parties have a degree of agency. A focus on harm caused, along with an understanding of contextual factors such as peer influence, inequality and power, capacity to consent, and nature and level of coercive control, are critical when responding to cases involving adolescent online solicitation rather than the simple apportioning of blame.

Assessment

When responding to issues relating to harmful sexual behaviour online, careful screening for whether the behaviour is genuinely problematic or abusive may be necessary. Some behaviour such as consensual sexting may technically be criminal but may not warrant anything further than advice about harm reduction in the context of risk-taking, but relatively normative, behaviour. For those young people involved with more concerning behaviour, risk assessment within the context of a comprehensive assessment of need will be necessary. It was highlighted earlier that some behaviour in relation to youth-produced sexual images and online harassment behaviour may have more in common with intimate partner violence than downloading and viewing child sexual exploitation material. Careful assessment of the behaviour will help to determine the most appropriate intervention, which may have to draw on models outside the harmful sexual behaviour field. It is also becoming apparent that a significant proportion of harmful sexual behaviour displayed by young people now has both online and offline dimensions. Hollis *et al.* (2017) found that, of 275 young people referred to NSPCC harmful sexual behaviour services in the UK between January and October 2015, 46% of those assessed displayed some form of online harmful sexual behaviour, and just 7% displayed online harmful sexual behaviour only. As with other experiences, online and offline realms seem to be converging in how harmful sexual behaviour manifests itself among adolescents.

Although there is some evidence of increasing numbers of young people involved with online harmful sexual behaviour being referred to specialist agencies (Hackett *et al.*, 2016), the practice literature around assessment and intervention is still limited. Henshaw *et al.* (2015), in a literature review in relation to adult online offending, suggest that risk assessment tools for sexual reoffending are likely to overestimate the risk of reoffending for downloading images of child sexual abuse. It is unclear whether this is the case with adolescents at this stage, and risk assessments should focus on identifying intervention goals and proportionate risk management measures rather than predicting risk. In the UK, the NSPCC and the AIM project recently collaborated to develop practice guidance – TA-HSB (Swann, 2017) – to assist practitioners in assessment formulation, building on the research of Hollis *et al.* (2017). This replaces previous guidance called iAIM (Swann, 2009), which – in making no reference to self-generated sexual images – is now obsolete. This shows how quickly this issue is evolving, and any guidance in relation to assessment will need to keep up-to-date with ongoing debates about how online harmful sexual behaviour is defined and conceptualised, and about emerging research and evidence, as well as about the rapidly changing cultural and technological environment.

Intervention

The heterogeneity of behaviour that may constitute problematic or abusive online sexual behaviour makes it difficult to establish any one single intervention approach. No specific treatment programmes have been evaluated as yet, although some resources, particularly in relation to early intervention, are emerging (e.g. Saint, 2014).

Nonetheless, a number of intervention principles arise from the research:

- The overlap and potential blurring of boundaries between online and offline realities and behaviour for children and young people may mean that an evaluation of online risk needs to be integrated into standard risk assessments of offline risk. Understanding a young person's online world will need to be an aspect of any assessment undertaken with young people involved with offline-only harmful sexual behaviour.
- Completing a timeline examining the experiences the young person has had online (first experience of the Internet, key positive and negative experiences, first exposure to sexual material online) in parallel with their offline experiences can be an important foundation in this work (Swann, 2009).
- Young people can be victims online as well as perpetrators. This needs to be explored in the course of an assessment and responded to in the context of interventions.
- There is some research suggesting that safe and confidential spaces for young people can support them to explore worries about their own

sexual thoughts and behaviour, particularly with respect to sexual attraction to younger children (Beier *et al.*, 2016). It is likely that online self-help resources may be especially valuable as young people may find this is a less stigmatising way of obtaining advice and support with these issues (McKibbin *et al.*, 2017).

- Assessment of sexual interests, preoccupation and compulsivity will be particularly relevant for those involved with downloading images of child sexual exploitation material. When relatively large collections of images and videos are found, screening for ASD/C may be indicated.

Conclusion

We live in a society where many complex aspects of adolescent development regarding relationships and healthy sexuality increasingly take place online. A small minority of young people are involved with technology-mediated sexual offending. However, there is growing evidence to suggest that adult paranoia about adolescent sexual expression is leading to some normative online behaviour being regarded as problematic or even criminalised. This, in turn, leads to considerable confusion among parents, carers and professionals about where adolescent sexual experimentation online ends and sexual exploitation online begins, especially when they feel outpaced in their understanding of new technologies by children. It is likely that online resources and, ultimately, interventions partly undertaken online may be particularly valuable in the future as young people may find this is a less stigmatising way of obtaining advice and support with these issues. It is likely that many of the future solutions to the problem of online harmful sexual behaviour are to be developed online.

Chapter 9

Prevention

Introduction

From the outset of this book we have been clear that our concern is ultimately with the prevention of child sexual abuse. This social issue represents a significant public health concern in the twenty-first century, and causes serious and long-term physical and psychological harm to countless victims every year. So far in this book, we have considered prevention in terms of identifying and preventing the recurrence of sexual abuse by children and young people. However, the majority of sexual abuse is never disclosed in the first place, and never comes to the attention of services. Most harmful sexual behaviour will not, therefore, be prevented by interventions focused on children who have already displayed this behaviour. As Seto comments:

> I'm swayed by the overwhelming evidence and logic behind the idea that it is better to intervene early than it is to intervene late, whatever the problem or target might be. Better in terms of more effective, more cost-efficient and morally superior (enhancing human potential instead of making the best of a bad situation) (Seto, cited in Tabachnick, 2013, p. 55).

Thinking about sexual abuse as a public health concern requires us to move beyond seeing it as a criminal justice issue to be dealt with solely by legal processes and statutory agencies. Smallbone *et al.* (2013, p. 61) argue that the basic 'chemistry' of child sexual abuse consists of:

- offenders (or potential offenders);
- victims (or potential victims);
- situations (the specific places and circumstances in which child sexual abuse occurs);
- communities (the social ecosystems in which child sexual abuse occurs).

Considering these elements provides a framework for identifying potential targets for prevention of harmful sexual behaviour in childhood. While the evidence regarding effective prevention strategies is still in its infancy, in this chapter we explore some promising approaches guided by this framework.

Children and young people at risk of displaying harmful sexual behaviour

In an Australian study, fourteen young people undertaking intervention programmes in relation to harmful sexual behaviour were asked whether there were any opportunities for adults to intervene that may have prevented their going on to abuse children in the first place (McKibbin et al., 2017). One nineteen year old young man reflected that:

> I think if I had sex education before everything had occurred, like obviously before I hit full on puberty, I think everything would have changed ... I'm not even sure if what had happened would have happened, because I would have known it was wrong, more so than what I did at the time. I would have known why it was wrong and why not to do it (McKibbin et al., 2017, p. 214).

Young people in this study remarked that education about healthy sexuality was inconsistent and did not address adolescent harmful sexual behaviour. It was also delivered too late. If the typical age of onset of harmful sexual behaviour is around 13–14, universal interventions about healthy sexuality need to be targeted at an earlier stage if they are to have an impact on the prevention of sexual abuse (Letourneau et al., 2017).

Three young people in McKibbin et al.'s (2017) study believed that access to pornography was a factor in the development of their harmful sexual behaviour, and adults being more proactive in helping them to manage pornography use and its impact would have made a difference. As we noted in the previous chapter, the majority of young people who view online pornography do not develop behavioural difficulties, but, for some, it can significantly influence both attitudes and their interactions with others. Several of the workers involved with these young people suggested that negative effects of pornography could be countered by teaching children and young people critical thinking skills about concepts of gender, power, age and consent. This accords with the emerging evidence about 'porn literacy' in adolescence (Crabbe and Corlett, 2011; Albury, 2014).

Another theme that emerges from McKibbin et al.'s (2017) research relates to the importance of interventions that help reduce the impact of young people's own victimisation experiences, particularly exposure to intimate partner violence. The young people in this study said that they wanted adults to intervene, both to hold their perpetrator(s) to account and to give the young person a 'language' to make sense of the abuse they had experienced. While there are various developmental pathways into harmful sexual behaviour in adolescence, young people who have displayed such behaviour often come from families where there are high levels and multiple sources of stress (Hackett, 2014). Interventions designed to promote a calmer, safer and more nurturing caregiving environment will have preventative potential, particularly for some young people where there may be a cluster of emerging risk factors. Where abuse has taken place and is known to services, integrating psycho-educational work around healthy sexuality and relationships into focused therapeutic and family support for children who have been maltreated could also have a preventative role.

Children as potential victims

The main focus of preventative strategies targeted at children as potential victims is on giving children skills in protective behaviour and helping them identify signs and indicators of situations that may be unsafe. These interventions tend to be school-based and can be offered at different stages in childhood. Providing information about appropriate and inappropriate interactions within relationships, including sexual interactions, may be an aspect of these interventions targeted at young adolescents, as will be delivering information about consent and how the law frames issues in relation to sexual conduct. Such school-based education programmes have been implemented on a large scale in some countries and tend to be integrated within programmes about healthy sexuality.

Walsh et al. (2015) reviewed twenty-four evaluations of such programmes conducted with a total of 5,802 participants in primary (elementary) and secondary (high) schools in the US, Canada, China, Germany, Spain, Taiwan and Turkey. The duration of programmes and methods used varied widely, but there were many common elements to programme content, including the teaching of safety rules, body ownership, private parts of the body, distinguishing types of touches and types of secrets, and who to tell. The review found evidence that programmes were effective in increasing participants' skills in protective behaviour and knowledge of sexual abuse prevention concepts, and knowledge gains were not significantly eroded up to six months later. There was no evidence that programmes increased or decreased children's social anxieties about abuse, and there was evidence of increased disclosure of current or past abuse further to the rollout of such programmes.

Crucially, however, the review found no evidence of these programmes reducing incidence of child sexual abuse (although under-reporting makes this challenging to measure). While some programmes consider peer-based sexual behaviour and what a respectful relationship might look like, the majority refer to risk presented by adults, and the notion of children or young people themselves presenting risks to other children is rarely considered. A holistic conceptualisation of prevention should address both the risks children face from other children and the risks that some children themselves may present (Letourneau *et al.*, 2017). This might involve teaching young people attending such programmes that noticing sexuality in children and even having sexual feelings towards children does not need to lead to abusive behaviour. These programmes could be further developed by involving parents in supporting their child's acquisition of both protective and self-regulation skills. This might also raise parents' awareness of how to become a more effective guardian, and the practical things they can do to prevent abuse, such as encouraging healthy communications within families about relationships and sex.

Situations

In Chapter 4, we argued that individual psychological factors are often over-emphasised and situational factors under-emphasised in theorising harmful sexual behaviour. As noted in Chapter 3, for children and young people the sites of abuse include domestic settings, public settings, organisational settings (such as schools or group-living environments) and virtual environments. Understanding the dynamics of abuse in these different settings could help in developing more targeted and effective preventative strategies that not only better protect children but also deter other children and adolescents from acting in sexually abusive ways.

Domestic settings

Around one-half of sexual abuse occurs in domestic settings involving close family relatives (Smallbone and Wortley, 2000). Such settings provide a child at risk of displaying harmful sexual behaviour with ready access to a victim (or victims), and a familiar environment with unsupervised spaces that they can control (McKillop *et al.*, 2015). The nature of family relationships ensures that victims are among the least likely to disclose (Paine and Hansen, 2002), and so preventing sexual abuse in domestic settings is, therefore, especially difficult. However, some basic strategies, including rules around keeping certain doors open, requiring privacy when bathing and undressing, and designing new houses with directly observable play areas, may contribute to prevention or early detection (McKillop *et al.*, 2015).

Recognising that harmful sexual behaviour may be more likely to be displayed by children and young people from families where abuse or other forms of stress are present suggests that information about sexual abuse prevention could usefully be integrated within other interventions designed to help such families. Education around how to support healthy sexual development in childhood may be a valuable addition to parenting programmes such as Triple P (Sanders, 1999), Incredible Years (Webster-Stratton, 1990) or Parents Plus (Sharry and Fitzpatrick, 1998), and a way of directing support to vulnerable families in a non-stigmatising manner.

Public settings

Public settings are social spaces such as parks, playgrounds, shopping centres, swimming pools and public transport, which are open and accessible to the community at large. Sexual abuse in public settings may involve victims who have no relationship with the abuser (Colombino *et al.*, 2011; McKillop *et al.*, 2012; Smallbone and Wortley, 2000; Gallagher *et al.*, 2008). However, as noted in Chapter 7, peer-on-peer sexual abuse involving individuals, gangs or groups may occur in settings where young people congregate and where there is low natural guardianship and formal surveillance (Tilley *et al.*, 2014).

The design and management of public settings along with scope for targeted policing make them conducive to place-based prevention. Eradicating secluded or private areas may help reduce opportunities for abuse. Training of professionals in relation to how they can contribute to sexual abuse prevention in the context of their role, such as security guards, park maintenance employees, swimming pool supervisors and staff at twenty-four-hour fast-food outlets, may reduce risk further. Improving natural surveillance (e.g. lighting and visibility) and introducing CCTV surveillance in places such as playgrounds, shopping centres, swimming areas and public amenities are useful preventative measures. Such measures will be more difficult to implement in larger, more open public spaces such as parks, and a balance needs to be struck between deterring offending and overly intrusive surveillance, which may engender unnecessary fear and suspicion (Smallbone *et al.*, 2013). The guardianship of parents and the vigilance of ordinary citizens can also be vitally important. Bystander-orientated, public information campaigns focusing on what practical steps adults can take when they are aware of inappropriate or harmful behaviour in their community may have a role to play.

Organisational settings

Risk of sexual abuse is often elevated in organisational settings where groups of children are supervised and cared for by unrelated adults, away from the direct care of parents and carers. While there have been some well-documented cases of abuse by adults in schools, churches, residential care units and sporting clubs, risks may also be presented by children and young people in such settings. This is evidenced by the growing public awareness of sexual harassment and sexual violence in schools and the emergence of peer-on-peer sexual abuse as a theme in historical inquiries into sexual abuse in residential care settings. One in six of the 6,875 survivors of childhood sexual abuse who gave evidence in private sessions to the Australian Royal Commission into Institutional Responses to Child Sexual Abuse reported child-on-child sexual abuse. The report also noted that of reports of child sexual abuse in institutional contexts between 2008 and 2013, children made up 67 per cent of those reported to police in Victoria; 76 per cent in New South Wales; and 93 per cent in Queensland (Royal Commission into Institutional Responses to Child Sexual Abuse, 2017).

A review of research regarding the prevention of harmful sexual behaviour in residential care settings concluded that modelling of respectful relationships, sexuality education and enhanced multi-agency practice responses to concerns is vital (McKibbin, 2017). Other research has focused on attitudes and knowledge of professionals, such as Green and Masson (2002), who conducted ethnographic studies in residential settings exploring the nature of sexual activity between children in group-living environments. They observed that staff often ignored power differences between children involved with sexual activity and typically normalised behaviour that the authors considered to be abusive. Staff had little training, support, guidelines or procedures that would assist them in responding appropriately to sexual behaviour that was concerning. Staff also described embarrassment, fear and worry about their own values, sexuality or gender getting in the way of being able to respond to concerns effectively. Green and Masson (2002) concluded that creating safer places for children to live together involves addressing organisational culture. Increasing 'natural observation', such as by introducing glass panels on doors to meeting rooms and communal spaces, or by allowing children into each other's bedrooms only on condition that doors remain open, may be important practical measures (Smallbone et al., 2013). However, guidance and training for staff on supporting children's healthy sexual and relational development are also essential, along with ensuring that children's rights are promoted so that children who have experienced disempowerment and abuse feel valued and respected, and can thrive in safe and nurturing environments where complaints and allegations are taken seriously.

An emphasis on organisational culture also has relevance for sexual abuse prevention in other settings. There is promising qualitative data in relation to 'whole school' interventions such as Mentors for Violence Prevention, Green Dot, and Bringing in the Bystander, which enhance school and college students' abilities to become active bystanders in the prevention of bullying, sexual harassment and teen dating abuse (Katz et al., 2011; Coker et al., 2011; Moynihan et al., 2011). There is some limited evidence that participants in school- and college-based sexual violence prevention programmes such as Coaching Boys into Men, Expect Respect, Rock and Water, and Shifting Boundaries are less likely to be identified as victims and perpetrators of sexual violence in comparison to control groups (DeGue et al., 2014; Miller et al., 2012; Taylor et al., 2013; de Graaf et al., 2016; Ball et al., 2012). Such programmes seem to be best introduced in early adolescence, and appear to show better outcomes when they focus on self-control, self-reflection, communication skills and social skills. Evaluations to date suggest that they need to be implemented as part of a comprehensive, multilevel strategy to reduce sexual violence. However, for some adolescents, harmful sexual behaviour may have its roots in problematic sexual behaviour in early childhood. Schools-based preventative efforts should not focus solely on secondary education, and so providing training for care providers such as nursery and primary school staff regarding normative sexual development and how to identify and manage concerning behaviour in young children is also key.

Virtual environments

As noted in the previous chapter, online harmful sexual behaviour takes many forms and is being recognised by specialist services as an increasing area of concern (Palmer, 2015). Guidance for providers of social media and interactive services has been developed in order to encourage the implementation of a number of measures to detect and prevent risks to children online (UKCCIS, 2015), but safety initiatives are as yet under-evaluated (Livingstone *et al.*, 2017). With the exception of sexting and sexual harassment they also tend to assume that most risks are presented by adults rather than coming potentially from other children and young people themselves.

Educating children, young people and parents in relation to 'e-safety' has an important role to play alongside public information and access to resources for professionals who work with children. There is limited evidence that some groups (such as lesbian, gay and bisexual youth; young people with learning disabilities and those diagnosed with ASD/C; and young people with mental health problems) may be at elevated risk online, and so preventative measures should be targeted accordingly (Palmer, 2015).

Safe and confidential spaces for young people can help them to explore worries about their own sexual thoughts or behaviour, particularly with respect to sexual attraction to younger children (Beier *et al.*, 2016). It is likely that online resources may be particularly valuable as a less stigmatising way of obtaining advice and support and projects such at Help Wanted! in the US are developing tools of this nature (Letourneau, 2016). However, alongside such specific measures, it may be that virtual environments should be con-ceptualised as extending – rather than separate from – children and young people's offline social interactions (Finkelhor, 2014). Online safety may be best achieved by adding specific components to existing programmes such as those highlighted in the previous section, which provide support around more generic life skills including emotional regulation, self-control, self-reflection and social skills.

Communities

Adolescence is a peak time for the emergence of harmful sexual behaviour, and also a time when child protection services struggle to engage with young people at risk. The nature of safeguarding issues for adolescents – going missing, truancy, sexual exploitation, substance misuse, bullying, risk-taking behaviour, negative peer influences, interpersonal violence with peers, threats and hostility in the community, self-harm and suicide attempts – are rarely measured in descriptive studies concerning young people who have displayed harmful sexual behaviour (Firmin, 2017).

The risks of harm young people face are often very different from those experienced by younger children, requiring distinctive safeguarding approaches that recognise the nature of young people's environments and experiences. This resonates with the finding that context and setting of abusive behaviour are important, and one of the key messages from research is that creating safer environments for children to live and grow up in may make a substantial contribution to the prevention of harmful sexual behaviour in childhood.

To be effective, therefore, prevention programmes need to target multiple risk and protective factors and incorporate strategies across the social ecology. Tilley *et al.* (2014) illustrate this principle when describing a community in Queensland, Australia, in which sexual violence among young people was prevalent, particularly within the indigenous population. Of special concern were reports of group rapes, girls drawn into under-age sex through peer associations, girls trading sex for money on the streets and the rape of girls while intoxicated. In one area, rates of reported sexual offences were almost seven times greater than the state average, and rates of sexually transmitted infections fifty-six times greater. These problems were compounded by a local context, in which many places were considered by locals to be unsafe (particularly at night), where there was a high frequency of missing school, low levels of family supervision, and a deep reluctance on the part of community members to intervene directly in problem behaviour or to contact the police with concerns.

An intervention strategy was delivered across various domains: public spaces, domestic spaces and in school and youth group spaces. Public spaces were targeted by fifteen-minute 'pulse patrols' staged at 'hot times' on 'hot days' of the week, with training provided to police in order to improve how they engaged with the young people they encountered. Extra lighting and CCTV supplemented this, and night patrols were undertaken by community members, who were better placed than police to enter into informal conversations and information-sharing about available services. Creating safer domestic spaces was achieved through professionals working closely with communities, sharing information about the problem through community forums and undertaking developmental work with parents focusing on parenting skills tailored to suit different community contexts and cultural backgrounds. Finally, a sex, ethics and guardianship programme for young people was developed in order to address attitudes that supported sexual violence towards girls and to improve their ability to interrupt risky situations. Therapy was provided to those who had experienced sexual violence to help prevent re-victimisation. All of this was achieved by a holistic and ecological conceptualisation of the problem and close consultation with affected communities.

Evaluation is ongoing, but the evidence to date indicates that fewer sexual offences are being reported to police and fewer general offences are being reported in locations where police did foot patrols. Parents say they have learnt new ways to keep children safe and could better identify risky situations for children. Teachers say that they now know how to identify worrying behaviour and are better able to respond to children who behave in worrying ways. These findings suggest that even seemingly intractable issues in relation to 'hot spots' for harmful sexual behaviour and youth violence can be tackled using a community approach (Griffiths University, 2017).

Conclusion

We have argued throughout this book that children and young people who have displayed harmful sexual behaviour are different from adults who sexually abuse and require a different set of responses, which are sensitive to their developmental needs as children. Understanding this behaviour demands an ecological and situational perspective rather than solely an individual psychological perspective to be taken. Sometimes, the anxiety provoked by children's harmful sexual behaviour, especially online behaviour, leads to punitive responses, drawing already troubled children into risk management and criminal justice systems that deny their rights and continue to blight their prospects throughout the course of their lives. While responses to children's harmful sexual behaviour need to manage and reduce genuine risks presented, we have argued that they must also respect and uphold children's rights, including their rights to safe and healthy sexual well-being and expression, and must continue to anchor the child as part of their community. Increasingly, the supports provided to children and young people who have displayed harmful sexual behaviour must address their online as well as their offline social worlds and recognise that these worlds are enmeshed. Rather than thinking narrowly about preventing recidivism, interventions need to consider the child's wider welfare and to support more positive life course trajectories.

Identifying harmful sexual behaviour when it occurs and intervening to reduce the likelihood of its recurrence are vital, but preventing it from happening in the first place is clearly preferable. Prevention strategies are in their infancy, but to be effective they need to operate at a number of levels. Universal education about healthy sexuality in schools, beginning with, but not confined to, primary schools, could usefully incorporate an understanding that not only adults but also children and young people themselves may present risks of sexual harm. Parenting programmes could include such materials, and supporting parents to provide calmer, safer and more nurturing caregiving environments may serve to attenuate some of the factors that characterise developmental pathways into harmful sexual behaviour. Situational prevention strategies, which extend guardianship and increase opportunities for natural observation, may also have a crucial role to play.

Ultimately, however, we need to recognise that harmful sexual behaviour exists within the context of a pervasive culture of legitimised, gendered power imbalances and of the condoning of more common and everyday forms of harassment, abuse and violence. This social problem is linked inextricably to the promotion of political, cultural and social messages that amplify power differences between genders and between adults and children. Changing family, organisational and community cultures may provide the first steps towards more sustainable long-term prevention of harmful sexual behaviour displayed by children and young people.

The task, then, is considerable – but also very simple. The most important actions we can take as adults – as parents, professionals and members of the community – to prevent harmful sexual behaviour in childhood and adolescence, involve helping children to grow up safely, upholding their rights and supporting their respect for the rights of others. For many of those we have described in this book, this will entail accessing appropriate and sufficient supports to help them move on from harm, and leave sources of hurt and pain behind them. However, prevention is always more desirable than cure, and the best outcomes for children are acheived when growing up means never having experienced or caused harm in the first place.

References

Abbey, A., Zawacki, T., Buck, P. O., Clinton, A. M. and McAuslan, P. (2004) 'Sexual assault and alcohol consumption: What do we know about their relationship and what types of research are still needed?', *Aggression and Violent Behavior*, Vol. 9, pp. 271–303

Abel, G. G., Becker, J. V. and Cunningham-Rathner, J. (1984) 'Complications, consent, and cognitions in sex between children and adults', *International Journal of Law and Psychiatry*, Vol. 7, pp. 89–103

Achenbach, T. M. and Edelbrock, C. (1991) *Manual for the Child Behavior Checklist/4–18 and 1991*, Burlington, VT: University of Vermont Department of Psychiatry

Aebi, M., Plattner, B., Ernest, M., Kaszynski, K. and Bessler, C. (2014) 'Criminal history and future offending of juveniles convicted of the possession of child pornography', *Sexual Abuse*, Vol. 26, pp. 375–90

Albury, K. (2014) 'Porn and sex education, porn as sex education', *Porn Studies*, Vol. 1, pp. 172–81

Allan, J. (2004) 'Mother blaming: a covert practice in therapeutic intervention', *Australian Social Work*, Vol. 57, pp. 57–70

Allardyce, S. (unpublished) 'Sexually harmful behaviour protocols in Scotland', Edinburgh: Centre for Criminal Justice Social Work, University of Edinburgh

Allardyce, S. and McAfee, J. (2016) *Ethical Decision Making with Young People Involved with Serious Offending*, Glasgow: Centre for Youth and Criminal Justice, University of Strathclyde

Allardyce, S. and Yates, P. (2009) 'The risks of young people abusing sexually at home, in the community or both: A comparative study of 34 boys in Edinburgh with harmful sexual behaviour', *Towards Effective Practice*, Vol. 8

Allardyce, S. and Yates, P. M. (2013) 'Assessing risk of victim crossover with children and young people who display harmful sexual behaviours', *Child Abuse Review*, Vol. 22, pp. 255–67

Allnock, D. and Miller, P. (2013) *No One Noticed, No One Heard: A Study of Disclosures of Childhood Abuse*, London: National Society for the Prevention of Cruelty to Children

Almond, L., Canter, D. and Gabrielle Salfati, C. (2006) 'Youths who sexually harm: A multivariate model of characteristics', *Journal of Sexual Aggression*, Vol. 12, pp. 97–114

Almond, T. J. (2014) 'Working with children and young people with harmful sexual behaviours: Exploring impact on practitioners and sources of support', *Journal of Sexual*

Aggression, Vol. 20, pp. 333–53

American Psychiatric Association (2013) *Diagnostic and Statistical Manual of Mental Disorders* (5th edn), Washington, DC: APA Andrews, D. A., Zinger, I., Hoge, R. D., Bonta, J., Gendreau, P. and Cullen, F. T. (1990) 'Does correctional treatment work? A clinically relevant and psychologically informed meta-analysis', *Criminology*, Vol. 28, pp. 369–404

Andrews, G., Corry, J., Slade, T., Issakidis, C. and Swanston, H. (2004) 'Child sexual abuse', in Ezzati, M., Lopez, A. D., Rodgers, A. and Murray, C. J. L. (eds) (2004) *Comparative Quantification of Health Risks: Global and Regional Burden of Disease Attributable to Selected Major Risk Factors*, Geneva: World Health Organization

Angelides, S. (2004) 'Feminism, child sexual abuse, and the erasure of child sexuality', *GLQ: A Journal of Lesbian and Gay Studies*, Vol. 10, pp. 141–77

Araji, S. K. (1997) *Sexually Aggressive Children: Coming To Understand Them, Thousand Oaks*, Thousand Oaks, CA, Sage

Araji, S. K. (2004) *Preadolescents and Adolescents: Evaluating Normative and Non-normative Sexual Behaviours and Development*, Abingdon, Taylor Francis

Arslan, M. M., Demirkiran, D. S., Akcan, R., Zeren, C. and Kokacya, M. H. (2016) 'General characteristics of child sexual offenders in Hatay, Turkey', *The Eurasian Journal of Medicine*, Vol. 48, pp. 6–9

ATSA (2017) 'Practice guidelines for assessment, treatment, and intervention with adolescents who have engaged in sexually abusive behaviour' (online). Available from URL: www.atsa.com/atsa-practice-guidelines (accessed 1 November 2017)

Australian Board of Statistics (2017) '4519.0 – Recorded Crime – Offenders, 2015–16' (online). Available from URL: www.abs.gov.au/AUSSTATS/abs@.nsf/DetailsPage/4519.02015–16?OpenDocument (accessed 29 November 2017)

Ayland, L. and West, B. (2006) 'The Good Way Model: A strengths-based approach for working with young people, especially those with intellectual difficulties, who have sexually abusive behaviour', *Journal of Sexual Aggression*, Vol. 12, pp. 189–201

Babchishin, K. M., Karl Hanson, R. and Hermann, C. A. (2011) 'The characteristics of online sex offenders: A meta-analysis', *Sexual Abuse*, Vol. 23, pp. 92–123

Bagley, C. (1992) 'Characteristics of 60 children and adolescents with a history of sexual assault against others: Evidence from a comparative study', *The Journal of Forensic Psychiatry*, Vol. 3, pp. 299–309

Bailey, R. (2011) *Letting Children Be Children: Report of an Independent Review of the Commercialisation and Sexualisation of Childhood*, London: Department of Education

Bak-Klimek, A., Karatzias, T., Elliott, L., Campbell, J., Pugh, R. and Laybourn, P. (2014) 'Nature of child sexual abuse and psychopathology in adult survivors: Results from a clinical sample in Scotland', *Journal of Psychiatric and Mental Health Nursing*, Vol. 21, pp. 550–7

Ball, B., Tharp, A. T., Noonan, R. K., Valle, L. A., Hamburger, M. E. and Rosenbluth, B. (2012) 'Expect respect support groups: Preliminary evaluation of a dating violence prevention program for at-risk youth', *Violence Against Women*, Vol. 18, pp. 746–62

Balogh, R., Bretherton, K., Whibley, S., Berney, T., Graham, S., Richold, P., Worsley, C. and Firth, H. (2001) 'Sexual abuse in children and adolescents with intellectual disability', *Journal of Intellectual Disability Research*, Vol. 45, pp. 194–201

Bancroft, J. (2003) *Sexual Development in Childhood*, Bloomington, IN: Indiana University Press

Bankes, N. (2006) 'The responsibility avoidance syndrome', in Erooga, M. and Masson, H. (eds) (2006) *Children and Young People Who Sexually Abuse Others: Current Developments and Practice Responses*, Abingdon: Routledge

Barbaree, H. E. and Marshall, W. L. (2006) *The Juvenile Sex Offender*, New York, NY: Guilford Press

Barker Robert, L. (1995) *The Social Work Dictionary* (3rd edn), Washington, DC: NASW Press

Barnardo's (2017) 'Police figures reveal rise of almost 80% in reports of child-on-child sex offences' (online). Available from URL: www.barnardos.org.uk/news/Police_figures_reveal_rise_of_almost_80_in_reports_of_child-onchild_sex_offences/latest-news.htm?ref=121581 (accessed 31 October 2017)

Barra, S., Bessler, C., Landolt, M. A. and Aebi, M. (2017) 'Patterns of adverse childhood experiences in juveniles who sexually offended', *Sexual Abuse*; doi:1079063217697135

Barter, C., Mccarry, M., Berridge, D. and Evans, K. (2009) *Partner Exploitation and Violence in Teenage Intimate Relationships*, London: National Society for the Prevention of Cruelty to Children

Basen-Engquist, K. and Parcel, G. S. (1992) 'Attitudes, norms, and self-efficacy: A model of adolescents' HIV-related sexual risk behavior', *Health Education Quarterly*, Vol. 19, pp. 263–77

Bass, L. B., Taylor, B. A., Knudson-Martin, C. and Huenergardt, D. (2006) 'Making sense of abuse: Case studies in sibling incest', *Contemporary Family Therapy*, Vol. 28, pp. 87–109

Bastian, B., Denson, T. F. and Haslam, N. (2013) 'The roles of dehumanization and moral outrage in retributive justice' (online); PLoS ONE 8(4): e61842; doi:10.1371/journal.pone.0061842

Bateman, J. and Milner, J. (2014) *Children and Young People Whose Behaviour is Sexually Concerning or Harmful: Assessing Risk and Developing Safety Plans*, London Jessica Kingsley

Bateman, T. (2017) *The State of Youth Justice 2017: An Overview of Trends and Developments*, London: National Association for Youth Justice

BBC (2015) 'School sex crime reports in UK top 5,500 in three years' (online). Available from URL: www.bbc.co.uk/news/education-34138287 (accessed 30 November 2017)

BBC (2017) 'Child-on-child sex offence reports "tip of the iceberg" ' (online). Available from URL: www.bbc.co.uk/news/uk-41504571 (accessed 27 November 2017)

Beckett, H., Brodie, I., Factor, F., Melrose, M., Pearce, J. J., Pitts, J., Shuker, L. and

Warrington, C. (2012) *Research into Gang-associated Sexual Exploitation and Sexual Violence: Interim Report*, Bedfordshire: University of Bedfordshire

Beckett, H., Brodie, I., Factor, F., Melrose, M., Pearce, J. J., Pitts, J., Shuker, L. and Warrington, C. (2013) *'It's Wrong But You Get Used to It': A Qualitative Study of Gang-associated Sexual Violence Towards, and Exploitation of, Young People in England*, Bedfordshire: University of Bedfordshire

Beckett, R. (2006) 'Risk prediction, decision making and evaluation of adolescent sexual abusers', in Erooga, M. and Masson, H. (eds) (2006) *Children and Young People Who Sexually Abuse Others: Current Developments and Practice Responses* (2nd edn), Abingdon: Routledge

Beier, K. M., Oezdemir, U. C., Schlinzig, E., Groll, A., Hupp, E. and Hellenschmidt, T. (2016) ' "Just dreaming of them": The Berlin Project for Primary Prevention of Child Sexual Abuse by Juveniles (PPJ)', *Child Abuse and Neglect*, Vol. 52, pp. 1–10

Belton, E. (2017) *Turn the Page: Manualised Treatment Programme*, London: National Society for the Prevention of Cruelty to Children

Bentley, H. (2017) *How Safe Are Our Children? The Most Comprehensive Overview of Child Protection in the UK*, London: National Society for the Prevention of Cruelty to Children

Berelowitz, S. (2013) *If Only Someone Had Listened: Office of the Children's Commissioner's Inquiry into Child Sexual Exploitation in Gangs and Groups. Final Report*, London: Office of the Children's Commissioner

Bhugra, D., Popelyuk, D. and Mcmullen, I. (2010) 'Paraphilias across cultures: Contexts and controversies', *Journal of Sex Research*, Vol. 47, pp. 242–56

Bijleveld, C. and Hendriks, J. (2003) 'Juvenile sex offenders: Differences between group and solo offenders', *Psychology, Crime and Law*, Vol. 9, pp. 237–45

Blanchard, R. (2010) 'The DSM diagnostic criteria for pedophilia', *Archives of Sexual Behavior*, Vol. 39, pp. 304–16

Bockting, W. (2008) 'Psychotherapy and the real-life experience: From gender dichotomy to gender diversity', *Sexologies*, Vol. 17, pp. 211–24

Boislard, M.-A., Van De Bongardt, D. and Blais, M. (2016) 'Sexuality (and lack thereof) in adolescence and early adulthood: A review of the literature', *Behavioral Sciences*, Vol. 6, p. 8

Boislard Pépin, M.-A. (2010) 'Précocité sexuelle et comportements sexuels à risque à l'adolescence: étude longitudinale des facteurs individuels, familiaux, dans le groupe d'amis et contextuels associés' (online), Université du Québec à Montréal. Available from URL: www.archipel.uqam.ca/3101/1/D1892.pdf (accessed 29 December 2017)

Boisvert, I., Tourigny, M., Lanctôt, N., Gagnon, M. M. and Tremblay, C. (2015) 'Psychosocial profiles of children referred for treatment for sexual behavior problems or for having been sexually abused', *Sexual Offender Treatment*, Vol. 10

Bonner, B. L., Walker, C. E. and Berliner, L. (2001) *Children with Sexual Behavior Problems: Assessment and Treatment*, Washington, DC, National Clearinghouse on *Child Abuse and Neglect* Information

Borduin, C., Henggeler, S., Blaske, D. and Stein, R. (1990) 'Multisystematic treatment of adolescent sexual offenders', *International Journal of Offender Therapy and Comparative Criminology*, Vol. 34, pp. 105–13

Borduin, C. M., Munschy, R. J., Wagner, D. V. and Taylor, E. K. (2011) 'Multisystemic therapy with juvenile sexual offenders: Development, validation, and dissemination', *International Perspectives on the Assessment and Treatment of Sexual Offenders: Theory, Practice, and Research*, pp. 263–85; doi:/10.1002/9781119990420.ch13

Borduin, C. M., Schaeffer, C. M. and Heiblum, N. (2009) 'A randomized clinical trial of multisystemic therapy with juvenile sexual offenders: Effects on youth social ecology and criminal activity', *Journal of Consulting and Clinical Psychology*, Vol. 77, p. 26

Boxer, A. M., Cohler, B. J., Herdt, G. and Irvin, F. (1993) 'Gay and lesbian youth', in Tolan, P. H. and Cohler, B. J. (eds) (1993) *Handbook of Clinical Research and Practice with Adolescents*, Oxford: John Wiley

Brady, A. and McCarlie, C. (2014) *Assessing and Reducing Risk: A Practice Framework for Working with Children and Young People Who Engage in Harmful Sexual Behaviour*, Glasgow: Glasgow City Council

Brämswig, J. and Dübbers, A. (2009) 'Disorders of pubertal development', *Deutsches Ärzteblatt International*, Vol. 106, pp. 295–303

Brannon, J. M., Larson, B. and Doggett, M. (1989) 'The extent and origins of sexual molestation and abuse among incarcerated adolescent males', *International Journal of Offender Therapy and Comparative Criminology*, Vol. 33, pp. 161–72

Bremer, J. F. (1998) 'Challenges in the assessment and treatment of sexually abusive adolescents', *The Irish Journal of Psychology*, Vol. 19, pp. 82–92

Brilleslijper-Kater, S. N. and Baartman, H. E. (2000) 'What do young children know about sex? Research on the sexual knowledge of children between the ages of 2 and 6 years', *Child Abuse Review*, Vol. 9, pp. 166–82

British Columbia Ministry of Education and Special Programs (1999) 'Responding to children's problem sexual behaviour in elementary schools: A resource for educators', Victoria, British Columbia Ministry of Education. Available from URL: www.icmec. org/wp-content/uploads/2015/10/Responding-to-Improper-Touching-CA.pdf (accessed 29 December 2017)

Bronfenbrenner, U. (1986) 'Ecology of the family as a context for human development: Research perspectives', *Developmental Psychology*, Vol. 22, pp. 723–42

Brook (2016) 'Brook traffic light system' (online). Available from URL: www.brook.org. uk/our-work/category/sexual-behaviours-traffic-light-tool (accessed 2 November 2017)

Brown, S. (2009) 'Attitudes towards sexual offenders and their rehabilitation: A special case', in Wood, S. and Gannon, T. (eds) (2009) *Public Opinion and Criminal Justice: Context, Practice, and Values*, Abingdon: Routledge

Brownlie, J. (2001) 'The "being-risky" child: Governing childhood and sexual risk', *Sociology*, Vol. 35, pp. 519–37

Buckingham, D. (2013) *Beyond Technology: Children's Learning in the Age of Digital Culture*, New York, NY: John Wiley

Bumby, K. M. and Bumby, N. H. (1997) 'Adolescent female sexual offenders', in Schwartz, B. K. and Cellini, H. R. (eds) (1997) *The Sex offender: New Insights, Treatment Innovations and Legal Developments*, Kingston, NJ: Civic Research Institute

Burman, M., Armstrong, S., Batchelor, S., Mcneill, F. and Nicholson, J. (2007) *Research and Practice in Risk Assessment and Risk Management of Children and Young People Engaging in Offending Behavior*, Paisley: Risk Management Authority

Burton, D. and Miner, M. (2016) 'Explaining male adolescent perpetration of sexual crimes', in Beech, A. and Ward, T. (eds) (2016) *The Wiley Handbook on the Theories, Assessment and Treatment of Sexual Offending*, Chichester, West Sussex: Wiley

Burton, D. and Schatz, R. (2003) 'Meta-analysis of the abuse rates of adolescent sexual abusers', 8th International Family Violence Conference, Portsmouth, NH

Burton, D. L. (2000) 'Were adolescent sexual offenders children with sexual behavior problems?', *Sexual Abuse*, Vol. 12, pp. 37–48

Burton, D. L., Miller, D. L. and Shill, C. T. (2002) 'A social learning theory comparison of the sexual victimization of adolescent sexual offenders and nonsexual offending male delinquents', *Child Abuse and Neglect*, Vol. 26, pp. 893–907

Butler, S. M. and Seto, M. C. (2002) 'Distinguishing two types of adolescent sex offenders', *Journal of the American Academy of Child and Adolescent Psychiatry*, Vol. 41, pp. 83–90

Caldwell, M. F. (2002) 'What we do not know about juvenile sexual reoffense risk', *Child Maltreatment*, Vol. 7, pp. 291–302

Caldwell, M. F. (2016) 'Quantifying the decline in juvenile sexual recidivism rates', *Psychology, Public Policy, and Law*, Vol. 22, No. 4, pp. 414–26; doi: 10.1037/law0000094

Campbell, F., Booth, A., Stepanova, E., Hackett, S., Sutton, A., Hynes, K., Sanderson, J. and Rogstad, K. (2016a) 'Draft guidance consultation: Harmful sexual behaviour in children: Evidence for identifying and assessing risk in children and young people who display harmful sexual behaviour' (online), London National Institute of Clinical Excellence/University of Sheffield/University of Durham. Available from URL: www.nice.org.uk/guidance/ng55/documents/evidence-review-2 (accessed 29 December 2017)

Campbell, F., Booth, A., Stepanova, E., Hackett, S., Sutton, A., Hynes, K., Sanderson, J. and Rogstad, K. (2016b). 'Evidence review 1 – interventions (harmful sexual behaviour in children: Evidence for identifying and helping children and young people who display harmful sexual behaviour' (online), London National Institute of Clinical Excellence/University of Sheffield/University of Durham. Available from URL: www.nice.org.uk/guidance/ng55/evidence/evidence-review-1-interventions-pdf-2660746285 (accessed 29 December 2017)

Carpentier, M. Y., Silovsky, J. F. and Chaffin, M. (2006) 'Randomized trial of treatment for children with sexual behavior problems: Ten-year follow-up', *Journal of Consulting and Clinical Psychology*, Vol. 74, pp. 482–8

Carson, C. (2007) *AIM Assessment and Interventions for under 12s*, Stockport: AIM

Carson, C. (2017) *Understanding and Managing Problematic and Harmful Sexual Behaviour in Education Settings* (3rd edn), Stockport: AIM

Carson, C. (unpublished) 'GEST Project on developing assessment criteria and intervention strategies for Primary School aged children with sexually inappropriate/abusive behaviours', Leeds: Leeds Education Department

Chaffin, M. (1996) 'Working with unsupportive mothers in incest cases', 12th Annual Midwest Conference on Child Sexual Abuse and Incest, Madison, WI

Chaffin, M., Letourneau, E. and Silovsky, J. F. (2002) 'Adults, adolescents, and children who sexually abuse children: A developmental perspective', in Myers, J. E. B., Berliner, L., Briere, J., Hendrix, C. T., Jenny, C. and Reid, T. A. (eds) (2002) *The APSAC Handbook on Child Maltreatment* (2nd edn), Thousand Oaks, CA: Sage

Chandra, A., Copen, C. E. and Mosher, W. D. (2013) 'Sexual behavior, sexual attraction, and sexual identity in the United States: Data from the 2006–2010 National Survey of Family Growth', in Baumie, A. K. (ed.) (2013) *International Handbook on the Demography of Sexuality*, New York, NY: Springer

Chang, H.-L. and Chow, C.-C. (2011) 'The treatment of fetishism in an adolescent with attention deficit hyperactivity disorder', *Chang Gung Medical Journal*, Vol. 34, pp. 440–3

Chassman, L., Kottler, J. and Madison, J. (2010) 'An exploration of counselor experiences of adolescents with sexual behavior problems', *Journal of Counseling and Development*, Vol. 88, pp. 269–76

Cherry, C. and O'Shea, D. (2006) 'Therapeutic work with families of young people who sexually abuse', in Erooga, M. and Masson, H. (eds) (2006) *Children and Young People Who Sexually Abuse Others*, Abingdon: Routledge, pp. 200–14

Childwise (2017) 'Childwise Monitor report 2017: Children's media use and purchasing' (online). Available from URL: www.saferinternet.org.uk/research/research-highlight-series/113-childwise-monitor-report-2017 (accessed 29 December 2017)

Cicchetti, D. and Toth, S. L. (1995) 'A developmental psychopathology perspective on child abuse and neglect', *Journal of the American Academy of Child and Adolescent Psychiatry*, Vol. 34, pp. 541–65

Clark, T. C., Lucassen, M. F. G., Bullen, P., Denny, S. J., Fleming, T. M., Robinson, E. M. and Rossen, F. V. (2014) 'The health and well-being of transgender High School students: Results from the New Zealand Adolescent Health Survey (Youth '12)', *Journal of Adolescent Health*, Vol. 55, pp. 93–9

Clayton, E., Jones, C., Brown, J. and Taylor, J. (2018, in press) 'The aetiology of child sexual abuse: A critical review of the empirical evidence'

Clements, K., Ryder, B., Mortimer, E. and Holmes, D. (2017) *Workforce Perspectives on Harmful Sexual Behaviour: Findings from the Local Authorities Research Consortium 7*, London: National Children's Bureau

Cohen, J. A., Mannarino, A. P. and Knudsen, K. (2005) 'Treating sexually abused children: 1 year follow-up of a randomized controlled trial', *Child Abuse and Neglect*, Vol. 29, pp.

135–45

Cohen-Kettenis, P. T. and Pfäfflin, F. (2003) *Transgenderism and Intersexuality in Childhood and Adolescence: Making Choices*, London: Sage

Coker, A. L., Cook-Craig, P. G., Williams, C. M., Fisher, B. S., Clear, E. R., Garcia, L. S. and Hegge, L. M. (2011) 'Evaluation of Green Dot: An active bystander intervention to reduce sexual violence on college campuses', *Violence Against Women*, Vol. 17, pp. 777–96

Cole, F. L. and Slocumb, E. M. (1995) 'Factors influencing safer sexual behaviors in heterosexual late adolescent and young adult collegiate males', *Journal of Nursing Scholarship*, Vol. 27, pp. 217–23

Colombino, N., Mercado, C. C., Levenson, J. and Jeglic, E. (2011) 'Preventing sexual violence: Can examination of offense location inform sex crime policy?', *International Journal of Law and Psychiatry*, Vol. 34, pp. 160–7

Cooper, A. (2005) 'Surface and depth in the Victoria Climbié inquiry report', *Child and Family Social Work*, Vol. 10, pp. 1–9

Cooper, C. L., Murphy, W. D. and Haynes, M. R. (1996) 'Characteristics of abused and nonabused adolescent sexual offenders', *Sexual Abuse*, Vol. 8, pp. 105–19

Cooper, K., Quayle, E., Jonsson, L. and Svedin, C. G. (2016) 'Adolescents and self-taken sexual images: A review of the literature', *Computers in Human Behavior*, Vol. 55, pp. 706–16

Coskun, M. and Ozturk, M. (2013) 'Sexual fetishism in adolescence: Report of two cases', *Dusunen Adam*, Vol. 26, pp. 199–205

Council of Europe (2007) 'Convention on the protection of children against sexual exploitation and sexual abuse'. CETS No. 201, 25 October 2007, Lanzarote

Cowburn, M. and Dominelli, L. (2001) 'Masking hegemonic masculinity: Reconstructing the paedophile as the dangerous stranger', *British Journal of Social Work*, Vol. 31, pp. 399–415

Crabbe, M. and Corlett, D. (2011) 'Eroticising inequality: Technology, pornography and young people', *Redress*, Vol. 20, p. 11

Craig, L. A. (2005) 'The impact of training on attitudes towards sex offenders', *Journal of Sexual Aggression*, Vol. 11, pp. 197–207

Craig, L. A. and Hutchinson, R. B. (2005) 'Sexual offenders with learning disabilities: Risk, recidivism and treatment', *Journal of Sexual Aggression*, Vol. 11, pp. 289–304

Crawford, M. and Popp, D. (2003) 'Sexual double standards: A review and methodological critique of two decades of research', *Journal of Sex Research*, Vol. 40, pp. 13–26

Creeden, K. (2009) 'How trauma and attachment can impact neurodevelopment: Informing our understanding and treatment of sexual behaviour problems', *Journal of Sexual Aggression*, Vol. 15, pp. 261–73

Criminal Justice Joint Inspection (2013) *Examining Multi-agency Responses to Children and Young People Who Sexually Offend: A Joint Inspection of the Effectiveness of Multi-agency Work with Children and Young People in England and Wales Who Have Committed Sexual Offences and Were Supervised in the Community*, London: HM Inspectorate of

Probation

Criminal Justice Statistics (2017) *Criminal Justice Statistics Outcomes by Offence 2006 to 2016: Pivot Table Analytical Tool for England and Wales,* London Ministry of Justice

Cunningham, C. and MacFarlane, K. (1991) *When Children Molest Children: Group Treatment Strategies for Young Sexual Abusers,* Orwell, VT: Safer Society Press

Curwen, T. (2011) 'A framework to assist in evaluating children's risk to repeat concerning sexual behaviour', in Calder, M. (ed.) (2011) *Contemporary Practice with Young People who Sexually Abuse: Evidence-based Developments,* Lyme Regis: Russell House

Curwen, T. and Costin, D. (2007) 'Toward assessing risk for repeated concerning sexual behaviour by children with sexual behaviour problems: What we know and what we can do with this knowledge', in Prescott, D. S. (ed.) (2007) *Knowledge and Practice: Challenges in the Treatment and Supervision of Sexual Abusers,* Bethany, OK: Wood N. Barnes

CYCJ (2017) 'A guide to youth justice in Scotland: Policy, Practice and Legislation; Chapter 7: Managing high risk' (online). Available from URL: www.cycj.org.uk/resource/youth-justice-in-scotland-guide (accessed 30 November 2017)

D'Andrea, W., Sharma, R., Zelechoski, A. D. and Spinazzola, J. (2011) 'Physical health problems after single trauma exposure: When stress takes root in the body', *Journal of the American Psychiatric Nurses Association,* Vol. 17, pp. 378–92

Da Costa, G., Spies, G. M. and Coetzee, L. (2014) 'Contributory factors to child on child sexual abuse: Perceptions of diverted female youth sex offenders', *Child Abuse Research in South Africa,* Vol. 15, pp. 35–50

Davidson, L. and Omar, H. A. (2014) 'Long-term consequences of childhood sexual abuse', *International Journal of Child and Adolescent Health,* Vol. 7, pp. 103–7

Davis, G. E. and Leitenberg, H. (1987) 'Adolescent sex offenders', *Psychological Bulletin,* Vol. 101, p. 417

Deacon, L. (2015) ' "Children's social care services": Response to children who display sexually harmful behaviour', doctoral dissertation, Durham University

De Graaf, H., Vanwesenbeeck, I., Meijer, S., Woertman, L. and Meeus, W. (2009) 'Sexual trajectories during adolescence: Relation to demographic characteristics and sexual risk', *Archives of Sexual Behavior,* Vol. 38, pp. 276–82

De Graaf, I., De Haas, S., Zaagsma, M. and Wijsen, C. (2016) 'Effects of rock and water: An intervention to prevent sexual aggression', *Journal of Sexual Aggression,* Vol. 22, pp. 4–19

DeGue, S. and DiLillo, D. (2004) 'Understanding perpetrators of nonphysical sexual coercion: Characteristics of those who cross the line', *Violence and Victims,* Vol. 19, pp. 673–88

DeGue, S., Valle, L. A., Holt, M. K., Massetti, G. M., Matjasko, J. L. and Tharp, A. T. (2014) 'A systematic review of primary prevention strategies for sexual violence perpetration', *Aggression and Violent Behavior,* Vol. 19, pp. 346–62

Denner, W. (2016) *The Student's Guide to an Epic Online Reputation … and Parents Too,* Warren Point, County Down: 10th Step Ltd

Department for Education (2017) *Definition and a Guide for Practitioners, Local Leaders and Decision Makers Working to Protect Children from Child Sexual Exploitation*, London: Department for Education

Derezotes, D. (2000) 'Evaluation of yoga and meditation trainings with adolescent sex offenders', *Child and Adolescent Social Work Journal*, Vol. 17, pp. 97–113

De Vries Robbé, M., Mann, R. E., Maruna, S. and Thornton, D. (2015) 'An exploration of protective factors supporting desistance from sexual offending', *Sexual Abuse*, Vol. 27, pp. 16–33

Dewhurst, A. M. and Nielsen, K. M. (1999) 'A resiliency-based approach to working with sexual offenders', *Sexual Addiction and Compulsivity: The Journal of Treatment and Prevention*, Vol. 6, pp. 271–9

Diamond, L. M. (2013) 'Sexual-minority, gender-nonconforming, and transgender youths', in Bromberg, D. and O'Donohue, W. T. (eds) (2012) *Handbook of Child and Adolescent Sexuality: Developmental and Forensic Psychology*, London: Elsevier

Dickson, N., Paul, C. and Herbison, P. (2003) 'Same-sex attraction in a birth cohort: Prevalence and persistence in early adulthood', *Social Science and Medicine*, Vol. 56, pp. 1607–15

Dodd, S. and Tolman, D. (2017) 'Reviving a positive discourse on sexuality within social work', *Social Work*, Vol. 62, No. 3, pp. 227–34; doi:10.1093/sw/swx016

DOH (2001) *Valuing People: A New Strategy for Learning Disability for the 21st Century*, London: Department of Health

Dombert, B., Schmidt, A. F., Banse, R., Briken, P., Hoyer, J., Neutze, J. and Osterheider, M. (2016) 'How common is men's self-reported sexual interest in prepubescent children?', *The Journal of Sex Research*, Vol. 53, pp. 214–23

Domhardt, M., Münzer, A., Fegert, J. M. and Goldbeck, L. (2015) 'Resilience in survivors of child sexual abuse: A systematic review of the literature', *Trauma, Violence, and Abuse*, Vol. 16, pp. 476–93

Doolin, E. J. (2011) 'Vagina: Diseases and treatment', in Mattei, P. (ed.) (2011) *Fundamentals of Pediatric Surgery*, New York, NY: Springer

Dopp, A. R., Borduin, C. M., Rothman, D. B. and Letourneau, E. J. (2017) 'Evidence-based treatments for youths who engage in illegal sexual behaviors', *Journal of Clinical Child and Adolescent Psychology*, Vol. 46, pp. 631–45

Dowden, C. and Andrews, D. A. (2004) 'The importance of staff practice in delivering effective correctional treatment: A meta-analytic review of core correctional practice', *International Journal of Offender Therapy and Comparative Criminology*, Vol. 48, pp. 203–14

Duane, Y. and Morrison, T. (2004) 'Families of young people who sexually abuse', in O'Reilly, G., Carr, A., Marshall, W. L. and Beckett, R. (eds) (2004) *The Handbook of Clinical intervention with Young People who Sexually Abuse*, Abingdon: Taylor Francis

Durham, A. (2006) *Young Men Who Have Sexually Abused: A Case Study Guide*, London: John Wiley

Duwe, G. and Kim, K. (2015) 'Out with the old and in with the new? An empirical comparison of supervised learning algorithms to predict ecidivism', *Criminal Justice Policy Review*, Vol. 28, pp. 570–600

Edgardh, K. and Ormstad, K. (2000) 'Prevalence and characteristics of sexual abuse in a national sample of Swedish seventeen-year-old boys and girls', *Acta paediatrica*, Vol. 89, pp. 310–19

Ellis, L. (1989) *Theories of Rape: Inquiries into the Causes of Sexual Aggression*, Abingdon: Taylor and Francis

Emerson, E. and Hatton, C. (2008) *CEDR Research Report 2008 (1): People with Learning Disabilities in England*, Lancaster: Lancaster University

End Violence against Women (2010) 'Sexual harassment in schools: A YouGov poll for EVAW' (online). Available from URL: www.endviolenceagainstwomen.org.uk/yougov-poll-exposes-high-levels-sexual-harassment-in-schools (accessed 7 February 2018)

Epperson, D. L., Ralston, C. A., Fowers, D. and Dewitt, J. (unpublished) 'Development of a sexual offense recidivism risk assessment tool – II (JSORRAT-II)', Ames, IA: University of Iowa

Evening Telegraph (2017) 'Youths the most likely age group in Tayside to be charged for indecent pictures of children' (online), 30 November 2017. Available from URL: www.eveningtelegraph.co.uk/fp/youths-likely-age-group-tayside-charged-indecent-pics-children (accessed 29 December 2017)

Ey, L.-A., McInnes, E. and Rigney, L. I. (2017) 'Educators' understanding of young children's typical and problematic sexual behaviour and their training in this area', *Sex Education*, Vol. 17, pp. 682–96

Fahy, B. (2011) 'Dilemmas for practitioners working with siblings under 10 years presenting with harmful sexual behaviours towards each other, with complex trauma histories. What are the challenges involved in how they should be placed in local authority care permanently?', in Calder, M. (ed.) (2011) *Contemporary Practice with Young People Who Sexually Abuse: Evidence-based developments*, Lyme Regis: Russell House

Falkenström, F., Granström, F. and Holmqvist, R. (2013) 'Therapeutic alliance predicts symptomatic improvement session by session', *Journal of Counseling Psychology*, Vol. 60, pp. 317–28

Fanniff, A. M. and Letourneau, E. J. (2012) 'Another piece of the puzzle: Psychometric properties of the J-SOAP-II', *Sexual Abuse*, Vol. 24, pp. 378–408

Fehrenbach, P. A., Smith, W., Monastersky, C. and Deisher, R. W. (1986) 'Adolescent sexual offenders: Offender and offense characteristics', *American Journal of Orthopsychiatry*, Vol. 56, pp. 225–33

Felitti, V. J. and Anda, R. F. (2010) 'The relationship of adverse childhood experiences to adult medical disease, psychiatric disorders and sexual behavior: Implications for healthcare', in Lanius, R. A., Eric, V. and Clare, P. (eds) (2010) *The Impact of Early Life Trauma on Health and Disease: The Hidden Epidemic*, Cambridge: Cambridge University Press

Fenichel, P. (2012) 'Delayed puberty', in Sultan, C. (ed.) (2012) *Pediatric and Adolescent Gynecology*, Basel: Karger

Finkelhor, D. (1984) *Child Sexual Abuse: New Theory and Research*, Washington, DC: Sage

Finkelhor, D. (1990) 'Early and long-term effects of child sexual abuse: An update', *Professional Psychology: Research and Practice*, Vol. 21, p. 325

Finkelhor, D. (2014) 'Commentary: Cause for alarm? Youth and internet risk research – a commentary on Livingstone and Smith (2014)', *Journal of Child Psychology and Psychiatry*, Vol. 55, pp. 655–8

Finkelhor, D. and Browne, A. (1985) 'The traumatic impact of child sexual abuse: a conceptualization', *American Journal of Orthopsychiatry*, Vol. 55, p. 530

Finkelhor, D. and Lewis, I. (1988) 'An epidemiologic approach to the study of child molestation', *Annals of the New York Academy of Sciences*, Vol. 528, pp. 64–78

Finkelhor, D., Ormrod, R. and Chaffin, M. (2009) 'Juveniles who commit sex offenses against minors' (online), *Juvenile Justice Bulletin*. Available from URL: www.unh.edu/ccrc/pdf/CV171.pdf (accessed 29 December 2017)

Finkelhor, D., Ormrod, R. K. and Turner, H. A. (2007) 'Poly-victimization: A neglected component in child victimization', *Child Abuse and Neglect*, Vol. 31, pp. 7–26

Finkelhor, D., Shattuck, A., Turner, H. A. and Hamby, S. L. (2014) 'The lifetime prevalence of child sexual abuse and sexual assault assessed in late adolescence', *Journal of Adolescent Health*, Vol. 55, pp. 329–33

Firmin, C. (2017) 'Contextual risk, individualised responses: An assessment of safeguarding responses to nine cases of peer-on-peer abuse', *Child Abuse Review*; doi:10.1002/car.2449

Firmin, C., Curtis, G., Fritz, D., Olatain, P., Latchford, L., Lloyd, J. and Larasi, I. (2016a) *Towards a Contextual Response to Peer-on-peer Abuse*, Luton: University of Bedfordshire

Firmin, C., Warrington, C. and Pearce, J. (2016b) 'Sexual exploitation and its impact on developing sexualities and sexual relationships: The need for contextual social work interventions', *The British Journal of Social Work*, bcw134

Fonagy, P., Butler, S., Baly, A., Seto, M., Anokhina, A., Kaminska, K. and Ellison, R. (2017) *Evaluation of Multisystemic Therapy for Adolescent Problematic Sexual Behaviour*, London: Department for Education. Available from URL: http://dera.ioe.ac.uk/29567/1/Evaluation_of_Multisystemic_Therapy_for_adolescent_problematic_sexual_behaviour.pdf (accessed 6 February 2018)

Fook, J. and Gardner, F. (2007) *Practising Critical Reflection: A Resource Handbook*, Maidenhead: McGraw-Hill Education

Fortenberry, J. D. (2013) 'Puberty and adolescent sexuality', *Hormones and Behavior*, Vol. 64, pp. 280–7

Fox, B. (2017) 'What makes a difference?: Evaluating the key distinctions and predictors of sexual and non-sexual offending among male and female juvenile offenders', *Journal of Criminal Psychology*, Vol. 7, pp. 134–50

Fox, B. and DeLisi, M. (2017) 'From criminological heterogeneity to coherent classes:

developing a typology of juvenile sex offenders', *Youth Violence and Juvenile Justice*; doi:1541204017699257

Fox, K. J. (2013) 'Incurable sex offenders, lousy judges and the media: Moral panic sustenance in the age of new media', *American Journal of Criminal Justice*, Vol. 38, pp. 160–81

Freund, K., Watson, R. and Dickey, R. (1990) 'Does sexual abuse in childhood cause pedophilia: An exploratory study', *Archives of Sexual Behavior*, Vol. 19, pp. 557–68

Friedrich, W. N. (2007) *Children with Sexual Behavior Problems: Family-based, Attachment-focused Therapy*, New York, NY: WW Norton

Friedrich, W. N., Davies, W., Feher, E. and Wright, J. (2003) 'Sexual behavior problems in preteen children', *Annals of the New York Academy of Sciences*, Vol. 989, pp. 95–104

Friedrich, W. N., Fisher, J., Broughton, D., Houston, M. and Shafran, C. R. (1998) 'Normative sexual behavior in children: A contemporary sample', *Pediatrics*, Vol. 101, e9

Friedrich, W. N., Fisher, J. L., Dittner, C. A., Acton, R., Berliner, L., Butler, J., Damon, L., Davies, W. H., Gray, A. and Wright, J. (2001) 'Child sexual behavior inventory: Normative, psychiatric, and sexual abuse comparisons', *Child Maltreatment*, Vol. 6, pp. 37–49

Friedrich, W. N., Gully, K. J. and Trane, S. T. (2005) 'Re: It is a mistake to conclude that sexual abuse and sexualized behavior are not related: A reply to Drach, Wientzen, and Ricci (2001)', *Child Abuse and Neglect*, Vol. 29, pp. 297–302

Friedrich, W. N., Jaworski, T. M., Huxsahl, J. E. and Bengtson, B. S. (1997) 'Dissociative and sexual behaviors in children and adolescents with sexual abuse and psychiatric histories', *Journal of Interpersonal Violence*, Vol. 12, pp. 155–71

Friedrich, W. N., Sandfort, T. G., Oostveen, J. and Cohen-Kettenis, P. T. (2000) 'Cultural differences in sexual behavior: 2–6 year old Dutch and American children', *Journal of Psychology and Human Sexuality*, Vol. 12, pp. 117–29

Fyson, R. (2007) 'Young people with learning disabilities who sexually harm others: the role of criminal justice within a multi-agency response', *British Journal of Learning Disabilities*, Vol. 35, pp. 181–6

Gallagher, B., Bradford, M. and Pease, K. (2008) 'Attempted and completed incidents of stranger-perpetrated child sexual abuse and abduction', *Child Abuse and Neglect*, Vol. 32, pp. 517–28

Geary, J., Lambie, I. and Seymour, F. (2006) *Turning Lives Around: A Process Evaluation of Community Adolescent Sexual Offender Treatment Programmes in New Zealand*, Wellington, New Zealand: Department of Child, Youth and Family

Geary, J., Lambie, I. and Seymour, F. (2011) 'Consumer perspectives of New Zealand community treatment programmes for sexually abusive youth', *Journal of Sexual Aggression*, Vol. 17, pp. 181–95

Gerber, J. (1994) 'The use of art therapy in juvenile sex offender specific treatment', *The Arts in Psychotherapy*, Vol. 21, pp. 367–74

Gil, E. and Johnson, T. C. (1993) *Sexualized Children: Assessment and Treatment of*

Sexualized Children and Children Who Molest, Rockville, MD: Launch Press

Gilby, R., Wolf, L. and Goldberg, B. (1989) 'Mentally retarded adolescent sex offenders: A survey and pilot study', *The Canadian Journal of Psychiatry*, Vol. 34, pp. 542–8

GIRFEC (2017) 'Getting It Right For Every Child' (online), Edinburgh: Scottish Government. Available from URL: www.gov.scot/Topics/People/Young-People/gettingitright (accessed 29 November 2017)

Gittins, D. (1998) *The Child in Question*, London: Macmillan

Glaser, D. (2014) 'The effects of child maltreatment on the developing brain', *Medico-Legal Journal*, Vol. 82, pp. 97–111

Gold, N., Benbenishty, R. and Osmo, R. (2001) 'A comparative study of risk assessments and recommended interventions in Canada and Israel', *Child Abuse and Neglect*, Vol. 25, pp. 607–22

Goldman, R. and Goldman, J. (1982) *Children's Sexual Thinking: A Comparative Study of Children Aged 5 to 15 Years in Australia, North America, Britain, and Sweden*, Boston, MA: Routledge & Kegan Paul

Gordon, B. N. and Schroeder, C. (1995) *Sexuality: A Developmental Approach to Problems*, New York, NY: Plenum Publishing

Graves, R., Openshaw, D. K. and Adams, G. R. (1992) 'Adolescent sex offenders and social skills training', *International Journal of Offender Therapy and Comparative Criminology*, Vol. 36, pp. 139–53

Gray, A., Busconi, A., Houchens, P. and Pithers, W. D. (1997) 'Children with sexual behavior problems and their caregivers: Demographics, functioning, and clinical patterns', *Sexual Abuse: A Journal of Research and Treatment*, Vol. 9, p. 267

Gray, C., White, A. L. and Mcandrew, S. (2002) *My Social Stories Book*, Philadelphia, PA: Jessica Kingsley

Green, L. and Masson, H. (2002) 'Adolescents who sexually abuse and residential accommodation: Issues of risk and vulnerability', *British Journal of Social Work*, Vol. 32, pp. 149–68

Greenberg, M. T., Speltz, M. L. and Deklyen, M. (1993) 'The role of attachment in the early development of disruptive behavior problems', *Development and Psychopathology*, Vol. 5, pp. 191–213

Griffin, H. L. and Vettor, S. (2012) 'Predicting sexual re-offending in a UK sample of adolescents with intellectual disabilities', *Journal of Sexual Aggression*, Vol. 18, pp. 64–80

Griffiths University (2017) 'The neighbourhoods project' (online). Available from URL: www2.griffith.edu.au/neighbourhoods-project/neighbourhoods-project (accessed 30 November 2017)

Grove, W. M. and Meehl, P. E. (1996) 'Comparative efficiency of informal (subjective, impressionistic) and formal (mechanical, algorithmic) prediction procedures: The clinical–statistical controversy', *Psychology, Public Policy, and Law*, Vol. 2, No. 2, pp. 293–323

Hackett, S. (2010) 'Children, young people and sexual violence', in Barter, C. and Berridge,

D. (eds) (2010) *Children Behaving Badly*, Chichester, West Sussex: Wiley

Hackett, S. (2014) *Children and Young People with Harmful Sexual Behaviours*, Dartington: Research in Practice

Hackett, S. (2016) 'Exploring the relationship between neglect and harmful sexual behaviours in children and young people: Evidence Scope 3' (online). Available from URL: www.nspcc.org.uk/globalassets/documents/research-reports/neglect-harmful-sexual-behaviours-evidence-scope-3.pdf (accessed 29 December 2017)

Hackett, S., Balfe, M., Masson, H. and Phillips, J. (2014) 'Family responses to young people who have sexually abused: Anger, ambivalence and acceptance', *Children and Society*, Vol. 28, pp. 128–39

Hackett, S., Holmes, D. and Branigan, P. (2016) *Harmful Sexual Behaviour Framework: An Evidence-informed Operational Framework for Children and Young People Displaying Harmful Sexual Behaviours*, London: National Society for the Prevention of Cruelty to Children

Hackett, S. and Masson, H. (2012) *Recidivism, Desistance and Life Course Trajectories of Young Sexual Abusers. An In-Depth Follow-Up Study, 10 Years On. ESRC End of Award Report, RES-062-23-0850*, Swindon: Economic and Social Research Council

Hackett, S., Masson, H., Balfe, M. and Phillips, J. (2015) 'Community reactions to young people who have sexually abused and their families: A shotgun blast, not a rifle shot', *Children and Society*, Vol. 29, pp. 243–54

Hackett, S., Phillips, J., Masson, H. and Balfe, M. (2012) *Recidivism, Desistance and Life Course Trajectories of Young Sexual Abusers. An In-depth Follow-up Study, 10 Years On*, SASS Research Briefing No. 7, Durham: School of Applied Social Sciences, Durham University

Hackett, S., Phillips, J., Masson, H. and Balfe, M. (2013) 'Individual, family and abuse characteristics of 700 British child and adolescent sexual abusers', *Child Abuse Review*, Vol. 22, pp. 232–45

Hackett, S., Print, B. and Dey, C. (1998) 'Brother nature? Therapeutic intervention with young men who sexually abuse their siblings', in Bannister, A. (ed.) (1998) *From Hearing to Healing: Working with the Aftermath of Child Sexual Abuse* (2nd edn), New York, NY: Wiley

Häggström-Nordin, E., Tydén, T., Hanson, U. and Larsson, M. (2009) 'Experiences of and attitudes towards pornography among a group of Swedish high school students', *The European Journal of Contraception and Reproductive Health Care*, Vol. 14, pp. 277–84

Hall, D. K., Mathews, F. and Pearce, J. (1998) 'Factors associated with sexual behavior problems in young sexually abused children', *Child Abuse and Neglect*, Vol. 22, pp. 1045–63

Hall, D. K., Mathews, F. and Pearce, J. (2002) 'Sexual behavior problems in sexually abused children: A preliminary typology', *Child Abuse and Neglect*, Vol. 26, pp. 289–312

Hall, G. and Hirschman, R. (1996) 'A quadripartite model of sexual aggression', in Hall, G. (ed.) (1996) *Theory-based Assessment, Treatment and Prevention of Sexual Aggression*, Oxford: Oxford University Press

Hamilton-Giachritsis, C., Hanson, E., Whittle, H. and Beech, A. (2017) *Everyone Deserves to Be Happy and Safe: A Mixed Methods Study Exploring How Online and Offline Child Sexual Abuse Impact Young People and How Respond to It*, London: National Society for the Prevention of Cruelty to Children

Hanson, R. K. and Thornton, D. (2000) 'Improving risk assessments for sex offenders: A comparison of three actuarial scales', *Law and Human Behavior*, Vol. 24, pp. 119–36

Harper, C. A. and Hogue, T. E. (2015) 'The emotional representation of sexual crime in the national British press', *Journal of Language and Social Psychology*, Vol. 34, pp. 3–24

Harris, A. J., Walfield, S. M., Shields, R. T. and Letourneau, E. J. (2016) 'Collateral consequences of juvenile sex offender registration and notification: Results from a survey of treatment providers', *Sexual Abuse*, Vol. 28, pp. 770–90

Harris, G. T., Rice, M. E. and Quinsey, V. L. (1998) 'Appraisal and management of risk in sexual aggressors: Implications for criminal justice policy', *Psychology, Public Policy, and Law*, Vol. 4, pp. 73–115

Harris, L., Blum, R. W. and Resnick, M. (1991) 'Teen females in Minnesota: A portrait of quiet disturbance', *Women and Therapy*, Vol. 11, pp. 119–35

Hart, A., Lane, D. and Doherty, G. (2017) *Report of the Historical Institutional Abuse Inquiry*, Belfast: The Inquiry into Historical Institutional Abuse 1922 to 1995 and The Executive Office

Hart-Kerkhoffs, L. 't, Jansen, L. M., Doreleijers, T. A., Vermeiren, R., Minderaa, R. B. and Hartman, C. A. (2009) 'Autism spectrum disorder symptoms in juvenile suspects of sex offenses', *The Journal of Clinical Psychiatry*, Vol. 70, pp. 266–72

Haugaard, J. (1996) 'Sexual behaviors between children: Professionals' opinions and undergraduates' recollections', *Families in Society: The Journal of Contemporary Social Services*, Vol. 77, pp. 81–9

Hazelwood, R. R. and Burgess, A. W. (2016) *Practical Aspects of Rape Investigation: A Multidisciplinary Approach*, Boca Raton, FL: CRC Press

Heffernan, R. and Ward, T. (2017) 'A comprehensive theory of dynamic risk and protective factors', *Aggression and Violent Behavior*, Vol. 37, pp. 129–41

Hellemans, H., Colson, K., Verbraeken, C., Vermeiren, R. and Deboutte, D. (2007) 'Sexual behavior in high-functioning male adolescents and young adults with autism spectrum disorder', *Journal of Autism and Developmental Disorders*, Vol. 37, pp. 260–9

Henshaw, M., Ogloff, J. R. and Clough, J. A. (2015) 'Looking beyond the screen: A critical review of the literature on the online child pornography offender', *Sexual Abuse*; doi:1079063215603690

Herdt, G. and McClintock, M. (2000) 'The magical age of 10', *Archives of Sexual Behavior*, Vol. 29, pp. 587–606

Hickey, N., McCrory, E., Farmer, E. and Vizard, E. (2008) 'Comparing the developmental and behavioural characteristics of female and male juveniles who present with sexually abusive behaviour', *Journal of Sexual Aggression*, Vol. 14, pp. 241–52

Hipwell, A. E., Keenan, K., Loeber, R. and Battista, D. (2010) 'Early predictors of sexually intimate behaviors in an urban sample of young girls', *Developmental Psychology*, Vol.

46, pp. 366–78

Hodges, C. (2002) 'A 5-step family therapy protocol to treat sibling on sibling sexual abuse', in Calder, M. (ed.) (2002) *Young People Who Sexually Abuse: Building the Evidence Base for Your Practice*, Lyme Regis: Russell House

Höglund, J., Jern, P., Sandnabba, N. K. and Santtila, P. (2014) 'Finnish women and men who self-report no sexual attraction in the past 12 months: Prevalence, relationship status, and sexual behavior history', *Archives of Sexual Behavior*, Vol. 43, pp. 879–89

Hogue, T. E. and Peebles, J. (1997) 'The influence of remorse, intent and attitudes toward sex offenders on judgments of a rapist', *Psychology, Crime and Law*, Vol. 3, pp. 249–59

Hollis, V., Belton, E. and Team, N. E. (2017) *Children and Young People who Engage in Technology-Assisted Harmful Sexual Behaviour*, London: National Society for the Prevention of Cruelty to Children

Horvath, M. A., Alys, L., Massey, K., Pina, A., Scally, M. and Adler, J. R. (2013) *Basically ... Porn Is Everywhere: A Rapid Evidence Assessment on the Effects That Access and Exposure to Pornography Has on Children and Young People*, London: Office of the Children's Commissioner

Hosser, D. and Bosold, C. (2006) 'A comparison of sexual and violent offenders in a German youth prison', *The Howard Journal of Crime and Justice*, Vol. 45, pp. 159–70

Houck, C. D., Barker, D., Rizzo, C., Hancock, E., Norton, A. and Brown, L. K. (2014) 'Sexting and sexual behavior in at-risk adolescents', *Pediatrics*, Vol. 133, e276–e282

Hsu, L. G. and Starzynski, J. (1990) 'Adolescent rapists and adolescent child sexual assaulters', *International Journal of Offender Therapy and Comparative Criminology*, Vol. 34, pp. 23–30

Hunter, J. A., Gilbertson, S. A., Vedros, D. and Morton, M. (2004) 'Strengthening community-based programming for juvenile sexual offenders: Key concepts and paradigm shifts', *Child Maltreatment*, Vol. 9, pp. 177–89

Hunter, J. A., Lexier, L. J., Goodwin, D. W., Browne, P. A. and Dennis, C. (1993) 'Psychosexual, attitudinal, and developmental characteristics of juvenile female sexual perpetrators in a residential treatment setting', *Journal of Child and Family Studies*, Vol. 2, pp. 317–26

Hutton, L. and Whyte, B. (2006) 'Children and young people with harmful sexual behaviours: First analysis of data from a Scottish sample', *Journal of Sexual Aggression*, Vol. 12, pp. 115–25

Ingevaldson, S., Goulding, A. and Tidefors, I. (2016) 'Experiences of intimate relationships in young men who sexually offended during adolescence: Interviews 10 years later', *Journal of Sexual Aggression*, Vol. 22, pp. 410–22

Irish, L., Kobayashi, I. and Delahanty, D. L. (2009) 'Long-term physical health consequences of childhood sexual abuse: A meta-analytic review', *Journal of Pediatric Psychology*, Vol. 35, pp. 450–61

Jakobovits, A. (2001) 'Fetal penile erection', *Ultrasound in Obstetrics and Gynecology*, Vol. 18, p. 405

James, A. and Neil, P. (1996) 'Juvenile sexual offending: One-year period prevalence study within Oxfordshire', *Child Abuse and Neglect*, Vol. 20, pp. 477–85

Janes, L. (2016) 'Is criminalising children's sexual behaviour counterproductive', *Child and Family Law Quarterly*, Vol. 28, p. 239

Jenkins, A. (1990) *Invitations to Responsibility: The Therapeutic Engagement of Men Who Are Violent and Abusive*, Adelaide, South Australia: Dulwich Centre Publications; doi:10.1002/j.1467-8438.1990.tb00796.x

Jenkins, A (2004a) 'Making it fair: Respectful and just intervention with disadvantaged young people who have abused', in Calder, M. C. (ed.) (2004) *Children and Young People Who Sexually Abuse: New Theory, Research and Practice Developments*, Lyme Regis: Russell House

Jenkins, A. (2004b) 'Knocking on shame's door: Facing shame without shaming disadvantaged young people who have abused', in Calder, M. C. (ed.) (2004) *Children and Young People Who Sexually Abuse: New Theory, Research and Practice Developments*, Lyme Regis: Russell House

Jenkins, A. (2009) *Becoming Ethical: A Parallel, Political Journey with Men who Have Abused*, Lyme Regis: Russell House

Jenks, C. (2005) *Childhood*, Abingdon: Routledge

Johnson, G. M. and Knight, R. A. (2000) 'Developmental antecedents of sexual coercion in juvenile sexual offenders', *Sexual Abuse*, Vol. 12, pp. 165–78

Johnson, T. C. (2015) 'Updated and expanded: Understanding children's sexual behaviors – what's natural and healthy' (online). Available from URL: www.tcavjohn.com (accessed 29 December 2017)

Johnson, T. C. and Feldmeth, J. (1993) 'Sexual behaviors: A continuum', in Gil, E. and Johnson, T. C. (eds) (1993) *Sexualized Children: Assessment and Treatment of Sexualized Children and Children Who Molest*, Rockville MD: Launch Press

Johnstone, L. and Cooke, D. (2008) *PRISM: Promoting Risk Intervention by Situational Management; Structured Professional Guidelines for Assessing Situational Risk Factors for Violence in Institutions*, Burnaby, BC: Law and Policy Institute, Simon Fraser University

Jones, L. M., Mitchell, K. J. and Finkelhor, D. (2013) 'Online harassment in context: Trends from three youth internet safety surveys (2000, 2005, 2010)', *Psychology of Violence*, Vol. 3, pp. 53–69

Jonsson, L. S., Priebe, G., Bladh, M. and Svedin, C. G. (2014) 'Voluntary sexual exposure online among Swedish youth – social background, Internet behavior and psychosocial health', *Computers in Human Behavior*, Vol. 30, pp. 181–90

Justice Analytics Service (2017) *Recorded Crime in Scotland: Other Sexual Crimes, 2013–14 and 2016–17. 26 September 2017*. Edinburgh: Scottish Government

Kaeser, F., Disalvo, C. and Moglia, R. (2000) 'Sexual behaviors of young children that occur in schools', *Journal of Sex Education and Therapy*, Vol. 25, pp. 277–85

Kahn, T. J. and Chambers, H. J. (1991) 'Assessing reoffense risk with juvenile sexual offenders', *Child Welfare: Journal of Policy, Practice, and Program*, Vol. 70, pp. 333–45

Katz, J., Heisterkamp, H. A. and Fleming, W. M. (2011) 'The social justice roots of the mentors in violence prevention model and its application in a High School setting', *Violence Against Women*, Vol. 17, pp. 684–702

Kaur, K. and Christie, C. (2018) *Local Commissioning of Services Addressing Child Sexual Abuse and Exploitation in England: A Rapid Review Incorporating Findings from Five Locations*, London: Centre of Expertise on Child Sexual Abuse and London Metropolitan University

Keane, M., Guest, A. and Padbury, J. (2013) 'A balancing act: A family perspective to sibling sexual abuse', *Child Abuse Review*, Vol. 22, pp. 246–54

Keelan, C. M. and Fremouw, W. J. (2013) 'Child versus peer/adult offenders: A critical review of the juvenile sex offender literature', *Aggression and Violent Behavior*, Vol. 18, pp. 732–44

Kelly, L. and Karsna, K. (2017) *Measuring the Scale and Changing Nature of Child Sexual Abuse and Child Sexual Exploitation: Scoping Report*, London: Centre of Expertise on Child Sexual Abuse and London Metropolitan University

Kemper, T. S. and Kistner, J. A. (2007) 'Offense history and recidivism in three victim-age-based groups of juvenile sex offenders', *Sexual Abuse*, Vol. 19, pp. 409–24

Kernsmith, P. D., Craun, S. W. and Foster, J. (2009) 'Public attitudes toward sexual offenders and sex offender registration', *Journal of Child Sexual Abuse*, Vol. 18, pp. 290–301

Kincaid, C., Jones, D. J., Sterrett, E. and McKee, L. (2012) 'A review of parenting and adolescent sexual behavior: The moderating role of gender', *Clinical Psychology Review*, Vol. 32, pp. 177–88

Kisiel, C., Fehrenbach, T., Liang, L.-J., Stolbach, B., McClelland, G., Griffin, G., Maj, N., Briggs, E. C., Vivrette, R. L. and Layne, C. M. (2014) 'Examining child sexual abuse in relation to complex patterns of trauma exposure: Findings from the National Child Traumatic Stress Network', *Psychological Trauma: Theory, Research, Practice, and Policy*, Vol. 6, S29–S39

Kjellgren, C., Priebe, G., Svedin, C. G. and Långström, N. (2010) 'Sexually coercive behavior in male youth: Population survey of general and specific risk factors', *Archives of Sexual Behavior*, Vol. 39, pp. 1161–9

Kjellgren, C., Wassberg, A., Carlberg, M., Långström, N. and Svedin, C. G. (2006) 'Adolescent sexual offenders: A total survey of referrals to social services in Sweden and subgroup characteristics', *Sexual Abuse*, Vol. 18, pp. 357–72

Klein, V., Yoon, D., Briken, P., Turner, D., Spehr, A. and Rettenberger, M. (2012) 'Assessment of accused juvenile sex offenders in Germany: A comparison of five different measures', *Behavioral Sciences and the Law*, Vol. 30, pp. 181–95

Kosson, D. S., Kelly, J. C. and White, J. W. (1997) 'Psychopathy-related traits predict self-reported sexual aggression among college men', *Journal of Interpersonal Violence*, Vol. 12, pp. 241–54

Kubik, E. K., Hecker, J. E. and Righthand, S. (2003) 'Adolescent females who have sexually offended: Comparisons with delinquent adolescent female offenders and adolescent males who sexually offend', *Journal of Child Sexual Abuse*, Vol. 11, pp. 63–83

Lamb, S. (2004) 'IV. Sexual tensions in girls' friendships', *Feminism and Psychology*, Vol. 14, pp. 376–82

Lamb, S. and Coakley, M. (1993) ' "Normal" childhood sexual play and games: Differentiating play from abuse', *Child Abuse and Neglect*, Vol. 17, pp. 515–26

Långström, N. and Grann, M. (2000) 'Risk for criminal recidivism among young sex offenders', *Journal of Interpersonal Violence*, Vol. 15, pp. 855–71

Langton, C. M. and Worling, J. R. (2015) 'Introduction to the special issue on factors positively associated with desistance for adolescents and adults who have sexually offended', *Sexual Abuse*, Vol. 27, p. 3

Larsson, I. (2000) 'Differences and similarities in sexual behaviour among pre-schoolers in Sweden and USA', *Nordic Journal of Psychiatry*, Vol. 54, pp. 251–7

Larsson, I. and Svedin, C. G. (2002) 'Teachers' and parents' reports on 3- to 6-year-old children's sexual behavior – a comparison', *Child Abuse and Neglect*, Vol. 26, pp. 247–66

Latzman, N. E., Viljoen, J. L., Scalora, M. J. and Ullman, D. (2011) 'Sexual offending in adolescence: A comparison of sibling offenders and nonsibling offenders across domains of risk and treatment need', *Journal of Child Sexual Abuse*, Vol. 20, pp. 245–63

Laumann, E. O., Gagnon, J., Michael, R. and Michaels, S. (1994) *Sex in America*, Boston, MA: Little, Brown

Leaper, C. and Friedman, C. K. (2007) 'The socialisation of gender', in Grusec, J. E. and Hastings, P. D. (eds) (2007) *Handbook of Socialization: Theory and research*, New York, NY: Guilford Press

Lee, M. and Crofts, T. (2015) 'Gender, pressure, coercion and pleasure: Untangling motivations for sexting between young people', *British Journal of Criminology*, Vol. 55, pp. 454–73

Leifer, M., Shapiro, J. P. and Kassem, L. (1993) 'The impact of maternal history and behavior upon foster placement and adjustment in sexually abused girls', *Child Abuse and Neglect*, Vol. 17, pp. 755–66

Lerner, R. M. and Galambos, N. L. (1998) 'Adolescent development: Challenges and opportunities for research, programs, and policies', *Annual Review of Psychology*, Vol. 49, pp. 413–46

Letourneau, E. J. (2016) 'Can programs like "Help Wanted" prevent child sexual abuse?', *Psychology Today*. Available from URL: www.psychologytoday.com/blog/prevention-now/201612/can-programs-help-wanted-prevent-child-sexual-abuse (accessed 5 February 2018)

Letourneau, E. J., Henggeler, S. W., Borduin, C. M., Schewe, P. A., Mccart, M. R., Chapman, J. E. and Saldana, L. (2009) 'Multisystemic therapy for juvenile sexual offenders: 1-year results from a randomized effectiveness trial', *Journal of Family Psychology*, Vol. 23, pp. 89–102

Letourneau, E. J. and Miner, M. H. (2005) 'Juvenile sex offenders: A case against the legal and clinical status quo', *Sexual Abuse*, Vol. 17, pp. 293–312

Letourneau, E. J., Schaeffer, C. M., Bradshaw, C. P. and Feder, K. A. (2017) 'Preventing the onset of child sexual abuse by targeting young adolescents with universal prevention programming', *Child Maltreatment*, Vol. 22, pp. 100–11

Leukfeldt, E. R., Jansen, J. and Stol, W. P. (2014) 'Child pornography, the Internet and juvenile suspects', *Journal of Social Welfare and Family Law*, Vol. 36, pp. 3–13

Lewis, T., McElroy, E., Harlaar, N. and Runyan, D. (2016) 'Does the impact of child sexual abuse differ from maltreated but non-sexually abused children? A prospective examination of the impact of child sexual abuse on internalizing and externalizing behavior problems', *Child Abuse and Neglect*, Vol. 51, pp. 31–40

Lindblad, F., Gustafsson, P. A., Larsson, I. and Lundin, B. (1995) 'Preschoolers' sexual behavior at daycare centers: An epidemiological study', *Child Abuse and Neglect*, Vol. 19, pp. 569–77

Lindsay, W. R. (2002) 'Research and literature on sex offenders with intellectual and developmental disabilities', *Journal of Intellectual Disability Research*, Vol. 46, pp. 74–85

Livingstone, S., Davidson, J., Bryce, J., Batool, S., Haughton, C. and Nandi, A. (2017) *Children's Online Activities, Risks and Safety: A Literature Review by the UKCCIS Evidence Group*, London: UK Council for Child Internet Safety

Longo, R. E. (1982) 'Sexual learning and experience among adolescent sexual offenders', *International Journal of Offender Therapy and Comparative Criminology*, Vol. 26, pp. 235–41

Lopez Sanchez, F., Del Campo, A. and Guijo, V. (2002) 'Prepubertal sexuality', *Sexologies*, Vol. 11, pp. 49–58

Lowenstein, L. (2002) 'Fetishes and their associated behavior', *Sexuality and Disability*, Vol. 20, pp. 135–47

Lucassen, M. F., Merry, S. N., Robinson, E. M., Denny, S., Clark, T., Ameratunga, S., Crengle, S. and Rossen, F. V. (2011) 'Sexual attraction, depression, self-harm, suicidality and help-seeking behaviour in New Zealand secondary school students', *Australian and New Zealand Journal of Psychiatry*, Vol. 45, pp. 376–83

Lunceford, B. (2011) 'The new pornographers: Legal and ethical considerations of sexting', in Drushel, B. and German, K. (2011) *The Ethics of Emerging Media: Information, Social Norms, and New Media Technology*, New York, NY: Continuum, pp. 99–118

Lussier, P. and Blokland, A. (2014) 'The adolescence–adulthood transition and Robins's continuity paradox: Criminal career patterns of juvenile and adult sex offenders in a prospective longitudinal birth cohort study', *Journal of Criminal Justice*, Vol. 42, pp. 153–63

Lussier, P., Van den Berg, C., Bijleveld, C. and Hendriks, J. (2012) 'A developmental taxonomy of juvenile sex offenders for theory, research, and prevention: The adolescent-limited and the high-rate slow desister', *Criminal Justice and Behaviour*, Vol. 39, pp. 1559–81

McAlinden, A.-M. (2012) *'Grooming' and the Sexual Abuse of Children: Institutional, Internet, and Familial Dimensions*, Oxford: Oxford University Press

McAlinden, A.-M. (2014) 'Deconstructing victim and offender identites in discourses on child sexual abuse hierarchies, blame and the good/evil dialectic', The British Journal of Criminology, Vol. 54, pp. 180–98

McAra, L. and McVie, S. (2010) 'Youth crime and justice: Key messages from the Edinburgh study of youth transitions and crime', Criminology and Criminal Justice, Vol. 10, pp. 179–209

McBride, R. S. and Schubotz, D. (2017) 'Living a fairy tale: The educational experiences of transgender and gender non-conforming youth in Northern Ireland', Child Care in Practice, Vol. 23, pp. 292–304

McCann, K. and Lussier, P. (2008) 'Antisociality, sexual deviance, and sexual reoffending in juvenile sex offenders: A meta-analytical investigation', Youth Violence and Juvenile Justice, Vol. 6, pp. 363–85

McCartan, K. (2010) 'Media constructions of, and reactions to, paedophilia in society', in Harrison, K. (ed.) (2010) Managing High-risk Sex Offenders in the Community: Risk Management, Treatment and Social Responsibility, Abingdon: Routledge

McCrory, E., De Brito, S. A. and Viding, E. (2012) 'The link between child abuse and psychopathology: A review of neurobiological and genetic research', Journal of the Royal Society of Medicine, Vol. 105, pp. 151–6

McCuish, E., Lussier, P. and Corrado, R. (2016) 'Criminal careers of juvenile sex and nonsex offenders: Evidence from a prospective longitudinal study', Youth Violence and Juvenile Justice, Vol. 14, pp. 199–224

McGrath, R. J., Cumming, G. F., Burchard, B. L., Zeoli, S. and Ellerby, L. (2009) Current Practices and Emerging Trends in Sexual Abuser Management, Brandon, VT: Safer Society Press

McGrath, R. J., Cumming, G. F., Burchard, B. L., Zeoli, S. and Ellerby, L. (2010) Current Practices and Emerging Trends in Sexual Abuser Management: The Safer Society 2009 North American Survey, Brandon, VT: Safer Society Press, p. 24

McGregor, K. (2013) 'Third of UK's social workers not currently receiving supervision' (online), Community Care. Available from URL: http://www.communitycare. co.uk/2013/06/18/third-of-uks-social-workers-not-currently-receiving-supervision (accessed 29 December 2017)

McGuire, R., Carlisle, J. U. and Young, B. (1964) 'Sexual deviations as conditioned behaviour: A hypothesis', Behaviour Research and Therapy, Vol. 2, pp. 185–90

McKibbin, G. (2017) 'Preventing harmful sexual behaviour and child sexual exploitation for children and young people living in residential care: A scoping review in the Australian context', Children and Youth Services Review, Vol. 82, pp. 373–82

McKibbin, G., Humphreys, C. and Hamilton, B. (2017) ' "Talking about child sexual abuse would have helped me": Young people who sexually abused reflect on preventing harmful sexual behaviour', Child Abuse and Neglect, Vol. 70, pp. 210–21

McKillop, N., Brown, S., Smallbone, S. and Pritchard, K. (2015) 'Similarities and differences in adolescence-onset versus adulthood-onset sexual abuse incidents', Child Abuse and Neglect, Vol. 46, pp. 37–46

McKillop, N., Smallbone, S., Wortley, R. and Andjic, I. (2012) 'Offenders' attachment and sexual abuse onset: A test of theoretical propositions', *Sexual Abuse*, Vol. 24, pp. 591–610

McManus, M. A., Long, M. L., Alison, L. and Almond, L. (2015) 'Factors associated with contact child sexual abuse in a sample of indecent image offenders', *Journal of Sexual Aggression*, Vol. 21, pp. 368–84

Malamuth, N. M. (1996) 'The confluence model of sexual aggression: Feminist and evolutionary perspectives', in Buss, D. (ed.) (1996) *Sex, Power, Conflict: Evolutionary and Feminist Perspectives*, Oxford: Oxford University Press

Manocha, K. F. and Mezey, G. (1998) 'British adolescents who sexually abuse: A descriptive study', *The Journal of Forensic Psychiatry*, Vol. 9, pp. 588–608

Marshall, W., Serran, G., Moulden, H., Mulloy, R., Fernández, Y., Mann, R. and Thornton, D. (2002) 'Therapist features in sexual offender treatment: Their reliable identification and influence on behaviour change', *Clinical Psychology and Psychotherapy*, Vol. 9, pp. 395–405

Marshall, W. L. and Barbaree, H. E. (1990) 'An integrated theory of the etiology of sexual offending', in Marshall, W. L. and Barbaree, H. E. (eds) (1990) *Handbook of Sexual Assault: Issues, Theories, and Treatment of the Offender*, Victoria, BC: Abe Books

Martellozzo, E., Monaghan, A., Adler, J. R., Davidson, J., Leyva, R. and Horvath, M. A. (2016) *'I Wasn't Sure It Was Normal to Watch It ...' A Quantitative and Qualitative Examination of the Impact of Online Pornography on the Values, Attitudes, Beliefs and Behaviours of Children and Young People*, London: Middlesex University

Martinez, G. M. and Abma, J. C. (2015) 'Sexual activity, contraceptive use, and childbearing of teenagers aged 15–19 in the United States', *NCHS Data Brief*, Vol. 209, pp. 1–8

Martinson, F. M. (1994) *The Sexual Life of Children*, Westport, CT: Greenwood

Mathews, R., Hunter, J. A. and Vuz, J. (1997) 'Juvenile female sexual offenders: Clinical characteristics and treatment issues', *Sexual Abuse*, Vol. 9, pp. 187–99

Meier, A. M. (2003) 'Adolescents' transition to first intercourse, religiosity, and attitudes about sex', *Social Forces*, Vol. 81, pp. 1031–52

Mercer, C. H., Tanton, C., Prah, P., Erens, B., Sonnenberg, P., Clifton, S., Macdowall, W., Lewis, R., Field, N. and Datta, J. (2013) 'Changes in sexual attitudes and lifestyles in Britain through the life course and over time: Findings from the National Surveys of Sexual Attitudes and Lifestyles (Natsal)', *The Lancet*, Vol. 382, pp. 1781–94

Messerschmidt, J. W. (2011) 'The struggle for heterofeminine recognition: Bullying, embodiment, and reactive sexual offending by adolescent girls', *Feminist Criminology*, Vol. 6, pp. 203–33

Messerschmidt, J. W. (2012) *Gender, Heterosexuality, and Youth Violence: The Struggle for Recognition*, Plymouth: Rowman and Littlefield

Metts, S. and Spitzberg, B. H. (1996) 'Sexual communication in interpersonal contexts: A script-based approach', *Annals of the International Communication Association*, Vol. 19, pp. 49–92

Miccio-Fonseca, L. (2000) 'Adult and adolescent female sex offenders: Experiences compared to other female and male sex offenders', *Journal of Psychology and Human Sexuality*, Vol. 11, pp. 75–88

Miccio-Fonseca, L. (2006) 'Multiplex empirically guided inventory of ecological aggregates for assessing sexually abusive children and adolescents (ages 4 to 19): MEGA♪ manual', San Diego, CA

Miccio-Fonseca, L. (2016) 'MEGA♪ cross-validation findings on sexually abusive females: Implications for risk assessment and clinical practice', *Journal of Family Violence*, Vol. 31, pp. 903–11

Miller, E., Tancredi, D. J., Mccauley, H. L., Decker, M. R., Virata, M. C. D., Anderson, H. A., Stetkevich, N., Brown, E. W., Moideen, F. and Silverman, J. G. (2012) ' "Coaching boys into men": A cluster-randomized controlled trial of a dating violence prevention program', *Journal of Adolescent Health*, Vol. 51, pp. 431–8

Milner, J., Myers, S. and O'Byrne, P. (2015) *Assessment in Social Work*, London: Palgrave Macmillan

Miniwatts Marketing Group (2017) 'Internet usage statistics' (online). Available from URL: www.internetworldstats.com/stats.htm (accessed 30 November 2017)

Minuchin, P. (1985) 'Families and individual development: Provocations from the field of family therapy', *Child Development*, Vol. 56, pp. 289–302

Mir, B. and Okotie, E. (2002) *Study of the Experiences of Black and Asian Young People Whose Behaviour is Sexually Harmful To Others*, Stockport: AIM Project

Mitchell, K. J., Jones, L. M., Finkelhor, D. and Wolak, J. (2014) *Trends in Unwanted Online Experiences and Sexting*, Durham, NH: Crimes Against Children Research Center

Money, J. (1976) 'Childhood: The last frontier in sex research', *The Sciences*, Vol. 16, pp. 12–27

Money, J. (1999) *The Lovemap Guidebook: A Definitive Statement*, New York, NY: Continuum International

Morgan, L. W., McClendon, L. S., McCarty, J. and Zinck, K. (2016) 'Supporting every child: School counselors' perceptions of juvenile sex offenders in schools', *Journal of School Counseling*, Vol. 14, pp. 1–37

Morrison, T. (2000) 'Working together to safeguard children: Challenges and changes for interagency coordination in child protection', *Journal of Interprofessional Care*, Vol. 14, pp. 363–73

Morrison, T. (2004) 'Preparing services and staff to work with young people who sexually abuse', in O'Reilly, G., Marshall, W. L., Carr, A. and Beckett, R. (eds) (2004) *The Handbook of Clinical Intervention with Young People Who Sexually Abuse*, Abingdon: Taylor Francis

Morrison, T. (2007) 'Emotional intelligence, emotion and social work. Context, characteristics, complications and contribution', *The British Journal of Social Work*, Vol. 37, pp. 245–63

Mosher, W. D., Chandra, A. and Jones, J. (2005) 'Sexual behaviour and selected health measures: men and women 15–44 years of age, United States, 2002', *Adv Data*, Vol.

362, pp. 1–55

Moultrie, D. (2006) 'Adolescents convicted of possession of abuse images of children: A new type of adolescent sex offender?', *Journal of Sexual Aggression*, Vol. 12, pp. 165–74

Moynihan, M. M., Banyard, V. L., Arnold, J. S., Eckstein, R. P. and Stapleton, J. G. (2011) 'Sisterhood may be powerful for reducing sexual and intimate partner violence: An evaluation of the Bringing in the Bystander in-person program with sorority members', *Violence Against Women*, Vol. 17, pp. 703–19

Mulholland, S. J. and McIntee, J. (1999) 'The significance of trauma in problematic sexual behaviour', in Calder, M. (ed.) (1999) *Working With Young People Who Sexually Abuse: New Pieces of the Jigsaw*, Lyme Regis: Russell House

Muncie, J. (2014) *Youth and Crime*, London: Sage

Munro, E. (2011) *The Munro review of child protection: Final report, a child-centred system*, London The Stationery Office

Murphy, G. H. (2003) 'Capacity to consent to sexual relationships in adults with learning disabilities', *Journal of Family Planning and Reproductive Healthcare*, Vol. 29, pp. 148–9

Myers, S. (2007) '(De)constructing the risk categories in the aim assessment model for children with sexually harmful behaviour', *Children and Society*, Vol. 21, pp. 365–77

Myles-Wright, A. and Nee, C. (2017) 'Holding the child (and practitioner) in mind?: Youth justice practitioners' experiences supervising young people displaying sexually harmful behaviour', *Journal of Interpersonal Violence*; doi:10.1177/0886260517701449

Napolitano, S. A. (1997) 'Depression, cognitive characteristics, and social functioning in adolescent sex offenders and conduct disordered adolescents in residential treatment', doctoral thesis, University of Texas

New, M. J., Stevenson, J. and Skuse, D. (1999) 'Characteristics of mothers of boys who sexually abuse', *Child Maltreatment*, Vol. 4, pp. 21–31

New Jersey Attorney General's Office (2006) 'Juvenile risk assessment scale manual' (online), New Jersey Attorney General's Office. Available from URL: www.state. nj.us/lps/dcj/megan/jras-manual-scale-606.pdf (accessed 30 November 2017)

Newman, B. M. and Newman, P. R. (2017) *Development Through Life: A Psychosocial Approach*, Boston, MA: Cengage Learning

NICE (2016) 'Harmful sexual behaviour among children and young people guidance' (online), London: National Institute of Clinical Excellence. Available from URL: www.nice.org.uk/guidance/ng55 (accessed 30 November 2017)

Norton, C. L., Tucker, A., Russell, K. C., Bettmann, J. E., Gass, M. A., Gillis, H. L. and Behrens, E. (2014) 'Adventure therapy with youth', *Journal of Experiential Education*, Vol. 37, pp. 46–59

O'Brien, M. and Bera, W. (1986) 'Adolescent sexual offenders: A descriptive typology', *Preventing Sexual Abuse*, Vol. 1, pp. 1–4

O'Brien, M. J. (1991) 'Taking sibling incest seriously', in Patton, M. Q. (ed.) (1991) *Family Sexual Abuse: Frontline Research and Evaluation*, Newsbury Park, CA: Sage

O'Callaghan, D. (1998) 'Practice issues in working with young abusers who have learning disabilities', *Child Abuse Review*, Vol. 7, pp. 435–48

O'Connor, R. and Waddell, S. (2015) *Preventing Gang Involvement and Youth Violence: Advice for Those Commissioning Mentoring Programmes*, London: Early Intervention Foundation

O'Connor, T. G. and Rutter, M. (2000) 'Attachment disorder behaviour following early severe deprivation: Extension and longitudinal follow-up', *Journal of the American Academy of Child and Adolescent Psychiatry*, Vol. 39, pp. 703–12

Ofcom (2016) 'Children and parents: Media use and attitudes report' (online). Available from URL: www.ofcom.org.uk/research-and-data/media-literacy-research/ childrens/children-parents-nov16 (accessed 29 December 2017)

Office for National Statistics (2017a) 'Crime in England and Wales: Year ending June 2017' (online). Available from URL: www.ons.gov.uk/peoplepopulationandcommunity/ crimeandjustice/bulletins/crimeinenglandandwales/june2017 (accessed 29 November 2017)

Office for National Statistics (2017b) 'Sexual Identity, UK: 2016' (online). Available from URL: www.ons.gov.uk/peoplepopulationandcommunity/culturalidentity/sexuality/ bulletins/sexualidentityuk/2016 (accessed 29 December 20176)

Office of the Children's Commissioner (2015) *Protecting Children from Harm: A Critical Assessment of Child Sexual Abuse in the Family Network in England and Priorities for Action*, London: Office of the Children's Commissioner

Oneal, B. J., Burns, G. L., Kahn, T. J., Rich, P. and Worling, J. R. (2008) 'Initial psychometric properties of a treatment planning and progress inventory for adolescents who sexually abuse', *Sexual Abuse*, Vol. 20, pp. 161–87

O'Neill, A. and Heaney, M. (2000) 'Restored or 'restoried': A consideration of the links between systemic family therapy and restorative justice', *Child Care in Practice*, Vol. 6, pp. 363–71

Onifade, E., Davidson, W. and Campbell, C. (2009) 'Risk assessment: The predictive validity of the youth level of service case management inventory with African Americans and girls', *Journal of Ethnicity in Criminal Justice*, Vol. 7, pp. 205–21

O'Reilly, G. and Carr, A. (2004) 'The clinical assessment of young people with sexually abusive behaviour', in O'Reilly, G., Marshall, W. L., Carr, A. and Beckett, R. (eds) (2004) *The Handbook of Clinical Intervention with Young People Who Sexually Abuse*, Abingdon: Taylor Francis

Orr, D. P., Wilbrandt, M. L., Brack, C. J., Rauch, S. P. and Ingersoll, G. M. (1989) 'Reported sexual behaviours and self-esteem among young adolescents', *American Journal of Diseases of Children*, Vol. 143, pp. 86–90

Oxnam, P. and Vess, J. (2006) 'A personality-based typology of adolescent sexual offenders using the Millon Adolescent Clinical Inventory', *New Zealand Journal of Psychology*, Vol. 35, pp. 36–44

Paine, M. L. and Hansen, D. J. (2002) 'Factors influencing children to self-disclose sexual abuse', *Clinical Psychology Review*, Vol. 22, pp. 271–95

Painter, K. and Scannapieco, M. (2013) 'Child maltreatment: The neurobiological aspects of posttraumatic stress disorder', *Journal of Evidence-based Social Work*, Vol. 10, pp. 276–84

Palmer, T. (2015) *Digital Dangers The Impact of Technology on the Sexual Abuse and Exploitation of Children and Young People*, Barkingside: Barnardo's

Papadopoulos, L. (2010) *Sexualisation of Young People Review*, London: Home Office

Papalia, N. L., Luebbers, S., Ogloff, J. R., Cutajar, M., Mullen, P. E. and Mann, E. (2017) 'Further victimization of child sexual abuse victims: A latent class typology of re-victimization trajectories', *Child Abuse and Neglect*, Vol. 66, pp. 112–29

Park, J. and Kim, S. (2016) 'Group size does matter: Differences among sexual assaults committed by lone, double, and groups of three or more perpetrators', *Journal of Sexual Aggression*, Vol. 22, pp. 342–54

Parker, I. (2014) *Young People, Sex and Relationships: The New Norms*, London: Institute for Public Policy Research

Pattatucci, A. M. and Hamer, D. H. (1995) 'Development and familiality of sexual orientation in females', *Behaviour Genetics*, Vol. 25, pp. 407–19

Pereda, N., Guilera, G., Forns, M. and Gómez-Benito, J. (2009a) 'The international epidemiology of child sexual abuse: A continuation of Finkelhor (1994)', *Child Abuse and Neglect*, Vol. 33, pp. 331–42

Pereda, N., Guilera, G., Forns, M. and Gómez-Benito, J. (2009b) 'The prevalence of child sexual abuse in community and student samples: A meta-analysis', *Clinical Psychology Review*, Vol. 29, pp. 328–38

Perry, B. D. (2009) 'Examining child maltreatment through a neurodevelopmental lens: Clinical applications of the neurosequential model of therapeutics', *Journal of Loss and Trauma*, Vol. 14, pp. 240–55

Peter, J. and Valkenburg, P. M. (2016) 'Adolescents and pornography: A review of 20 years of research', *The Journal of Sex Research*, Vol. 53, pp. 509–31

Pierce, M. and Hardy, R. (2012) 'Commentary: The decreasing age of puberty – as much a psychosocial as biological problem?', *International Journal of Epidemiology*, Vol. 41, pp. 300–2

Pinkerton, S. D., Bogart, L. M., Cecil, H. and Abramson, P. R. (2003) 'Factors associated with masturbation in a collegiate sample', *Journal of Psychology and Human Sexuality*, Vol. 14, pp. 103–21

Pithers, W. D., Gray, A., Busconi, A. and Houchens, P. (1998) 'Children with sexual behaviour problems: Identification of five distinct child types and related treatment considerations', *Child Maltreatment*, Vol. 3, pp. 384–406

Pittman, N. (2013) *Raised on the Registry: The Irreparable Harm of Placing Children on Sex Offender Registries in the US*, Washington, DC: Human Rights Watch

Porter, L. E. and Alison, L. J. (2006) 'Examining group rape: A descriptive analysis of offender and victim behaviour', *European Journal of Criminology*, Vol. 3, pp. 357–81

Powell, A. and Henry, N. (2014) 'Blurred lines? Responding to "sexting" and gender-based violence among young people', *Children Australia*, Vol. 39, pp. 119–24

Prentky, R. and Righthand, S. (2003) *Juvenile Sex Offender Assessment Protocol-II*

(J-SOAP-II) Manual, Bridgewater, MA: Justice Resource Institute

Prescott, D. S. (2009) *Building Motivation for Change in Sexual Offenders*, Brandon, VT: Safer Society Press

Print, B. (2013) *The Good Lives Model for Adolescents Who Sexually Harm*, Brandon, VT: Safer Society Foundation

Print, B., Griffin, H., Beech, A., Quayle, J., Bradshaw, H., Henniker, J. and Morrison, T. (2007) *AIM2: An Initial Assessment Model for Young People Who Display Sexually Harmful Behaviour*, Stockport: AIM Project

Pritchard, D., Graham, N., Penney, H., Owen, G., Peters, S. and Mace, F. C. (2016) 'Multicomponent behavioural intervention reduces harmful sexual behaviour in a 17-year-old male with autism spectrum disorder: A case study', *Journal of Sexual Aggression*, Vol. 22, pp. 368–78

Radford, L., Corral, S., Bradley, C., Fisher, H., Bassett, C., Howat, N. and Collishaw, S. (2011) *Child Abuse and Neglect in the UK Today*, London: National Society for the Prevention of Cruelty to Children

Ramírez, W. (2002) 'Caracterización de ofensores sexuales juveniles: experiencia de la Clínica de Adolescentes del Hospital Nacional de Niños', *Acta pediátrica Costarricense*, Vol. 16, pp. 69–74

Rasmussen, L. A., Burton, J. E. and Christopherson, B. J. (1992) 'Precursors to offending and the trauma outcome process in sexually reactive children', *Journal of Child Sexual Abuse*, Vol. 1, pp. 33–48

Rasmussen, L. A. and Miccio-Fonseca, L. (2007) 'Paradigm shift: Implementing MEGA, a new tool proposed to define and assess sexually abusive dynamics in youth ages 19 and under', *Journal of Child Sexual Abuse*, Vol. 16, pp. 85–106

Ray, F., Marks, C. and Bray-Garretson, H. (2004) 'Challenges to treating adolescents with Asperger's Syndrome who are sexually abusive', *Sexual Addiction and Compulsivity*, Vol. 11, pp. 265–85

Ray, J. A. and English, D. J. (1995) 'Comparison of female and male children with sexual behaviour problems', *Journal of Youth and Adolescence*, Vol. 24, pp. 439–51

Reitzel, L. R. and Carbonell, J. L. (2006) 'The effectiveness of sexual offender treatment for juveniles as measured by recidivism: A meta-analysis', *Sexual Abuse*, Vol. 18, pp. 401–21

Restrepo, E. M. (2013) 'Factores de riesgo y protección en los agresores sexuales infantiles', *Skopein: La justicia en manos de la Ciencia*, Vol. 2, p. 2.

Reynolds, M., Herbenick, D. and Bancroft, J. (2003) *Sexual Development in Childhood*, Bloomington, IN: Indiana University Press

Rich, P. (2003) *Understanding, Assessing, and Rehabilitating Juvenile Sexual Offenders*, New York, NY: John Wiley

Rich, P. (2009) *Juvenile Sexual Offenders: A Comprehensive Guide to Risk Evaluation*, New York, NY: John Wiley

Rich, P. (2017a) A contemporary approach to the assessment of risk in sexually abusive youth', in Wilcox, D., Donathy, M., Gray, R. and Baim, C. (eds) *Working with Sex*

Offenders: A Guide for Practitioners. Abingdon: Routledge

Rich, P. (2017b) 'J-RAT: Juvenile Risk Assessment Tool (v4)' (online). Available from URL: www.philrich.net/risk-assessment-instruments.html (accessed 30 November 2017)

Richardson, G. (2009) 'Sharp practice: The Sexually Harmful Adolescent Risk Protocol (SHARP)', in Calder, M. (ed.) (2009) *Sexual Abuse Assessments: Using and Developing Frameworks for Practice*, Lyme Regis: Russell House

Richardson, G., Kelly, T. P., Graham, F. and Bhate, S. R. (2004) 'A personality-based taxonomy of sexually abusive adolescents derived from the Millon Adolescent Clinical Inventory (MACI)', *British Journal of Clinical Psychology*, Vol. 43, pp. 285–98

Richardson, J. and Schuster, M. A. (2004) *Everything You Never Wanted Your Kids to Know About Sex (But Were Afraid They'd Ask): The Secrets to Surviving Your Child's Sexual Development from Birth to the Teens*, New York, NY: Harmony Books

Rigby, P., Whyte, B. and Schinkel, M. (2013) *Young People and MAPPA in Scotland*. Edinburgh: Criminal Justice Social Work Development Centre, University of Edinburgh

Righthand, S., Prentky, R., Knight, R., Carpenter, E., Hecker, J. E. and Nangle, D. (2005) 'Factor structure and validation of the juvenile sex offender assessment protocol (J-SOAP)', *Sexual Abuse*, Vol. 17, No. 1, pp. 13–30

Ringrose, J. (2010) 'Sluts, whores, fat slags and Playboy bunnies: Teen girls' negotiations of "sexy" on social networking sites and at school', in Jackson, C., Paechter, C. and Renold, E. (eds) (2010) *Girls and Education 3–16: Continuing Concerns, New Agenda*, Basingstoke: Open University Press

Ringrose, J., Gill, R., Livingstone, S. and Harvey, L. (2012) *A Qualitative Study of Children, Young People and 'Sexting': A Report Prepared for the NSPCC*, London: National Society for the Prevention of Cruelty to Children

RMA (2017) 'Risk assessment tool evaluation directory (RATED) – youth assessment/ sexual violence risk' (online), Paisley: Risk Management Authority. Available from URL: http://rated.rmascotland.gov.uk/risk-tools/youth-assessment-sexuviolence-risk (accessed 30 November 2017)

Robinson, S. (2005) 'Considerations for the assessment of female sexually abusive youth', in Calder, M. (ed.) (2005) *Children and Young People Who Sexually Abuse: New Theory, Research and Practice Developments*, Lyme Regis: Russell House

Robinson, S. (2009) 'The core assessment of young females who sexually abuse', in Calder, M. (ed.) (2009) *Sexual Abuse Assessment: Using and Developing Frameworks for Practice*, Lyme Regis: Russell House

Rogers, D. L. and Ferguson, C. J. (2011) 'Punishment and rehabilitation attitudes towards sex offenders versus non-sexual offenders', *Journal of Aggression, Maltreatment and Trauma*, Vol. 20, pp. 395–414

Rojas, E. Y. and Gretton, H. M. (2007) 'Background, offence characteristics, and criminal outcomes of Aboriginal youth who sexually offend: A closer look at Aboriginal youth intervention needs', *Sexual Abuse*, Vol. 19, pp. 257–83

Rosenfield, R. L., Lipton, R. B. and Drum, M. L. (2009) 'Thelarche, pubarche, and menarche attainment in children with normal and elevated body mass index', *Pediatrics*, Vol. 123, pp. 84–8

Royal Commission into Institutional Responses to Child Sexual Abuse (2017) 'Final report recommendations: Children with harmful sexual behaviour, Vol. 10' (online), Commonwealth of Australia. Available from URL: www.childabuseroyalcommission. gov.au/children-harmful-sexual-behaviours (accessed 6 February 2018)

Rozmus, C. L. and Edgil, A. E. (1993) 'Values, knowledge, and attitudes about acquired immunodeficiency syndrome in rural adolescents', *Journal of Pediatric Healthcare*, Vol. 7, pp. 167–73

Ryan, G. and Blum, J. (1994) *Childhood Sexuality: A Guide for Parents*, Denver, CO: developed and distributed by Kempe Children's Center with Families First

Ryan, G., Miyoshi, T. J., Metzner, J. L., Krugman, R. D. and Fryer, G. E. (1996) 'Trends in a national sample of sexually abusive youths', *Journal of the American Academy of Child and Adolescent Psychiatry*, Vol. 35, pp. 17–25

Sahlstrom, K. J. and Jeglic, E. L. (2008) 'Factors affecting attitudes towards juvenile sex offenders', *Journal of Child Sexual Abuse*, Vol. 17, pp. 180–96

Saint, L. (2014) 'The inform young people programme', in Hackett, S. (ed.) (2014) *Children and Young People with Harmful Sexual Behaviours*, Dartington: Research in Practice

Salerno, J. M., Najdowski, C. J., Stevenson, M. C., Wiley, T. R., Bottoms, B. L., Vaca, R. and Pimentel, P. S. (2010) 'Psychological mechanisms underlying support for juvenile sex offender registry laws: Prototypes, moral outrage, and perceived threat', *Behavioural Sciences and the Law*, Vol. 28, pp. 58–83

Sanders, M. R. (1999) 'Triple P-positive parenting program: Towards an empirically validated multilevel parenting and family support strategy for the prevention of behaviour and emotional problems in children', *Clinical Child and Family Psychology Review*, Vol. 2, pp. 71–90

Sandfort, T. G. and Cohen-Kettenis, P. T. (2000) 'Sexual behaviour in Dutch and Belgian children as observed by their mothers', *Journal of Psychology and Human Sexuality*, Vol. 12, pp. 105–15

Sandler, J. C., Letourneau, E. J., Vandiver, D. M., Shields, R. T. and Chaffin, M. (2017) 'Juvenile sexual crime reporting rates are not influenced by juvenile sex offender registration policies', *Psychology, Public Policy, and Law*, Vol. 23, p. 131

Sandnabba, N. K., Santtila, P., Wannäs, M. and Krook, K. (2003) 'Age and gender specific sexual behaviours in children', *Child Abuse and Neglect*, Vol. 27, pp. 579–605

Savin-Williams, R. C. (2011) 'Identity development among sexual-minority youth', in Schwartz, S. J., Luyckx, K., and Vignoles, V. L. (eds) (2011) *Handbook of Identity, Theory and Research*, New York, NY: Springer

Sawyerr, A. and Bagley, C. (2017) 'Child sexual abuse and adolescent and adult adjustment: A review of British and world evidence, with implications for social work, and mental health and school counselling', *Advances in Applied Sociology*, Vol. 7, pp. 1–15

Schmidt, S. R. (2008) 'Adolescent girls with illegal sexual behaviour', *APSAC Advisor*, Vol. 20, pp. 12–13

Schoentjes, E., Deboutte, D. and Friedrich, W. (1999) 'Child sexual behaviour inventory: A Dutch-speaking normative sample', *Pediatrics*, Vol. 104, pp. 885–93

Scottish Government (2014) *Framework for Risk Assessment Management and Evaluation (FRAME) for Local Authorities and Partners – Incorporating Care and Risk Management Guidance – for Children and Young People Under 18*, Edinburgh: Scottish Government

Scottish Social Services Council (2014) 'Codes of practice for social service workers and employers' (online). Available from URL: www.sssc.uk.com/about-the-sssc/codes-of-practice/what-are-the-codes-of-practice (accessed 29 November 2017)

Scourfield, J., Allely, C., Coffey, A. and Yates, P. (2016) 'Working with fathers of at-risk children: Insights from a qualitative process evaluation of an intensive group-based intervention', *Children and Youth Services Review*, Vol. 69, pp. 259–67

Seguino, S. (2007) '*Plus ça change?* Evidence on global trends in gender norms and stereotypes', *Feminist Economics*, Vol. 13, pp. 1–28

Seto, M. (2008) *Pedophilia and Sexual Offending Children: Theory, Assessment and Intervention*, Washington, DC: American Psychology Association

Seto, M. C. (2004) 'Pedophilia and sexual offenses against children', *Annual Review of Sex Research*, Vol. 15, pp. 321–61

Seto, M. C., Hermann, C. A., Kjellgren, C., Priebe, G., Svedin, C. G. and Långström, N. (2015) 'Viewing child pornography: Prevalence and correlates in a representative community sample of young Swedish men', *Archives of Sexual Behaviour*, Vol. 44, pp. 67–79

Seto, M. C. and Lalumière, M. L. (2010) 'What is so special about male adolescent sexual offending? A review and test of explanations through meta-analysis', *Psychological Bulletin*, Vol. 136, No. 4, 526–75

Seto, M. C., Lalumière, M. L. and Blanchard, R. (2000) 'The discriminative validity of a phallometric test for pedophilic interests among adolescent sex offenders against children', *Psychological Assessment*, Vol. 12, p. 319

Seto, M. C., Murphy, W. D., Page, J. and Ennis, L. (2003) 'Detecting anomalous sexual interests in juvenile sex offenders', *Annals of the New York Academy of Sciences*, Vol. 989, pp. 118–30

Shannon, D. (2008) 'Online sexual grooming in Sweden – Online and offline sex offences against children as described in Swedish police data', *Journal of Scandinavian Studies in Criminology and Crime Prevention*, Vol. 9, pp. 160–80

Sharry, J. and Fitzpatrick, C. (1998) *Parents Plus Programme: A Practical and Positive Video-based Course for Managing and Solving Discipline Problems in Children*, manual and videos, Dublin: Mater Hospital

Shaw, J. A., Lewis, J. E., Loeb, A., Rosado, J. and Rodriguez, R. A. (2000) 'Child on child sexual abuse: Psychological perspectives', *Child Abuse and Neglect*, Vol. 24, pp. 1591–1600

Sigurdsson, J. F., Gudjonsson, G., Asgeirsdottir, B. B. and Sigfusdottir, I. D. (2010) 'Sexually abusive youth: What are the background factors that distinguish them from other youth?', *Psychology, Crime and Law*, Vol. 16, pp. 289–303

Silovsky, J. F., Niec, L., Bard, D. and Hecht, D. B. (2007) 'Treatment for preschool children with interpersonal sexual behaviour problems: A pilot study', *Journal of Clinical Child and Adolescent Psychology*, Vol. 36, pp. 378–91

Simmons, R. (2002) *Odd Girl Out: The Hidden Culture of Aggression in Girls*, San Diego, CA: Houghton Mifflin Harcourt

Skuse, D., Bentovim, A., Hodges, J., Stevenson, J., Andreou, C., Lanyado, M., New, M., Williams, B. and McMillan, D. (1998) 'Risk factors for development of sexually abusive behaviour in sexually victimised adolescent boys: cross sectional study', *Bmj*, Vol. 317, pp. 175–9

Smallbone, S. (2016) 'Situational prevention approaches', in Jeglic, E. L. and Calkins, C. (eds) (2016) *Sexual Violence*, New York, NY: Springer

Smallbone, S., Marshall, W. L. and Wortley, R. (2013) *Preventing Child Sexual Abuse: Evidence, Policy and Practice*, Cullompton: Willan

Smallbone, S. and Wortley, R. K. (2000) *Child sexual abuse in Queensland: Offender Characteristics and Modus Operandi*, Brisbane: Queensland Crime Commission and the Criminology Research Council; doi:10.1.1.421.9382&rep=rep1&type=pdf

Smith, C., Bradbury-Jones, C., Lazenbatt, A. and Taylor, J. (2013) *Provision for Young People Who Have Displayed Harmful Sexual Behaviour*, London: National Society for the Prevention of Cruelty to Children

Smith, W. R., Monastersky, C. and Deisher, R. M. (1987) 'MMPI-based personality types among juvenile sexual offenders', *Journal of Clinical Psychology*, Vol. 43, pp. 422–30

Somervell, J. and Lambie, I. (2009) 'Wilderness therapy within an adolescent sexual offender treatment programme: A qualitative study', *Journal of Sexual Aggression*, Vol. 15, pp. 161–77

Soothill, K. and Walby, S. (1991) *Sex Crime in the News*, London: Routledge

South Australia Department for Education and Child Development (2013) 'Responding to problem sexual behaviour in children and young people: Guidelines for staff in education and care settings' (online). Available from URL: www.decd.sa.gov.au/sites/g/files/net691/f/responding_to_problem_sexual_behaviour_in_children_and_young_people.pdf (accessed 29 December 2017)

Spice, A., Viljoen, J. L., Latzman, N. E., Scalora, M. J. and Ullman, D. (2013) 'Risk and protective factors for recidivism among juveniles who have offended sexually', *Sexual Abuse*, Vol. 25, pp. 347–69

Spiegel, D. R., Shaukat, A. M., McCroskey, A. L., Chatterjee, A., Ahmadi, T., Simmelink, D., Oldfield, E. C., Pryor, C. R., Faschan, M. and Raulli, O. (2016) 'Conceptualizing a subtype of patients with chronic pain: the necessity of obtaining a history of sexual abuse', *The International Journal of Psychiatry in Medicine*, Vol. 51, pp. 84–103

St Amand, A., Bard, D. E. and Silovsky, J. F. (2008) 'Meta-analysis of treatment for child sexual behaviour problems: Practice elements and outcomes', *Child Maltreatment*,

Vol. 13, pp. 145–66

Stanley, N., Barter, C., Wood, M., Aghtaie, N., Larkins, C., Lanau, A. and Överlien, C. (2016) 'Pornography, sexual coercion and abuse and sexting in young people's intimate relationships: A European study', *Journal of Interpersonal Violence*; doi:0886260516633204

Stermac, L. and Sheridan, P. (1993) *The Developmentally Disabled Adolescent Sex Offender*, New York, NY: Guilford Press

Stevens, P., Hutchin, K., French, L. and Craissati, J. (2013) 'Developmental and offence-related characteristics of different types of adolescent sex offender: A community sample', *Journal of Sexual Aggression*, Vol. 19, pp. 138–57

Stevenson, M. C., Malik, S. E., Totton, R. R. and Reeves, R. D. (2015) 'Disgust sensitivity predicts punitive treatment of juvenile sex offenders: The role of empathy, dehumanization, and fear', *Analyses of Social Issues and Public Policy*, Vol. 15, pp. 177–97

Stillman, S. (2016) 'The list: When juveniles are found guilty of sexual misconduct, the sex-offender registry can be a life sentence' (online), *The New Yorker*. Available from URL: www.newyorker.com/magazine/2016/03/14/when-kids-are-accused-of-sex-crimes (accessed 29 November 2017)

Stoltenborgh, M., Van Ijzendoorn, M. H., Euser, E. M. and Bakermans-Kranenburg, M. J. (2011) 'A global perspective on child sexual abuse: Meta-analysis of prevalence around the world', *Child Maltreatment*, Vol. 16, pp. 79–101

Štulhofer, A., Buško, V. and Landripet, I. (2010) 'Pornography, sexual socialisation, and satisfaction among young men', *Archives of Sexual Behaviour*, Vol. 39, pp. 168–78

Sullivan, P. M. and Knutson, J. F. (2000) 'Maltreatment and disabilities: A population-based epidemiological study', *Child Abuse and Neglect*, Vol. 24, pp. 1257–73

Svedin, C. G., Åkerman, I. and Priebe, G. (2011) 'Frequent users of pornography: A population-based epidemiological study of Swedish male adolescents', *Journal of Adolescence*, Vol. 34, pp. 779–88

Swann, R. (2009) *Internet Assessment Intervention and Moving On: iAIM Practice Guidance for Young People Who Display Harmful Sexual Behaviour On-line Using New Technologies*, Stockport, AIM Project

Swann, R. (2017) *Technology-assisted Harmful Sexual Behaviours Practice Guidance*, Stockport: National Society for the Prevention of Cruelty to Children and AIM

Swanson, C. K. and Garwick, G. B. (1990) 'Treatment for low-functioning sex offenders: Group therapy and interagency coordination', *Mental Retardation*, Vol. 28, p. 155

Swisher, L. M., Silovsky, J. F., Stuart, J. R. H. and Pierce, K. (2008) 'Children with sexual behaviour problems', *Juvenile and Family Court Journal*, Vol. 59, pp. 49–69

Tabachnick, J. (2013) 'Why prevention? Why now?', *International Journal of Behavioural Consultation and Therapy*, Vol. 8, p. 55

Taith (2016) *Girl's Talk: Supporting Girls to Develop Healthy Sexual Relationships*, Barkingside: Barnardo's

Tanner, J. (1967) 'Puberty', *Advances in Reproductive Physiology*, Vol. 2, p. 311

Taylor, B. G., Stein, N. D., Mumford, E. A. and Woods, D. (2013) 'Shifting boundaries: An experimental evaluation of a dating violence prevention program in middle schools', *Prevention Science*, Vol. 14, pp. 64–76

Tenbergen, G., Wittfoth, M., Frieling, H., Ponseti, J., Walter, M., Walter, H., Beier, K. M., Schiffer, B. and Kruger, T. H. (2015) 'The neurobiology and psychology of pedophilia: recent advances and challenges', *Frontiers in Human Neuroscience*, Vol. 9, pp. 1–20

Ter Beek, E., Spruit, A., Kuiper, C. H. Z., Van Der Rijken, R. E. A., Hendriks, J. and Stams, G. J. J. M. (2017) 'Treatment effect on recidivism for juveniles who have sexually offended: A multilevel meta-analysis', *Journal of Abnormal Child Psychology*; doi:10.1007/s10802-017-0308-3

Thibaut, F., Bradford, J. M., Briken, P., De La Barra, F., Hässler, F. and Cosyns, P. (2016) 'The World Federation of Societies of Biological Psychiatry (WFSBP) guidelines for the treatment of adolescent sexual offenders with paraphilic disorders', *The World Journal of Biological Psychiatry*, Vol. 17, pp. 2–38

Thigpen, J. W., Pinkston, E. M. and Mayefsky, J. H. (2003) *Normative Sexual Behaviour of African American Children: Sexual Development in Childhood*, Bloomington, IN: Indiana University Press, pp. 241–54

Thomas, J. and Viar, C. (2005) 'Family reunification in cases of sibling incest', in Calder, M. (ed.) (2005) *Children and Young People Who Sexually Abuse: New Theory, Research and Practice Developments*, Lyme Regis: Russell House

Thornton, J. A., Stevens, G., Grant, J., Indermaur, D., Chamarette, C. and Halse, A. (2008) 'Intrafamilial adolescent sex offenders: Family functioning and treatment', *Journal of Family Studies*, Vol. 14, pp. 362–75

Tidefors, I., Arvidsson, H., Ingevaldson, S. and Larsson, M. (2010) 'Sibling incest: A literature review and a clinical study', *Journal of Sexual Aggression*, Vol. 16, pp. 347–60

Tilley, N., Rayment-McHugh, S., Smallbone, S., Wardell, M., Smith, D., Allard, T., Wortley, R., Findlater, D., Stewart, A. and Homel, R. (2014) 'On being realistic about reducing the prevalence and impacts of youth sexual violence and abuse in two Australian indigenous communities', *Learning Communities: International Journal of Learning in Social Contexts*, Vol. 14, pp. 6–27

Timms, S. and Goreczny, A. J. (2002) 'Adolescent sex offenders with mental retardation: Literature review and assessment considerations', *Aggression and Violent Behaviour*, Vol. 7, pp. 1–19

Tolman, D. L. and McClelland, S. I. (2011) 'Normative sexuality development in adolescence: A decade in review, 2000–2009', *Journal of Research on Adolescence*, Vol. 21, pp. 242–55

Tomaszewska, P. and Krahé, B. (2016) 'Predictors of sexual aggression victimization and perpetration among Polish university students: A longitudinal study', *Archives of Sexual Behaviour*, pp. 1–13; doi:10.1007/s10508-016-0823-2

Torres, R. and Fernández, F. (1995) 'Self-esteem and value of health as determinants of adolescent health behaviour', *Journal of Adolescent Health*, Vol. 16, pp. 60–3

Trowell, J. (1997) 'The psychodynamics of incest', in Welldon, E. and Van Velsen, C. (eds) (1997) *Practical Guide to Forensic Psychotherapy*, London: Jessica Kingsley

Tudiver, J. and Griffin, J. (1992) 'Treating developmentally disabled adolescents who have committed sexual abuse', *SIECCAN Newsletter*, Vol. 27, pp. 5–10

UKCCIS (2015) *Child Safety Online: A Practical Guide for Providers of Social Media and Interactive Services*, London: UK Council for Child Internet Safety

Ullman, S. E. (2007) 'Comparing gang and individual rapes in a community sample of urban women', *Violence and Victims*, Vol. 22, p. 43

UNICEF (1989) 'Convention on the rights of the child' (online). Available from URL: www.unicef.org/crc (accessed 6 February 2018)

UNICEF (2017) *A Familiar Face: Violence in the Lives of Children and Adolescents*, New York, NY: UNICEF

Van den Berg, C., Bijleveld, C., Hendriks, J. and Mooi-Reci, I. (2014) 'The juvenile sex offender: The effect of employment on offending', *Journal of Criminal Justice*, Vol. 42, pp. 145–52

Van der Put, C. E. (2015) 'Female adolescent sexual and non-sexual violent offenders: A comparison of the prevalence and impact of risk and protective factors for general recidivism', *BMC Psychiatry*, Vol. 15, p. 236

Van der Put, C. E., Deković, M., Stams, G. J. J., Van Der Laan, P. H., Hoeve, M. and Van Amelsfort, L. (2011) 'Changes in risk factors during adolescence: Implications for risk assessment', *Criminal Justice and Behaviour*, Vol. 38, pp. 248–62

Vandiver, D. M. and Teske Jr, R. (2006) 'Juvenile female and male sex offenders: A comparison of offender, victim, and judicial processing characteristics', *International Journal of Offender Therapy and Comparative Criminology*, Vol. 50, pp. 148–65

Van Royen, K., Vandebosch, H. and Poels, K. (2015) 'Severe sexual harassment on social networking sites: Belgian adolescents' views', *Journal of Children and Media*, Vol. 9, pp. 472–91

Van Wijk, A. P., Mali, B. R., Bullens, R. A. and Vermeiren, R. R. (2007) 'Criminal profiles of violent juvenile sex and violent juvenile non-sex offenders: An explorative longitudinal study', *Journal of Interpersonal Violence*, Vol. 22, pp. 1340–55

Vaswani, N. and Simpson, S. (2015) 'The use of Safer Lives in Scotland with young people displaying sexually harmful behaviours' (online), Glasgow Centre for Youth and Criminal Justice, University of Strathclyde. Available from URL: www.cycj.org.uk/wp-content/uploads/2015/05/The-use-of-safer-lives-in-Scotland-report.pdf (accessed 29 December 2017)

Veneziano, C., Veneziano, L. and Legrand, S. (2000) 'The relationship between adolescent sex offender behaviours and victim characteristics with prior victimization', *Journal of Interpersonal Violence*, Vol. 15, pp. 363–74

Viki, G. T., Fullerton, I., Raggett, H., Tait, F. and Wiltshire, S. (2012) 'The role of dehumanization in attitudes towards the social exclusion and rehabilitation of sex offenders', *Journal of Applied Social Psychology*, Vol. 42, pp. 2349–67

Viljoen, J. L., Mordell, S. and Beneteau, J. L. (2012) 'Prediction of adolescent sexual reoffending: a meta-analysis of the J-SOAP-II, ERASOR, J-SORRAT-II, and Static-99', *Law and Human Behavior*, Vol. 36, pp. 423–8; doi:10.1037/h0093938

Viner, R. M., Ozer, E. M., Denny, S., Marmot, M., Resnick, M., Fatusi, A. and Currie, C. (2012) 'Adolescence and the social determinants of health', *The Lancet*, Vol. 379, pp. 1641–52

Vizard, E. (2002) 'The assessment of young sexual abusers', in Calder, M. (ed.) (2002) *Young People Who Sexually Abuse: Building the Evidence Base for Your Practice*, Lyme Regis: Russell House

Vosmer, S., Hackett, S. and Callanan, M. (2009) ' "Normal" and "inappropriate" childhood sexual behaviours: Findings from a Delphi study of professionals in the United Kingdom', *Journal of Sexual Aggression*, Vol. 15, pp. 275–88

Wallien, M. S. and Cohen-Kettenis, P. T. (2008) 'Psychosexual outcome of gender-dysphoric children', *Journal of the American Academy of Child and Adolescent Psychiatry*, Vol. 47, pp. 1413–23

Walsh, K., Zwi, K., Woolfenden, S. and Shlonsky, A. (2015) 'School-based education programmes for the prevention of child sexual abuse', *Cochrane Database of Systematic Reviews*, Vol. 4; doi:10.1002/14651858.CD004380.pub3

Ward, T. and Beech, A. (2006) 'An integrated theory of sexual offending', *Aggression and Violent Behaviour*, Vol. 11, pp. 44–63

Ward, T. and Gannon, T. A. (2006) 'Rehabilitation, etiology, and self-regulation: The comprehensive good lives model of treatment for sexual offenders', *Aggression and Violent Behaviour*, Vol. 11, pp. 77–94

Ward, T., Vess, J., Collie, R. M. and Gannon, T. A. (2006) 'Risk management or goods promotion: The relationship between approach and avoidance goals in treatment for sex offenders', *Aggression and Violent Behaviour*, Vol. 11, pp. 378–93

Wastell, D. and White, S. (2012) 'Blinded by neuroscience: Social policy, the family and the infant brain', *Families, Relationships and Societies*, Vol. 1, pp. 397–414

Webster-Stratton, C. (1990) *The Incredible Years parent training program manual: Effective communication, anger management and problem-solving (ADVANCE)*, Seattle, WA: Incredible Years

Wellings, K., Collumbien, M., Slaymaker, E., Singh, S., Hodges, Z., Patel, D. and Bajos, N. (2006) 'Sexual behaviour in context: a global perspective', *The Lancet*, Vol. 368, pp. 1706–28

Wheeler, J. G., George, W. H. and Dahl, B. J. (2002) 'Sexually aggressive college males: Empathy as a moderator in the "Confluence Model" of sexual aggression', *Personality and Individual Differences*, Vol. 33, pp. 759–75

White, J. W. and Smith, P. H. (2004) 'Sexual assault perpetration and reperpetration: From adolescence to young adulthood', *Criminal Justice and Behaviour*, Vol. 31, pp. 182–202

Whyte, B. (2008) *Youth Justice in Practice: Making a Difference*, Bristol: Policy Press

Wiggins, J., Hepburn, S. and Rossiter, R. (2013) 'Reducing harmful sexual behaviour in adolescents: Joshua Wiggins and colleagues discuss the work of a therapy group for young people with learning disabilities who have behaved inappropriately', *Learning*

Disability Practice, Vol. 16, pp. 16–23

Wijkman, M., Weerman, F., Bijleveld, C. and Hendriks, J. (2015) 'Group sexual offending by juvenile females', *Sexual Abuse*, Vol. 27, pp. 335–56

Willis, G. M. and Levenson, J. S. (2016) 'The relationship between childhood adversity and adult psychosocial outcomes in females who have sexually offended: implications for treatment', *Journal of Sexual Aggression*, Vol. 22, pp. 355–67

Wilson, C. P. and Chaud, M. I. S. (2013) 'Agresiones sexuales infanto-juveniles: una aproximación a víctimas de agresores menores de edad', *Salud & Sociedad: investigaciones en psicologia de la salud y psicologia social*, Vol. 4, pp. 266–82

Wilson, D. and Andrews, C. (2004) *Internet Traders of Child Pornography and Other Censorship Offenders in New Zealand: Updated Statistics*, Wellington, New Zealand: Department of Internal Affairs

Wilson, D. C. and Silverman, I. (2002) *Innocence betrayed: Paedophilia, The Media and Society*, Cambridge: Polity Press

Wilson, R. J. and Burns, M. (2011) *Intellectual Disability and Problems in Sexual Behaviour: Assessment, Treatment, and Promotion of Healthy Sexuality*, Holuyoke, MA: Neari Press

Winokur, M., Rozen, D., Batchelder, K. and Valentine, D. (2006) *Juvenile Sexual Offender Treatment: A Systematic Review of Evidence-Based Research*, Fort Collins, CO: Colorado State University, Applied Research in Child Welfare Project, Social Work Research Center, School of Social Work, College of Applied Human Sciences

Wolak, J. and Finkelhor, D. (2011) *Sexting: A Typology*, Durham, NH: Crimes Against Children Research Center, University of New Hampshire

Wolak, J. and Finkelhor, D. (2013) 'Are crimes by online predators different from crimes by sex offenders who know youth in-person?', *Journal of Adolescent Health*, Vol. 53, pp. 736–41

Wolak, J., Finkelhor, D. and Mitchell, K. (2011) 'Child pornography possessors: Trends in offender and case characteristics', *Sexual Abuse*, Vol. 23, pp. 22–42

Wolak, J., Finkelhor, D., Walsh, W. and Treitman, L. (2018) 'Sextortion of minors: Characteristics and dynamics', *Journal of Adolescent Health*, Vol. 62, pp. 72–9

Wolf, R. M. and Long, D. (2016) 'Pubertal development', *Pediatrics in Review*, Vol. 37, pp. 292–300

Wood, C., Welman, M. and Netto, L. (2000) 'A profile of young sex offenders in South Africa', *Southern African Journal of Child and Adolescent Mental Health*, Vol. 12, pp. 45–58

Wood, M., Barter, C., Stanley, N., Aghtaie, N. and Larkins, C. (2015) 'Images across Europe: The sending and receiving of sexual images and associations with interpersonal violence in young people's relationships', *Children and Youth Services Review*, Vol. 59, pp. 149–60

Woodiwiss, J. (2014) 'Beyond a single story: The importance of separating "harm" from "wrongfulness" and "sexual innocence" from "childhood" in contemporary narratives of childhood sexual abuse', *Sexualities*, Vol. 17, pp. 139–58

World Health Organization (2003) *Guidelines for Medico-legal Care of Victims of Sexual*

Violence, Geneva: World Health Organization

Worling, J. R. (1995) 'Adolescent sibling incest offenders: Differences in family and individual functioning when compared to adolescent nonsibling sex offenders', *Child Abuse and Neglect*, Vol. 19, pp. 633–43

Worling, J. R. (2001) 'Personality-based typology of adolescent male sexual offenders: Differences in recidivism rates, victim-selection characteristics, and personal victimization histories', *Sexual Abuse*, Vol. 13, pp. 149–66

Worling, J. R. (2006) 'Assessing sexual arousal with adolescent males who have offended sexually: Self-report and unobtrusively measured viewing time', *Sexual Abuse*, Vol. 18, pp. 383–400

Worling, J. R. (2013) "Desistence for adolescents who sexually harm (DASH-13)' (online). Available from URL: www.drjamesworling.com/dash-13.html (accessed 30 November 2017)

Worling, J. R. (2017) 'Protective + Risk Observations For Eliminating Sexual Offense Recidivism (PROFESOR) – History and rationale' (online). Available from URL: www.profesor.ca/history--rationale.html (accessed 30 November 2017)

Worling, J. R., Bookalam, D. and Litteljohn, A. (2012) 'Prospective validity of the estimate of risk of adolescent sexual offense recidivism (ERASOR)', *Sexual Abuse*, Vol. 24, pp. 203–23

Worling, J. R. and Curwen, T. (2001) 'Estimate of risk of adolescent sexual offense recidivism (ERASOR; Version 2.0)', in Calder, M. (ed.) (2001) *Juveniles and Children Who Sexually Abuse: Frameworks for Assessment*, Lyme Regis: Russell House

Worling, J. R. and Långström, N. (2006) 'Risk of sexual recidivism in adolescents who offend sexually', in Barbaree, H. E. and Marshall, W. L. (eds) (2006) *The Juvenile Sex Offender*, New York, NY: Guilford Press

Worling, J. R. and Langton, C. M. (2016) 'Assessment of adolescents who have sexually offended', in Craig, L. A. and Rettenberger, M. (eds) (2016) *The Wiley Handbook on the Theories, Assessment and Treatment of Sexual Offending*, Chichester, West Sussex: Wiley

Worling, J. R., Litteljohn, A. and Bookalam, D. (2010) '20-year prospective follow-up study of specialized treatment for adolescents who offended sexually', *Behavioural Sciences and the Law*, Vol. 28, pp. 46–57

Wright, R. and West, D. (1981) 'Rape: A comparison of group offences and lone assaults', *Medicine, Science and the Law*, Vol. 21, pp. 25–30

Yang, M. L., Fullwood, E., Goldstein, J. and Mink, J. W. (2005) 'Masturbation in infancy and early childhood presenting as a movement disorder: 12 cases and a review of the literature', *Pediatrics*, Vol. 116, pp. 1427–32

Yates, P. (2017a) 'Sibling sexual abuse: Why don't we talk about it?', *Journal of Clinical Nursing*, Vol. 26, pp. 2482–94

Yates, P. (2017b) ' "Siblings as better together": Social worker decision-making in cases involving sibling sexual behaviour', *The British Journal of Social Work*, bcz018

Yates, P., Allardyce, S. and MacQueen, S. (2012) 'Children who display harmful sexual behaviour: Assessing the risks of boys abusing at home, in the community or across both settings', *Journal of Sexual Aggression*, Vol. 18, pp. 23–35

Yates, P. (2015) ' "Better Together": A grounded theory study of social worker decision making in cases involving sexual behaviour between siblings', PhD thesis in social work, University of Edinburgh, p. 370. Available from URL: www.era.lib.ed.ac.uk/handle/1842/16446 (accessed 6 February 2018)

Ybarra, M. L., Espelage, D. L. and Mitchell, K. J. (2007) 'The co-occurrence of Internet harassment and unwanted sexual solicitation victimization and perpetration: Associations with psychosocial indicators', *Journal of Adolescent Health*, Vol. 41, S31–S41

Ybarra, M. L., Mitchell, K. J. and Korchmaros, J. D. (2011) 'National trends in exposure to and experiences of violence on the Internet among children', *Pediatrics*; doi:10.1542/peds.2011–0118

Ybarra, M.L. and Thompson, R.E., (2017) Predicting the emergence of sexual violence in adolescence. *Prevention Science*, pp.1–13.

Young, A. M., Grey, M. and Boyd, C. J. (2009) 'Adolescents' experiences of sexual assault by peers: Prevalence and nature of victimization occurring within and outside of school', *Journal of Youth and Adolescence*, Vol. 38, pp. 1072–83

Youth Justice Board (2008) *Young People Who Sexually Abuse: Key Elements of Effective Practice*, London: Youth Justice Board for England and Wales

Youth Justice Board/Ministry of Justice (2018) *Youth Justice Statistics 2016/17, England and Wales*, London: Ministry of Justice

Zeanah, C. H., Smyke, A. T. and Dumitrescu, A. (2002) 'Attachment disturbances in young children. II: Indiscriminate behaviour and institutional care', *Journal of the American Academy of Child and Adolescent Psychiatry*, Vol. 41, pp. 983–9

Zeng, G., Chu, C. M., Koh, L. L. and Teoh, J. (2015a) 'Risk and criminogenic needs of youth who sexually offended in Singapore: An examination of two typologies', *Sexual Abuse*, Vol. 27, pp. 479–95

Zeng, G., Chu, C. M. and Lee, Y. (2015b) 'Assessing protective factors of youth who sexually offended in Singapore: Preliminary evidence on the utility of the DASH-13 and the SAPROF', *Sexual Abuse*, Vol. 27, pp. 91–108

Zimmer-Gembeck, M. J., Hughes, N., Kelly, M. and Connolly, J. (2012) 'Intimacy, identity and status: Measuring dating goals in late adolescence and emerging adulthood', *Motivation and Emotion*, Vol. 36, pp. 311–22

Zimring, F. E. (2009) *An American Travesty: Legal Responses to Adolescent Sexual Offending*, New York, NY: University of Chicago Press

Zucker, K. J. and Bradley, S. J. (1995) *Gender Identity Disorder and Psychosexual Problems in Children and Adolescents*, New York, NY: Guilford Press

Zuroff, D. C., Kelly, A. C., Leybman, M. J., Blatt, S. J. and Wampold, B. E. (2010) 'Between-therapist and within-therapist differences in the quality of the therapeutic relationship: effects on maladjustment and self-critical perfectionism', *Journal of Clinical Psychology*, Vol. 66, pp. 681–97

Index

Note: page numbers in *italics* denote figures or tables